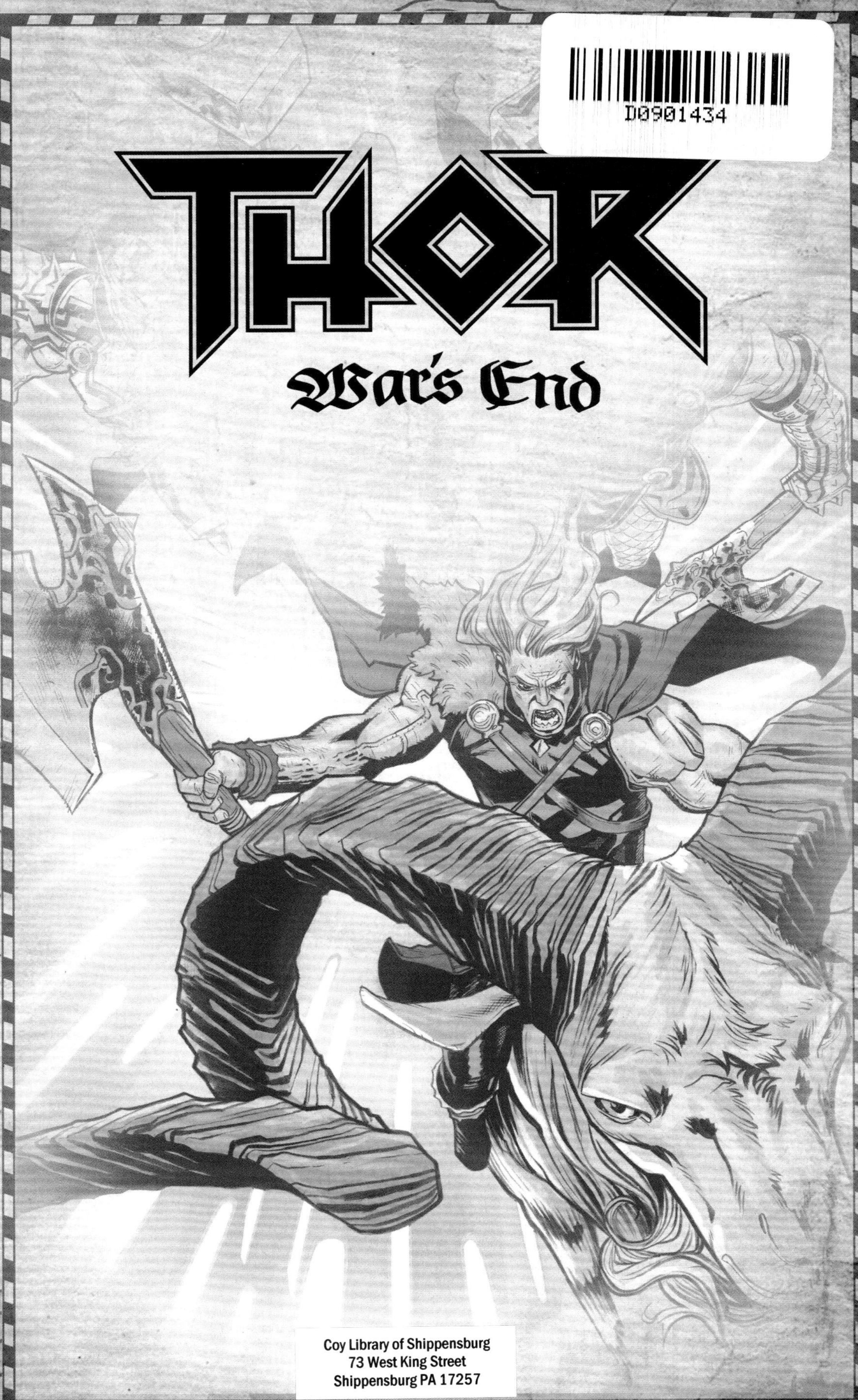
THOR
War's End

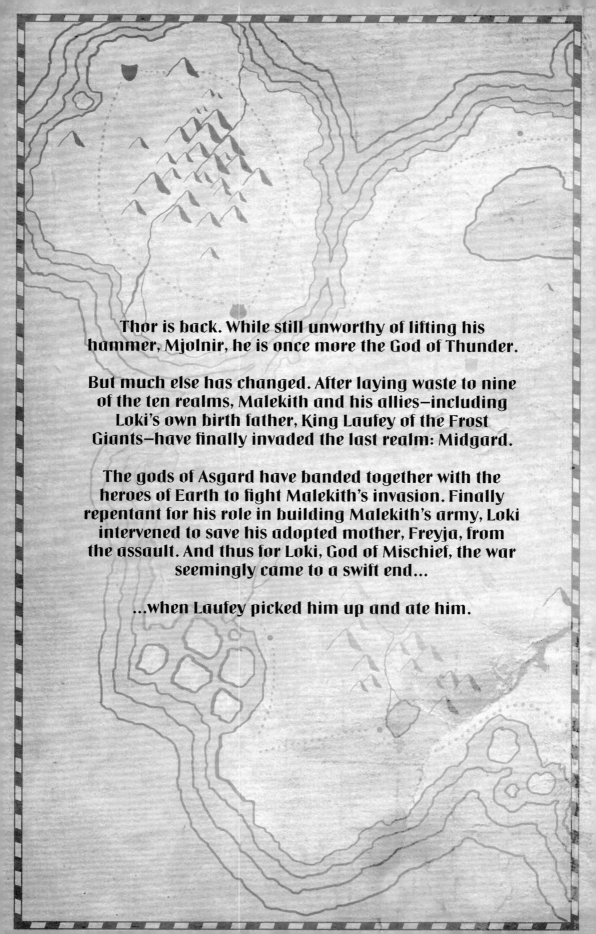

Thor is back. While still unworthy of lifting his
hammer, Mjolnir, he is once more the God of Thunder.

But much else has changed. After laying waste to nine
of the ten realms, Malekith and his allies—including
Loki's own birth father, King Laufey of the Frost
Giants—have finally invaded the last realm: Midgard.

The gods of Asgard have banded together with the
heroes of Earth to fight Malekith's invasion. Finally
repentant for his role in building Malekith's army, Loki
intervened to save his adopted mother, Freyja, from
the assault. And thus for Loki, God of Mischief, the war
seemingly came to a swift end...

...when Laufey picked him up and ate him.

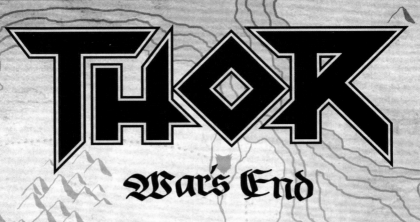

THOR

War's End

JASON AARON
WRITER

#12-13 & #15-16

MIKE DEL MUNDO
ARTIST

MIKE DEL MUNDO
WITH **MARCO D'ALFONSO**
(#13, #15-16)
COLOR ARTISTS

#14

SCOTT HEPBURN
ARTIST

MATTHEW WILSON
COLOR ARTIST

VC's JOE SABINO
LETTERER

MIKE DEL MUNDO
COVER ART

SARAH BRUNSTAD
ASSOCIATE EDITOR

WIL MOSS
EDITOR

TOM BREVOORT
EXECUTIVE EDITOR

THOR CREATED BY
STAN LEE, LARRY LIEBER & JACK KIRBY

COLLECTION EDITOR: JENNIFER GRÜNWALD • ASSISTANT EDITOR: CAITLIN O'CONNELL
ASSOCIATE MANAGING EDITOR: KATERI WOODY • EDITOR, SPECIAL PROJECTS: MARK D. BEAZLEY
VP PRODUCTION & SPECIAL PROJECTS: JEFF YOUNGQUIST • BOOK DESIGNERS: STACIE ZUCKER WITH JAY BOWEN

SVP PRINT, SALES & MARKETING: DAVID GABRIEL • DIRECTOR, LICENSED PUBLISHING: SVEN LARSEN
EDITOR IN CHIEF: C.B. CEBULSKI • CHIEF CREATIVE OFFICER: JOE QUESADA
PRESIDENT: DAN BUCKLEY • EXECUTIVE PRODUCER: ALAN FINE

THOR VOL. 3: WAR'S END. Contains material originally published in magazine form as THOR #12-16. First printing 2019. ISBN 978-1-302-91445-5. Published by MARVEL WORLDWIDE, INC., a subsidiary of MARVEL ENTERTAINMENT, LLC. OFFICE OF PUBLICATION: 135 West 50th Street, New York, NY 10020. **Printed in Canada.** DAN BUCKLEY, President, Marvel Entertainment; JOHN NEE, Publisher; JOE QUESADA, Chief Creative Officer; TOM BREVOORT, SVP of Publishing; DAVID BOGART, Associate Publisher & SVP of Talent Affairs; DAVID GABRIEL, SVP of Sales & Marketing, Publishing; JEFF YOUNGQUIST, VP of Production & Special Projects; DAN CARR, Executive Director of Publishing Technology; ALEX MORALES, Director of Publishing Operations; DAN EDINGTON, Managing Editor; SUSAN CRESPI, Production Manager; STAN LEE, Chairman Emeritus. For information regarding advertising in Marvel Comics or on Marvel.com, please contact Vit DeBellis, Custom Solutions & Integrated Advertising Manager, at vdebellis@marvel.com. For Marvel subscription inquiries, please call 888-511-5480. **Manufactured between 9/6/2019 and 10/8/2019 by SOLISCO PRINTERS, SCOTT, QC, CANADA.**

10 9 8 7 6 5 4 3 2 1

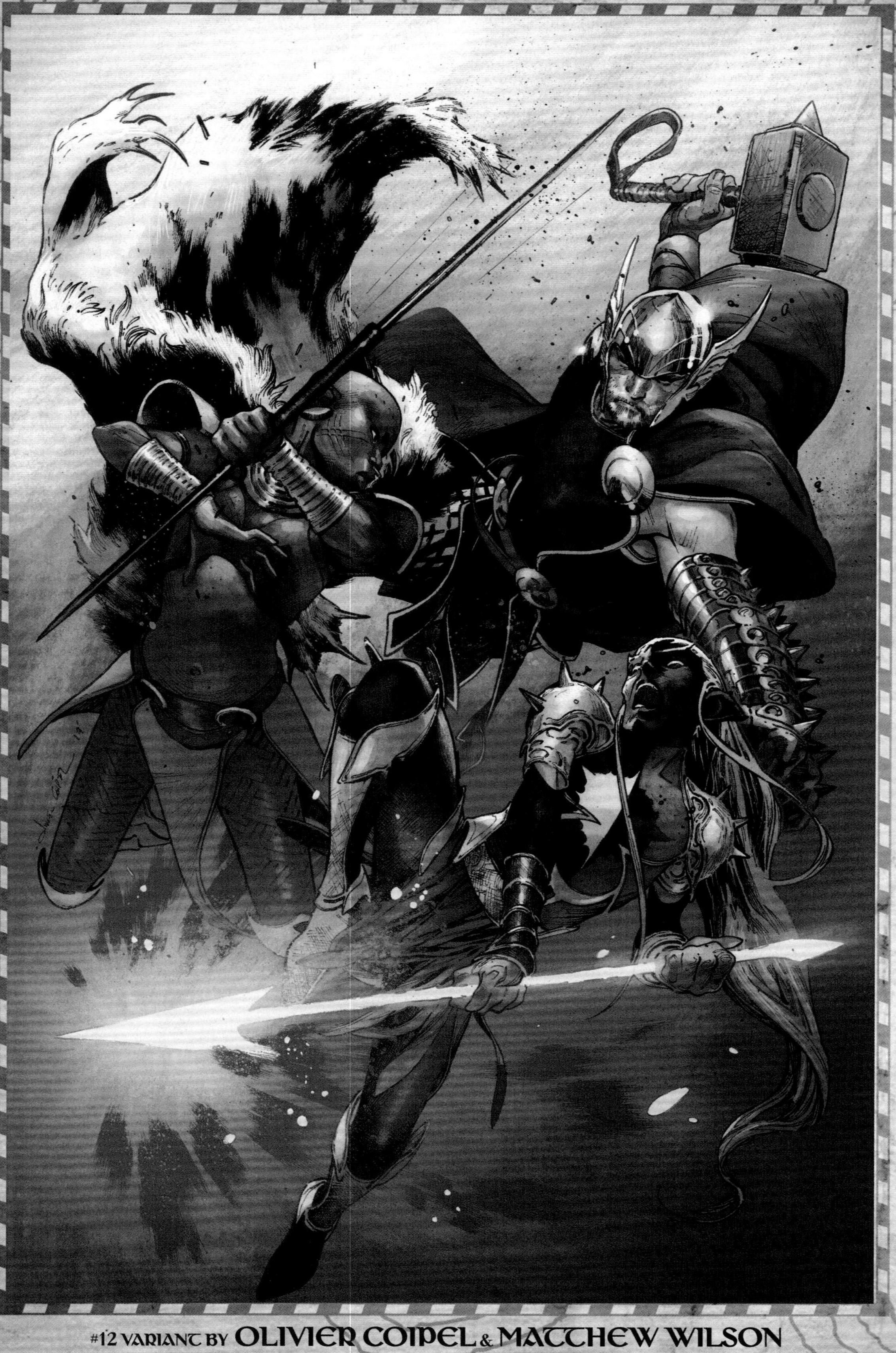

#12 VARIANT BY OLIVIER COIPEL & MATTHEW WILSON

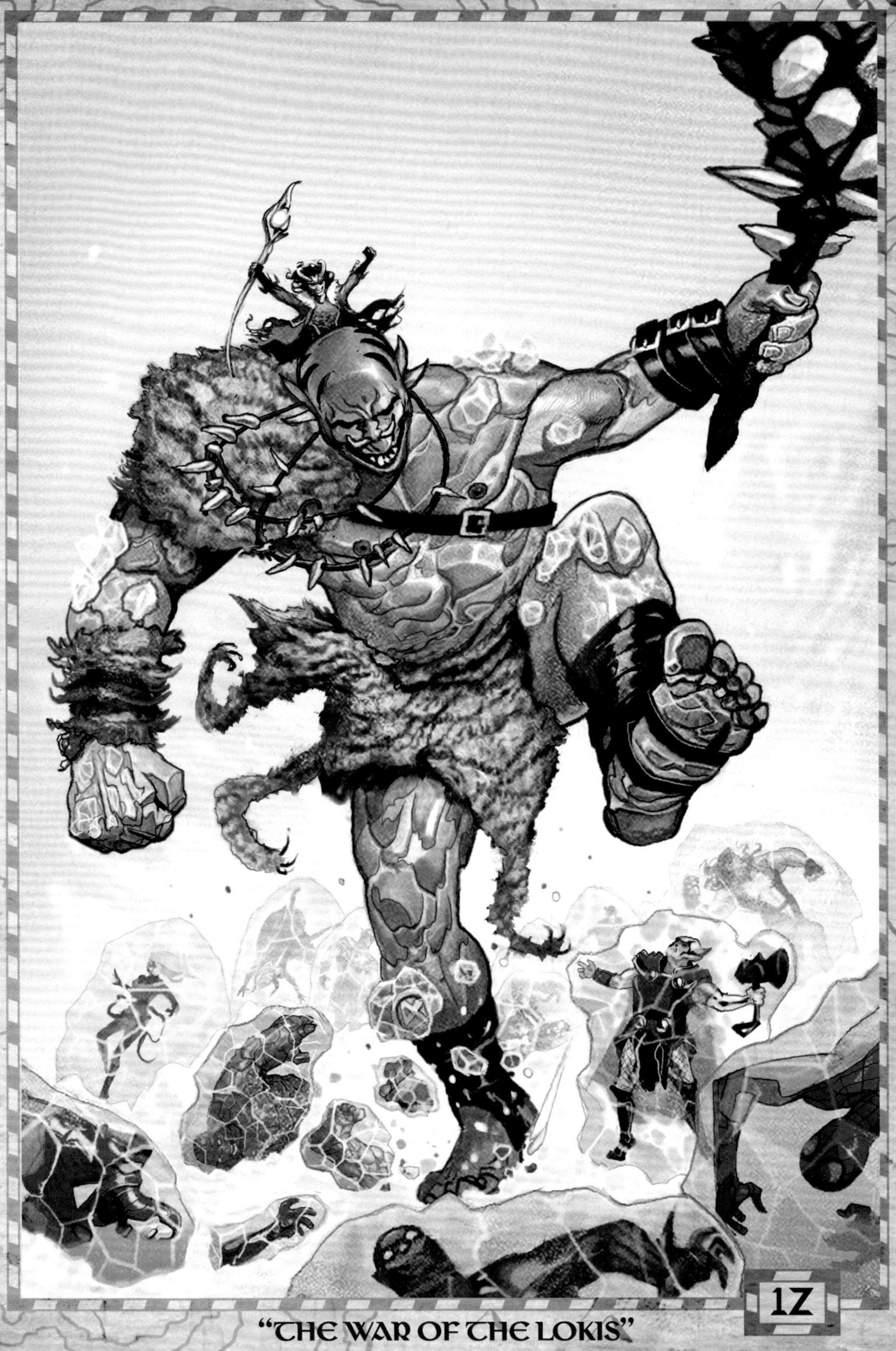

"THE WAR OF THE LOKIS"

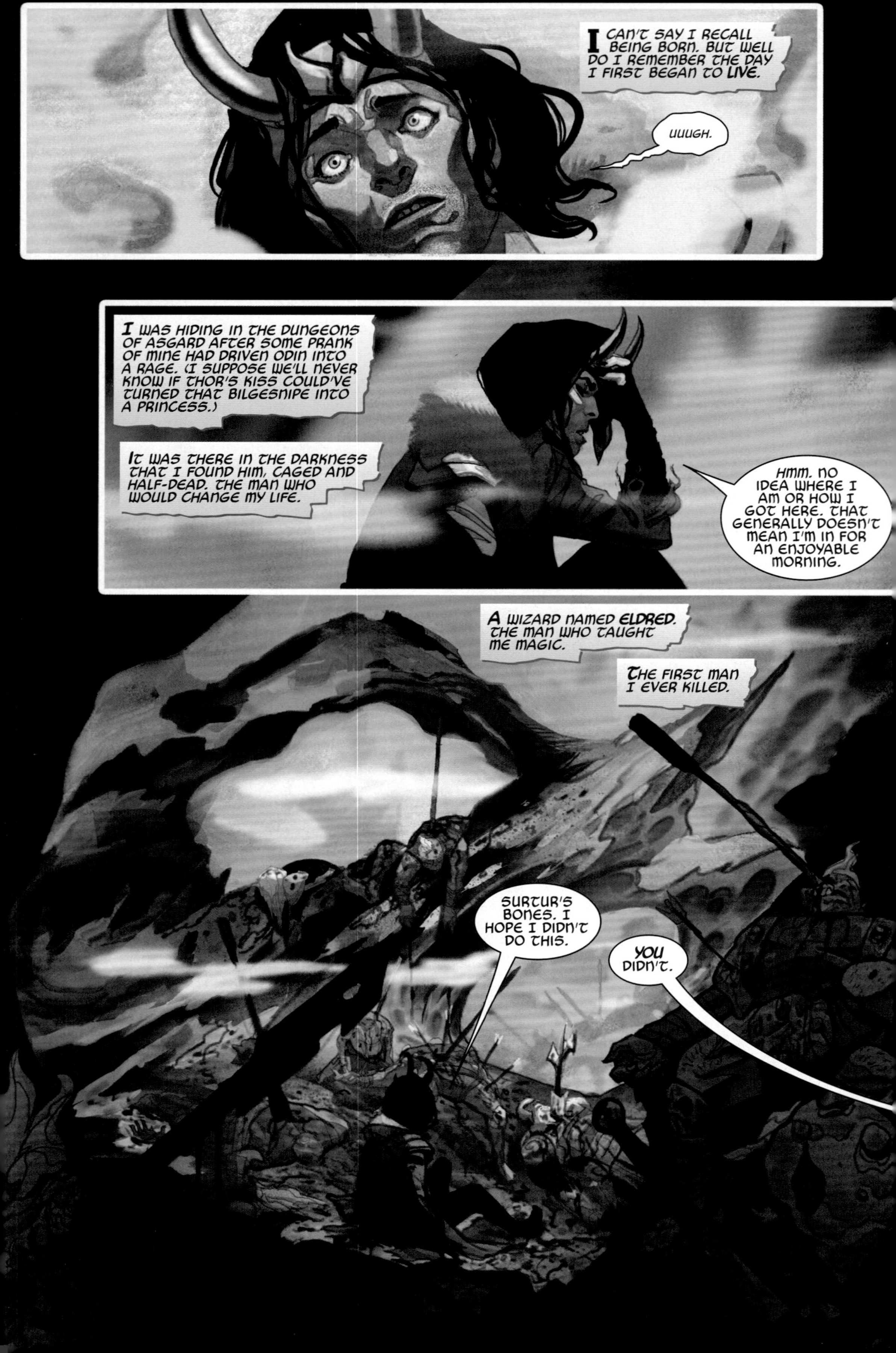
I CAN'T SAY I RECALL BEING BORN. BUT WELL DO I REMEMBER THE DAY I FIRST BEGAN TO LIVE.
UUUGH.
I WAS HIDING IN THE DUNGEONS OF ASGARD AFTER SOME PRANK OF MINE HAD DRIVEN ODIN INTO A RAGE. (I SUPPOSE WE'LL NEVER KNOW IF THOR'S KISS COULD'VE TURNED THAT BILGESNIPE INTO A PRINCESS.)
IT WAS THERE IN THE DARKNESS THAT I FOUND HIM, CAGED AND HALF-DEAD. THE MAN WHO WOULD CHANGE MY LIFE.
HMM. NO IDEA WHERE I AM OR HOW I GOT HERE. THAT GENERALLY DOESN'T MEAN I'M IN FOR AN ENJOYABLE MORNING.
A WIZARD NAMED ELDRED. THE MAN WHO TAUGHT ME MAGIC.
THE FIRST MAN I EVER KILLED.
SURTUR'S BONES. I HOPE I DIDN'T DO THIS.
YOU DIDN'T.

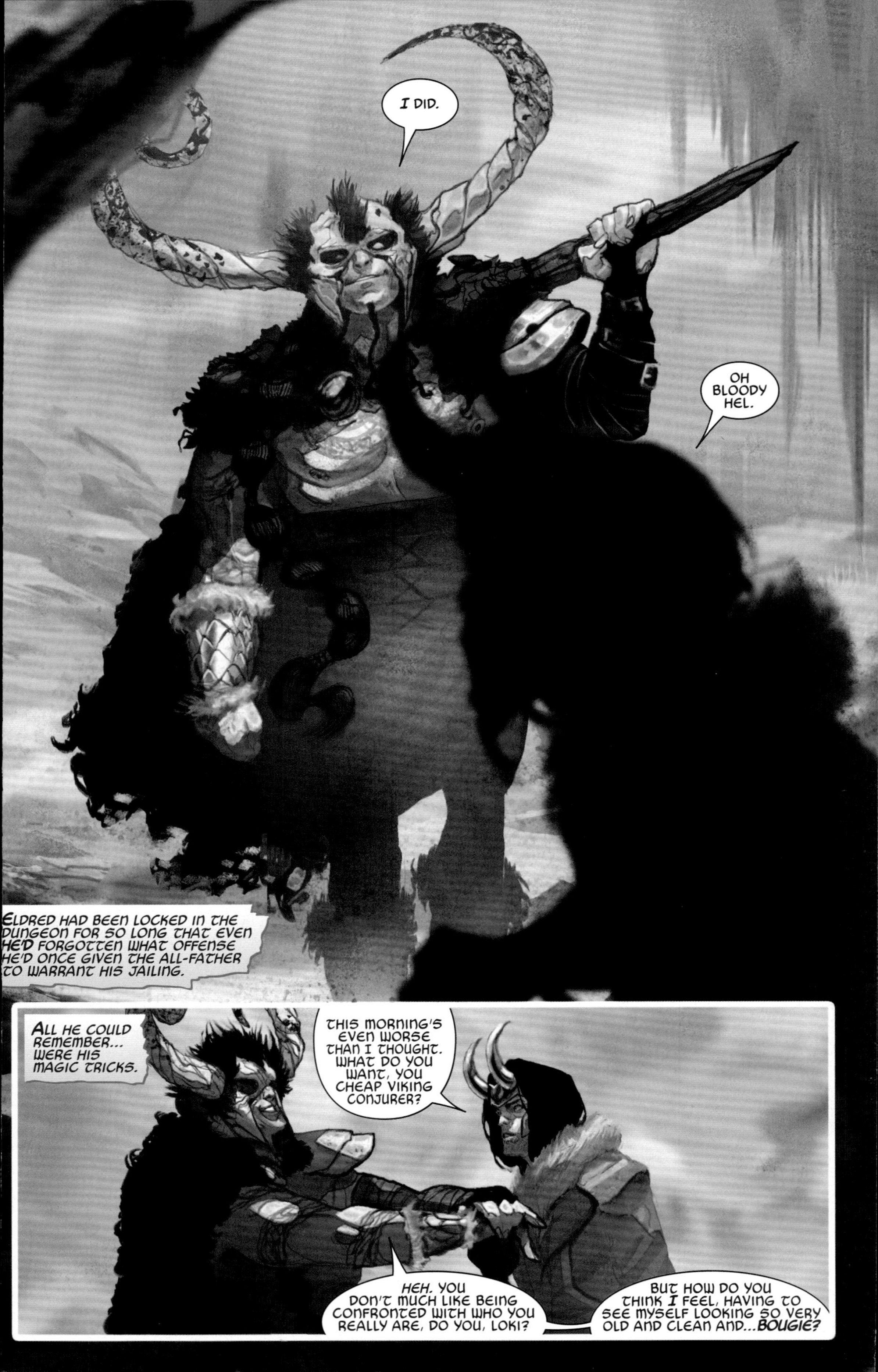
I DID.
OH BLOODY HEL.
ELDRED HAD BEEN LOCKED IN THE DUNGEON FOR SO LONG THAT EVEN **HE'D** FORGOTTEN WHAT OFFENSE HE'D ONCE GIVEN THE ALL-FATHER TO WARRANT HIS JAILING.
ALL HE COULD REMEMBER... WERE HIS MAGIC TRICKS.
THIS MORNING'S EVEN WORSE THAN I THOUGHT. WHAT DO YOU WANT, YOU CHEAP VIKING CONJURER?
HEH. YOU DON'T MUCH LIKE BEING CONFRONTED WITH WHO YOU REALLY ARE, DO YOU, LOKI?
BUT HOW DO YOU THINK *I* FEEL, HAVING TO SEE MYSELF LOOKING SO VERY OLD AND CLEAN AND...***BOUGIE?***

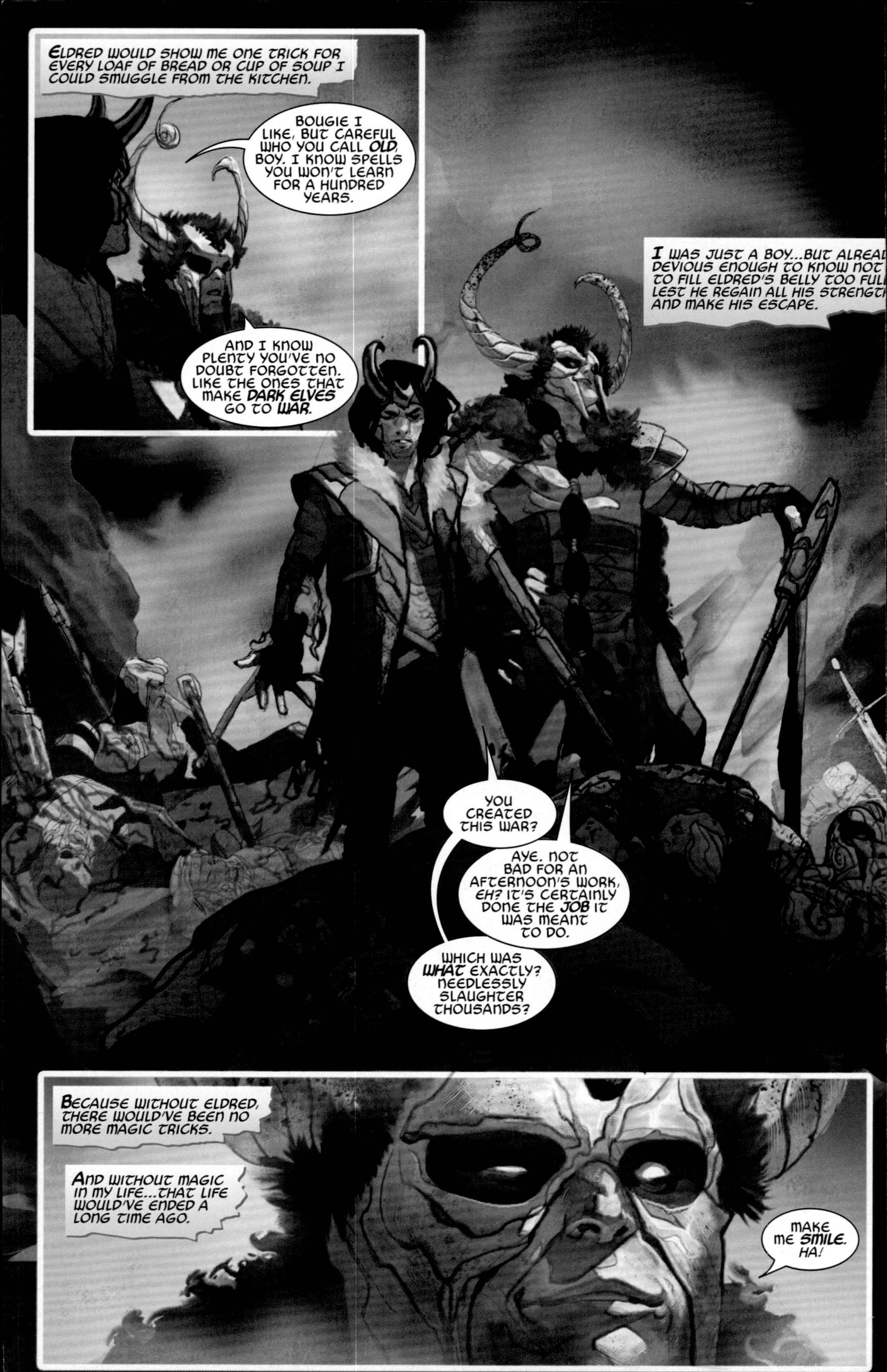
ELDRED WOULD SHOW ME ONE TRICK FOR EVERY LOAF OF BREAD OR CUP OF SOUP I COULD SMUGGLE FROM THE KITCHEN.
BOUGIE I LIKE, BUT CAREFUL WHO YOU CALL OLD, BOY. I KNOW SPELLS YOU WON'T LEARN FOR A HUNDRED YEARS.
AND I KNOW PLENTY YOU'VE NO DOUBT FORGOTTEN. LIKE THE ONES THAT MAKE DARK ELVES GO TO WAR.
I WAS JUST A BOY...BUT ALREAD DEVIOUS ENOUGH TO KNOW NOT TO FILL ELDRED'S BELLY TOO FULL LEST HE REGAIN ALL HIS STRENGTH AND MAKE HIS ESCAPE.
YOU CREATED THIS WAR?
AYE. NOT BAD FOR AN AFTERNOON'S WORK, EH? IT'S CERTAINLY DONE THE JOB IT WAS MEANT TO DO.
WHICH WAS WHAT EXACTLY? NEEDLESSLY SLAUGHTER THOUSANDS?
BECAUSE WITHOUT ELDRED, THERE WOULD'VE BEEN NO MORE MAGIC TRICKS.
AND WITHOUT MAGIC IN MY LIFE...THAT LIFE WOULD'VE ENDED A LONG TIME AGO.
MAKE ME SMILE. HA!

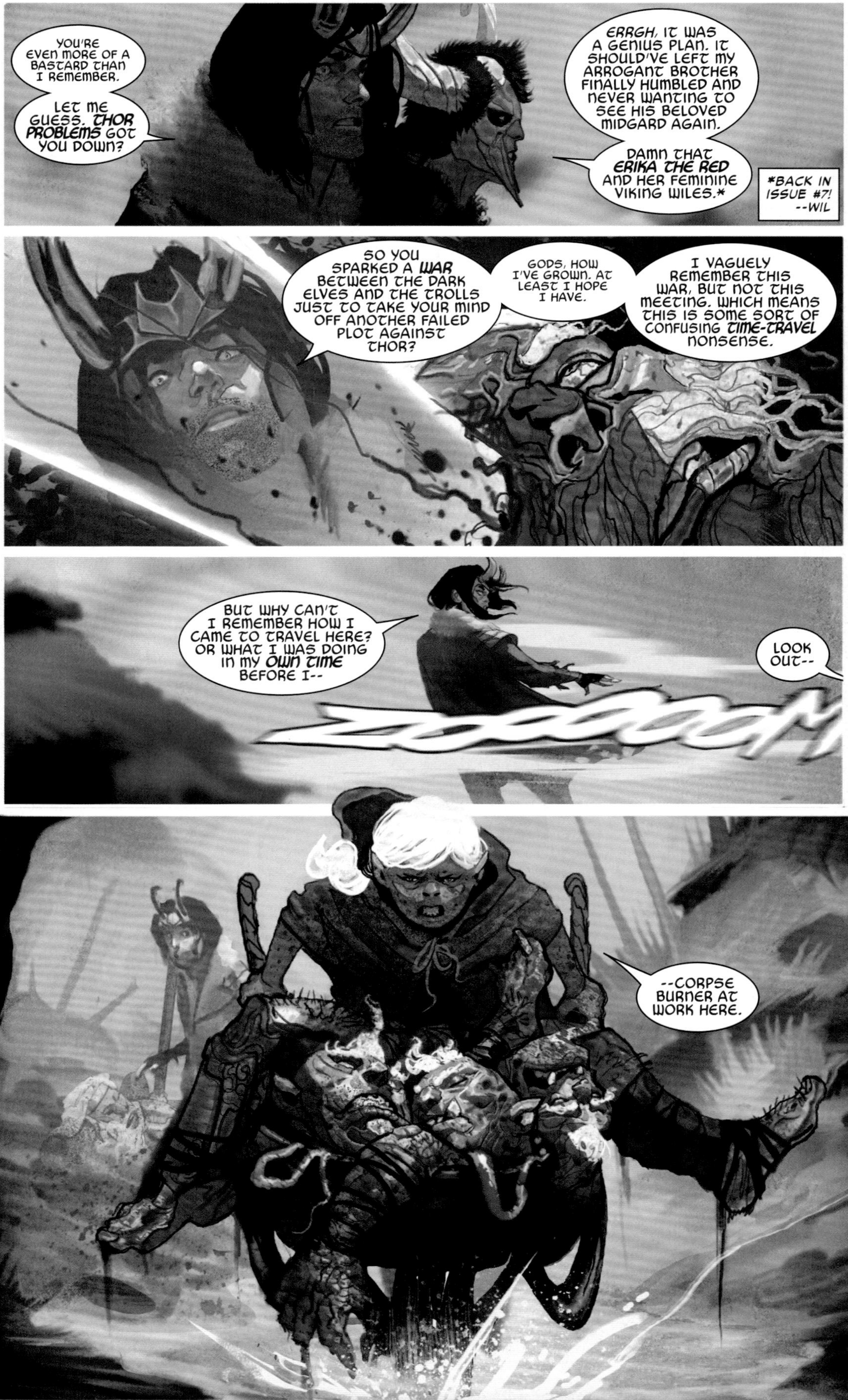
YOU'RE EVEN MORE OF A BASTARD THAN I REMEMBER.
LET ME GUESS. THOR PROBLEMS GOT YOU DOWN?
ERRGH, IT WAS A GENIUS PLAN. IT SHOULD'VE LEFT MY ARROGANT BROTHER FINALLY HUMBLED AND NEVER WANTING TO SEE HIS BELOVED MIDGARD AGAIN.
DAMN THAT ERIKA THE RED AND HER FEMININE VIKING WILES.*
*BACK IN ISSUE #7! --WIL
SO YOU SPARKED A WAR BETWEEN THE DARK ELVES AND THE TROLLS JUST TO TAKE YOUR MIND OFF ANOTHER FAILED PLOT AGAINST THOR?
GODS, HOW I'VE GROWN. AT LEAST I HOPE I HAVE.
I VAGUELY REMEMBER THIS WAR, BUT NOT THIS MEETING. WHICH MEANS THIS IS SOME SORT OF CONFUSING TIME-TRAVEL NONSENSE.
BUT WHY CAN'T I REMEMBER HOW I CAME TO TRAVEL HERE? OR WHAT I WAS DOING IN MY OWN TIME BEFORE I--
LOOK OUT--
ZOOOOOM
--CORPSE BURNER AT WORK HERE.

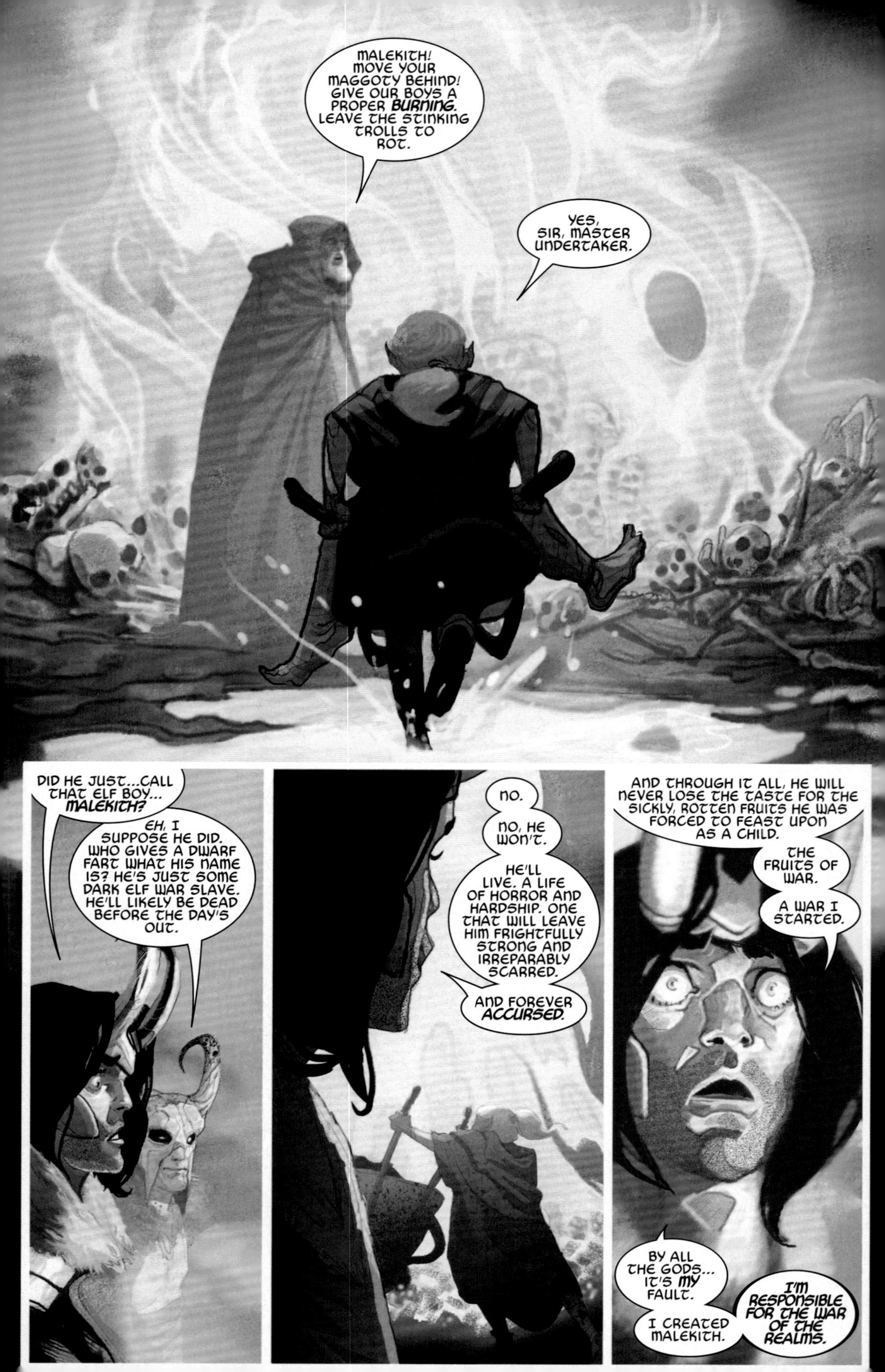

MALEKITH! MOVE YOUR MAGGOTY BEHIND! GIVE OUR BOYS A PROPER *BURNING*. LEAVE THE STINKING TROLLS TO ROT.
YES, SIR, MASTER UNDERTAKER.
DID HE JUST...CALL THAT ELF BOY... *MALEKITH?*
EH, I SUPPOSE HE DID. WHO GIVES A DWARF FART WHAT HIS NAME IS? HE'S JUST SOME DARK ELF WAR SLAVE. HE'LL LIKELY BE DEAD BEFORE THE DAY'S OUT.
NO.
NO, HE WON'T.
HE'LL LIVE. A LIFE OF HORROR AND HARDSHIP. ONE THAT WILL LEAVE HIM FRIGHTFULLY STRONG AND IRREPARABLY SCARRED.
AND FOREVER *ACCURSED*.
AND THROUGH IT ALL, HE WILL NEVER LOSE THE TASTE FOR THE SICKLY, ROTTEN FRUITS HE WAS FORCED TO FEAST UPON AS A CHILD.
THE FRUITS OF WAR.
A WAR I STARTED.
BY ALL THE GODS... IT'S *MY* FAULT.
I CREATED MALEKITH.
I'M RESPONSIBLE FOR THE WAR OF THE REALMS.

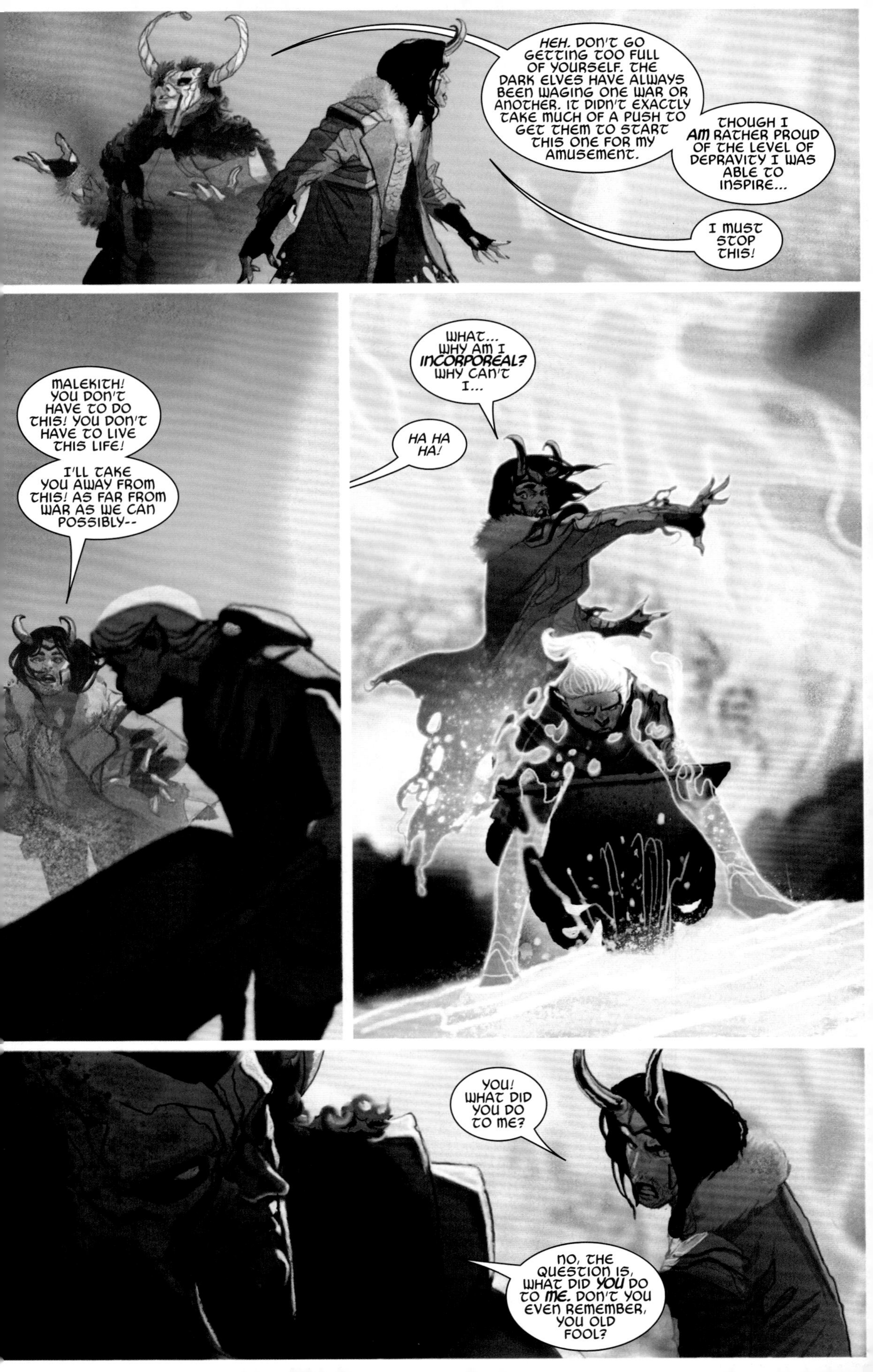
HEH. DON'T GO GETTING TOO FULL OF YOURSELF. THE DARK ELVES HAVE ALWAYS BEEN WAGING ONE WAR OR ANOTHER. IT DIDN'T EXACTLY TAKE MUCH OF A PUSH TO GET THEM TO START THIS ONE FOR MY AMUSEMENT.
THOUGH I AM RATHER PROUD OF THE LEVEL OF DEPRAVITY I WAS ABLE TO INSPIRE...
I MUST STOP THIS!
MALEKITH! YOU DON'T HAVE TO DO THIS! YOU DON'T HAVE TO LIVE THIS LIFE!
I'LL TAKE YOU AWAY FROM THIS! AS FAR FROM WAR AS WE CAN POSSIBLY--
WHAT... WHY AM I INCORPOREAL? WHY CAN'T I...
HA HA HA!
YOU! WHAT DID YOU DO TO ME?
NO, THE QUESTION IS, WHAT DID YOU DO TO ME. DON'T YOU EVEN REMEMBER, YOU OLD FOOL?

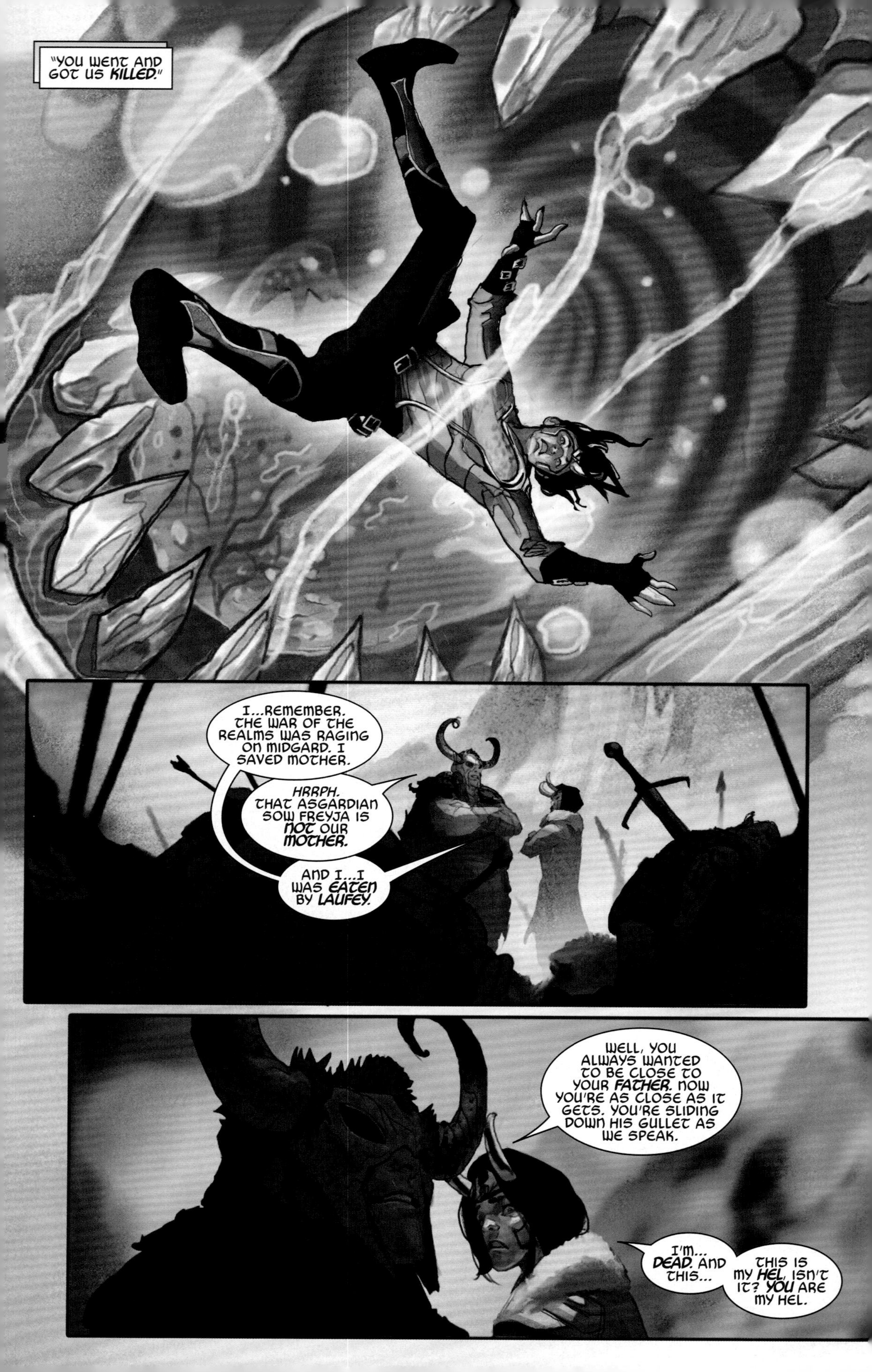
"YOU WENT AND GOT US KILLED."
I...REMEMBER. THE WAR OF THE REALMS WAS RAGING ON MIDGARD. I SAVED MOTHER.
HRRPH. THAT ASGARDIAN SOW FREYJA IS NOT OUR MOTHER.
AND I...I WAS EATEN BY LAUFEY.
WELL, YOU ALWAYS WANTED TO BE CLOSE TO YOUR FATHER. NOW YOU'RE AS CLOSE AS IT GETS. YOU'RE SLIDING DOWN HIS GULLET AS WE SPEAK.
I'M... DEAD. AND THIS...
THIS IS MY HEL, ISN'T IT? YOU ARE MY HEL.

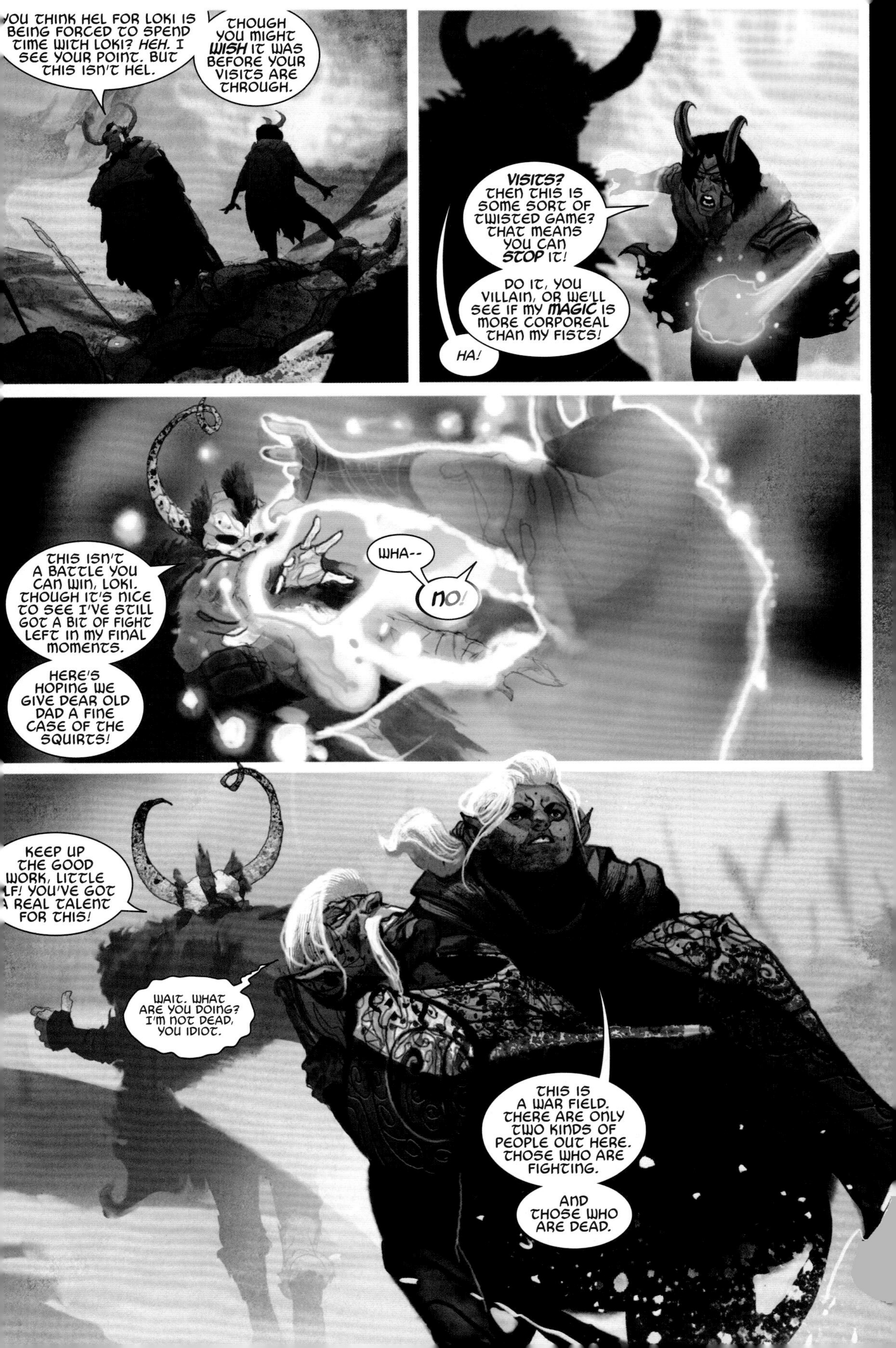
YOU THINK HEL FOR LOKI IS BEING FORCED TO SPEND TIME WITH LOKI? HEH. I SEE YOUR POINT. BUT THIS ISN'T HEL.
THOUGH YOU MIGHT WISH IT WAS BEFORE YOUR VISITS ARE THROUGH.
VISITS? THEN THIS IS SOME SORT OF TWISTED GAME? THAT MEANS YOU CAN STOP IT!
DO IT, YOU VILLAIN, OR WE'LL SEE IF MY MAGIC IS MORE CORPOREAL THAN MY FISTS!
HA!
THIS ISN'T A BATTLE YOU CAN WIN, LOKI. THOUGH IT'S NICE TO SEE I'VE STILL GOT A BIT OF FIGHT LEFT IN MY FINAL MOMENTS.
HERE'S HOPING WE GIVE DEAR OLD DAD A FINE CASE OF THE SQUIRTS!
WHA--
NO!
KEEP UP THE GOOD WORK, LITTLE LF! YOU'VE GOT REAL TALENT FOR THIS!
WAIT. WHAT ARE YOU DOING? I'M NOT DEAD, YOU IDIOT.
THIS IS A WAR FIELD. THERE ARE ONLY TWO KINDS OF PEOPLE OUT HERE. THOSE WHO ARE FIGHTING.
AND THOSE WHO ARE DEAD.

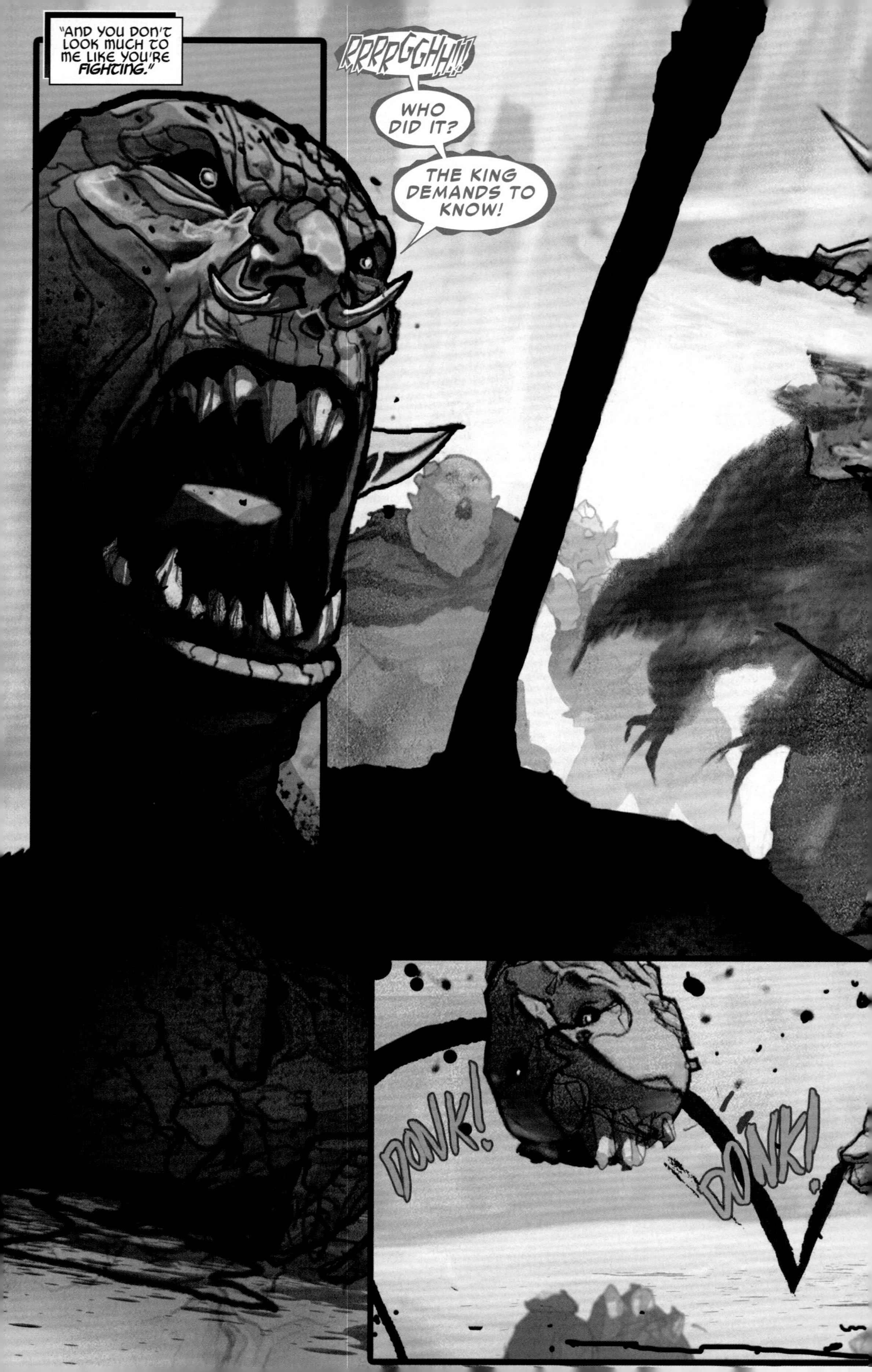
"AND YOU DON'T LOOK MUCH TO ME LIKE YOU'RE FIGHTING."
RRRRGGHH!!!
WHO DID IT?
THE KING DEMANDS TO KNOW!
DONK!
DONK!

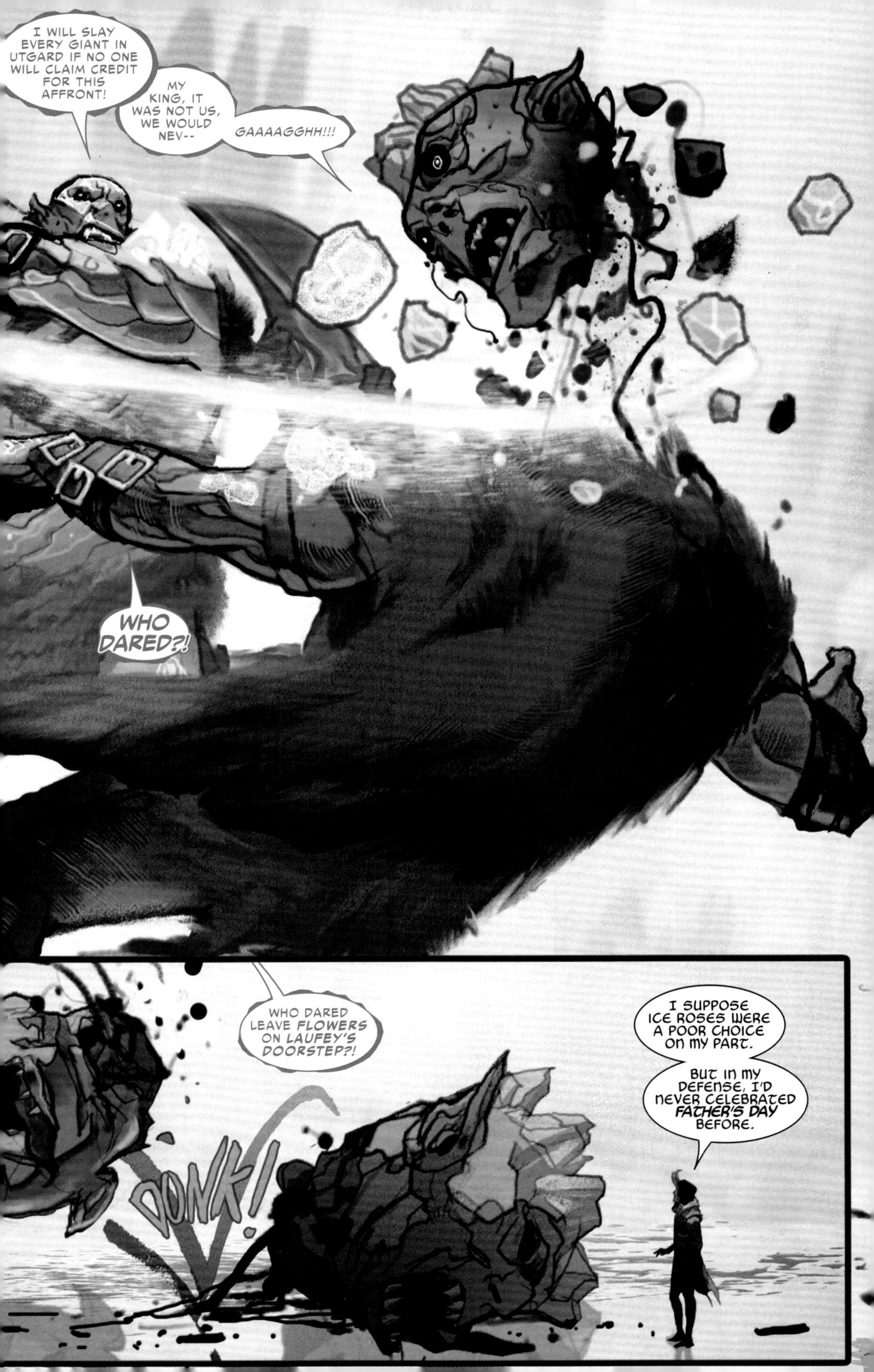
I WILL SLAY EVERY GIANT IN UTGARD IF NO ONE WILL CLAIM CREDIT FOR THIS AFFRONT!
MY KING, IT WAS NOT US, WE WOULD NEV--
GAAAAGGHH!!!
WHO DARED?!
WHO DARED LEAVE FLOWERS ON LAUFEY'S DOORSTEP?!
DONK!
I SUPPOSE ICE ROSES WERE A POOR CHOICE ON MY PART.
BUT IN MY DEFENSE, I'D NEVER CELEBRATED FATHER'S DAY BEFORE.

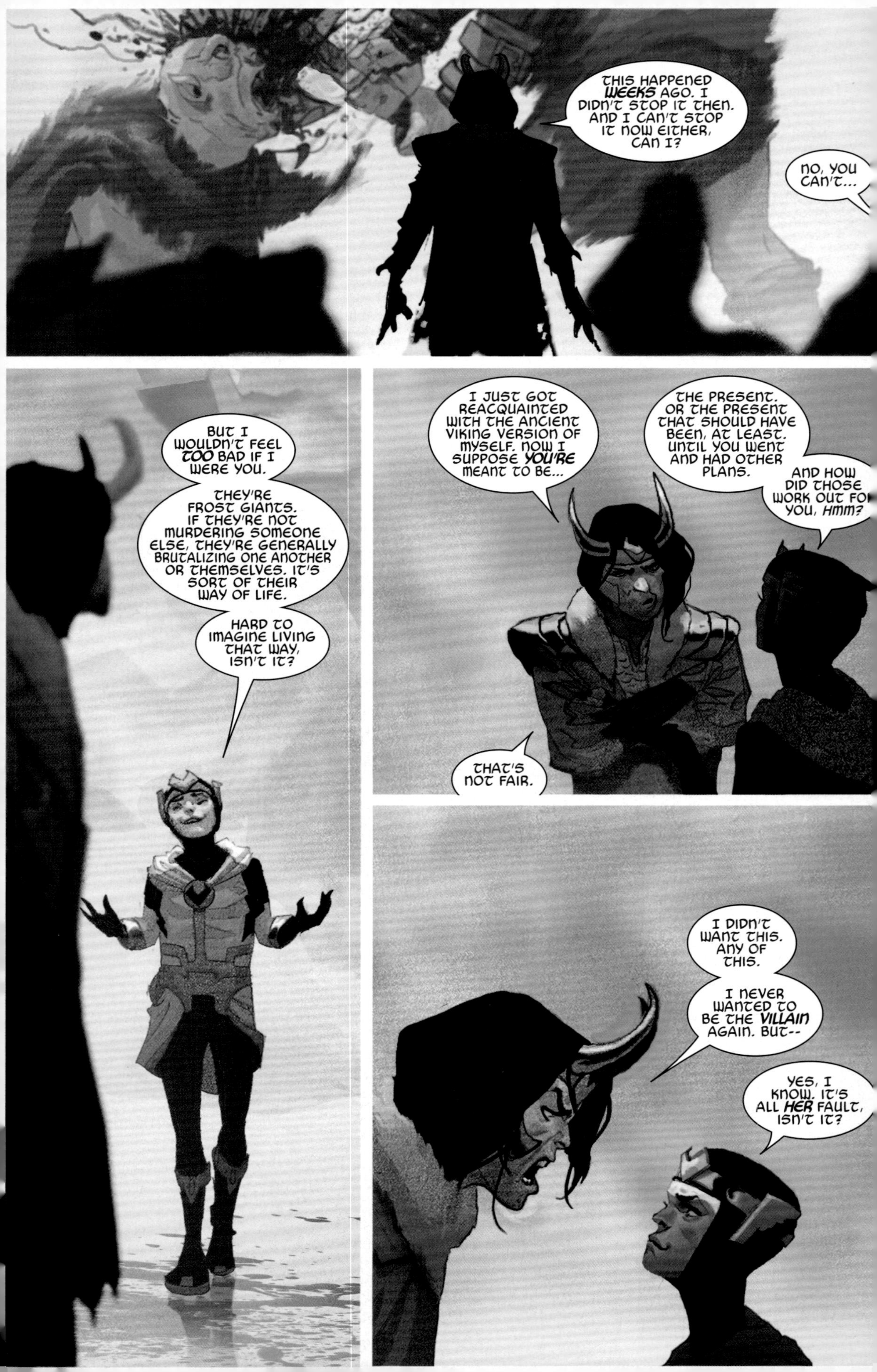
THIS HAPPENED WEEKS AGO. I DIDN'T STOP IT THEN. AND I CAN'T STOP IT NOW EITHER, CAN I?
NO, YOU CAN'T...
BUT I WOULDN'T FEEL TOO BAD IF I WERE YOU.
THEY'RE FROST GIANTS. IF THEY'RE NOT MURDERING SOMEONE ELSE, THEY'RE GENERALLY BRUTALIZING ONE ANOTHER OR THEMSELVES. IT'S SORT OF THEIR WAY OF LIFE.
HARD TO IMAGINE LIVING THAT WAY, ISN'T IT?
I JUST GOT REACQUAINTED WITH THE ANCIENT VIKING VERSION OF MYSELF. NOW I SUPPOSE YOU'RE MEANT TO BE...
THE PRESENT. OR THE PRESENT THAT SHOULD HAVE BEEN, AT LEAST. UNTIL YOU WENT AND HAD OTHER PLANS.
AND HOW DID THOSE WORK OUT FO YOU, HMM?
THAT'S NOT FAIR.
I DIDN'T WANT THIS. ANY OF THIS.
I NEVER WANTED TO BE THE VILLAIN AGAIN. BUT--
YES, I KNOW. IT'S ALL HER FAULT, ISN'T IT?

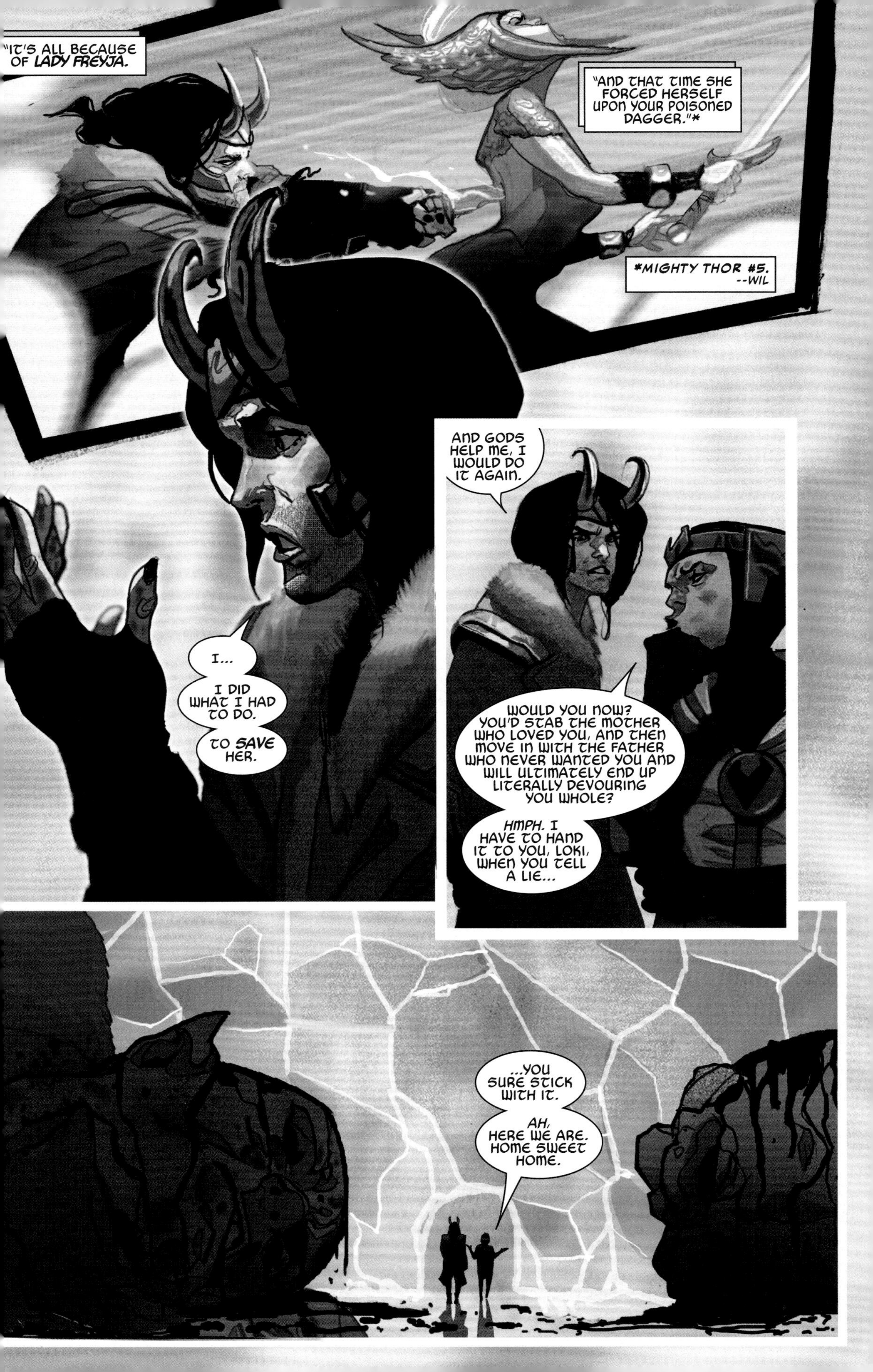
"IT'S ALL BECAUSE OF LADY FREYJA.
"AND THAT TIME SHE FORCED HERSELF UPON YOUR POISONED DAGGER."*
*MIGHTY THOR #5. --WIL
I...
I DID WHAT I HAD TO DO.
TO SAVE HER.
AND GODS HELP ME, I WOULD DO IT AGAIN.
WOULD YOU NOW? YOU'D STAB THE MOTHER WHO LOVED YOU, AND THEN MOVE IN WITH THE FATHER WHO NEVER WANTED YOU AND WILL ULTIMATELY END UP LITERALLY DEVOURING YOU WHOLE?
HMPH. I HAVE TO HAND IT TO YOU, LOKI, WHEN YOU TELL A LIE...
...YOU SURE STICK WITH IT.
AH, HERE WE ARE. HOME SWEET HOME.

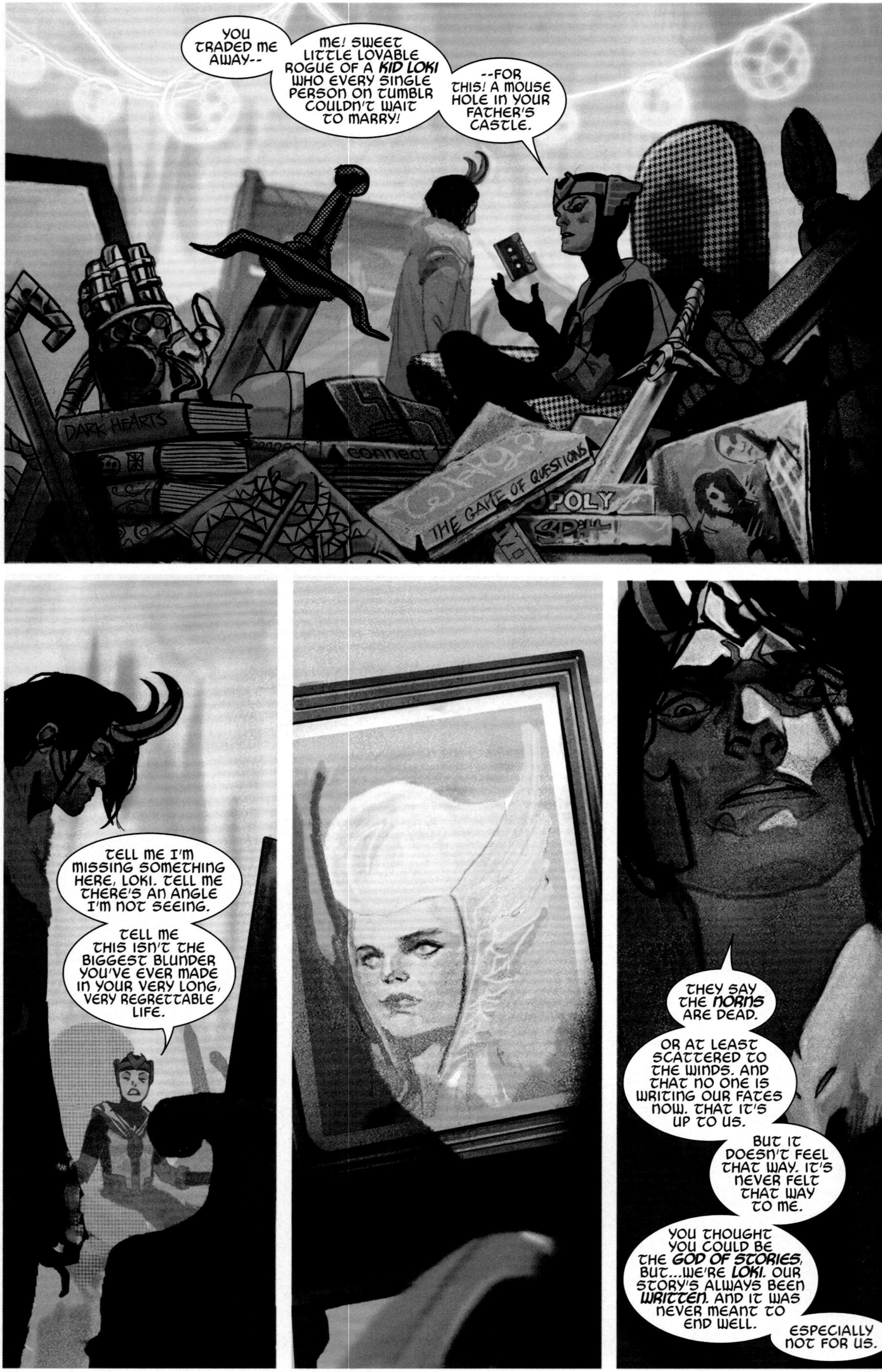
YOU TRADED ME AWAY--
ME! SWEET LITTLE LOVABLE ROGUE OF A KID LOKI WHO EVERY SINGLE PERSON ON TUMBLR COULDN'T WAIT TO MARRY!
--FOR THIS! A MOUSE HOLE IN YOUR FATHER'S CASTLE.
DARK HEARTS
connect
THE GAME OF QUESTIONS
POLY
TELL ME I'M MISSING SOMETHING HERE, LOKI. TELL ME THERE'S AN ANGLE I'M NOT SEEING.
TELL ME THIS ISN'T THE BIGGEST BLUNDER YOU'VE EVER MADE IN YOUR VERY LONG, VERY REGRETTABLE LIFE.
THEY SAY THE NORNS ARE DEAD.
OR AT LEAST SCATTERED TO THE WINDS. AND THAT NO ONE IS WRITING OUR FATES NOW. THAT IT'S UP TO US.
BUT IT DOESN'T FEEL THAT WAY. IT'S NEVER FELT THAT WAY TO ME.
YOU THOUGHT YOU COULD BE THE GOD OF STORIES, BUT...WE'RE LOKI. OUR STORY'S ALWAYS BEEN WRITTEN. AND IT WAS NEVER MEANT TO END WELL.
ESPECIALLY NOT FOR US.

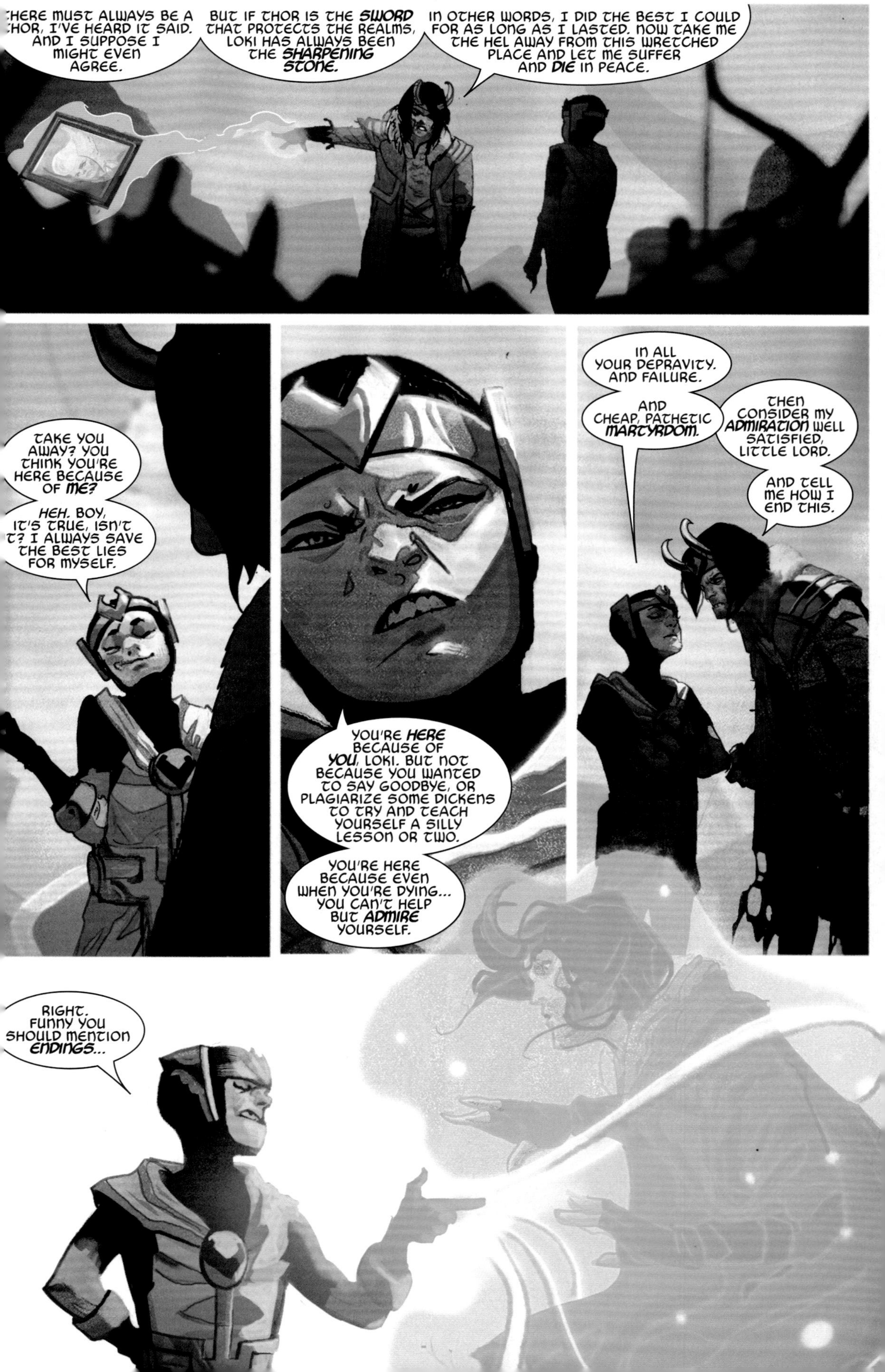
THERE MUST ALWAYS BE A THOR, I'VE HEARD IT SAID. AND I SUPPOSE I MIGHT EVEN AGREE.
BUT IF THOR IS THE SWORD THAT PROTECTS THE REALMS, LOKI HAS ALWAYS BEEN THE SHARPENING STONE.
IN OTHER WORDS, I DID THE BEST I COULD FOR AS LONG AS I LASTED. NOW TAKE ME THE HEL AWAY FROM THIS WRETCHED PLACE AND LET ME SUFFER AND DIE IN PEACE.
TAKE YOU AWAY? YOU THINK YOU'RE HERE BECAUSE OF ME?
HEH. BOY, IT'S TRUE, ISN'T IT? I ALWAYS SAVE THE BEST LIES FOR MYSELF.
YOU'RE HERE BECAUSE OF YOU, LOKI. BUT NOT BECAUSE YOU WANTED TO SAY GOODBYE, OR PLAGIARIZE SOME DICKENS TO TRY AND TEACH YOURSELF A SILLY LESSON OR TWO.
YOU'RE HERE BECAUSE EVEN WHEN YOU'RE DYING... YOU CAN'T HELP BUT ADMIRE YOURSELF.
IN ALL YOUR DEPRAVITY. AND FAILURE.
AND CHEAP, PATHETIC MARTYRDOM.
THEN CONSIDER MY ADMIRATION WELL SATISFIED, LITTLE LORD.
AND TELL ME HOW I END THIS.
RIGHT. FUNNY YOU SHOULD MENTION ENDINGS...

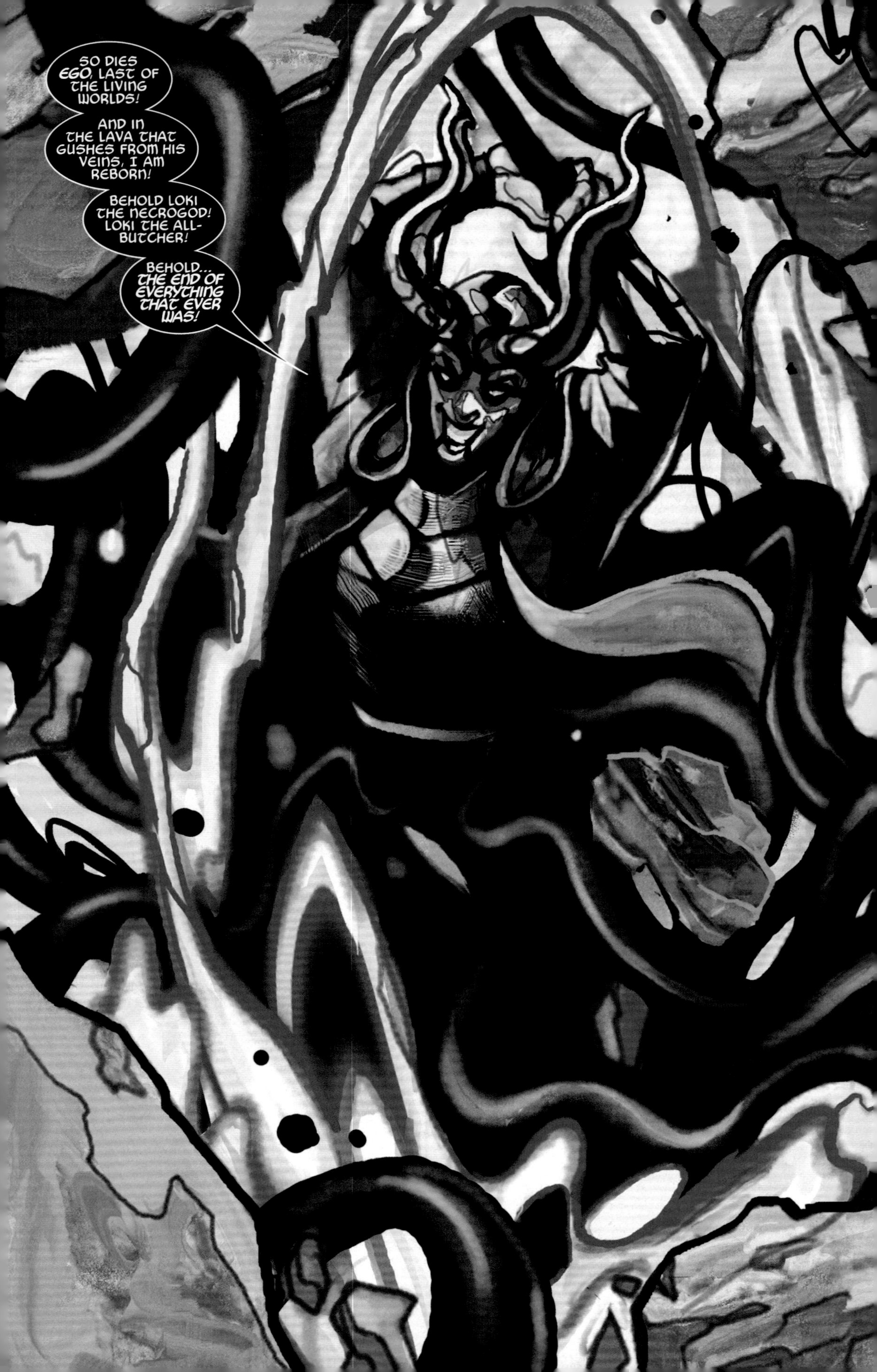
SO DIES EGO, LAST OF THE LIVING WORLDS!
AND IN THE LAVA THAT GUSHES FROM HIS VEINS, I AM REBORN!
BEHOLD LOKI THE NECROGOD! LOKI THE ALL-BUTCHER!
BEHOLD... THE END OF EVERYTHING THAT EVER WAS!

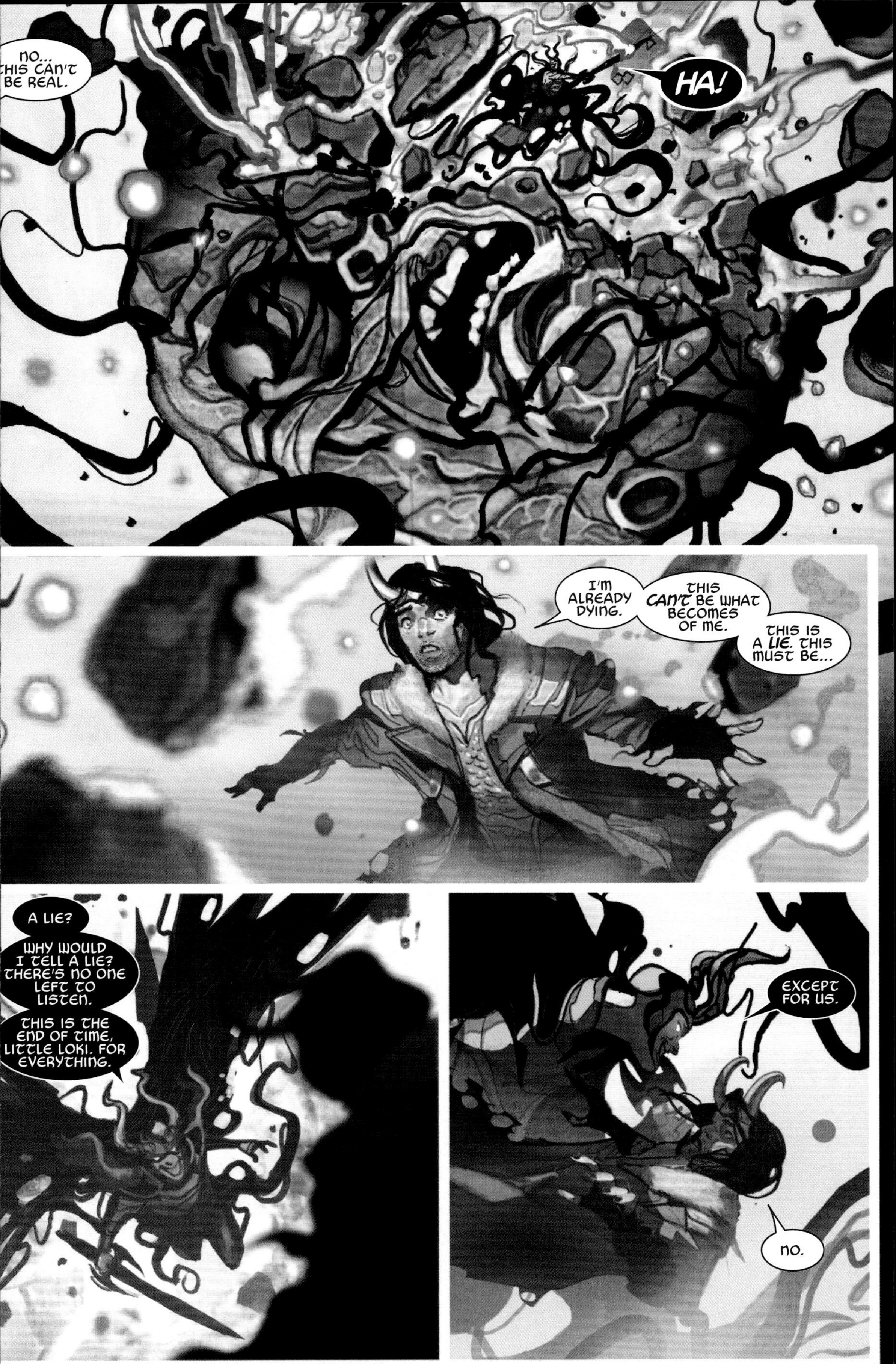

NO... THIS CAN'T BE REAL.
HA!
I'M ALREADY DYING.
THIS CAN'T BE WHAT BECOMES OF ME.
THIS IS A LIE. THIS MUST BE...
A LIE?
WHY WOULD I TELL A LIE? THERE'S NO ONE LEFT TO LISTEN.
THIS IS THE END OF TIME, LITTLE LOKI. FOR EVERYTHING.
EXCEPT FOR US.
NO.

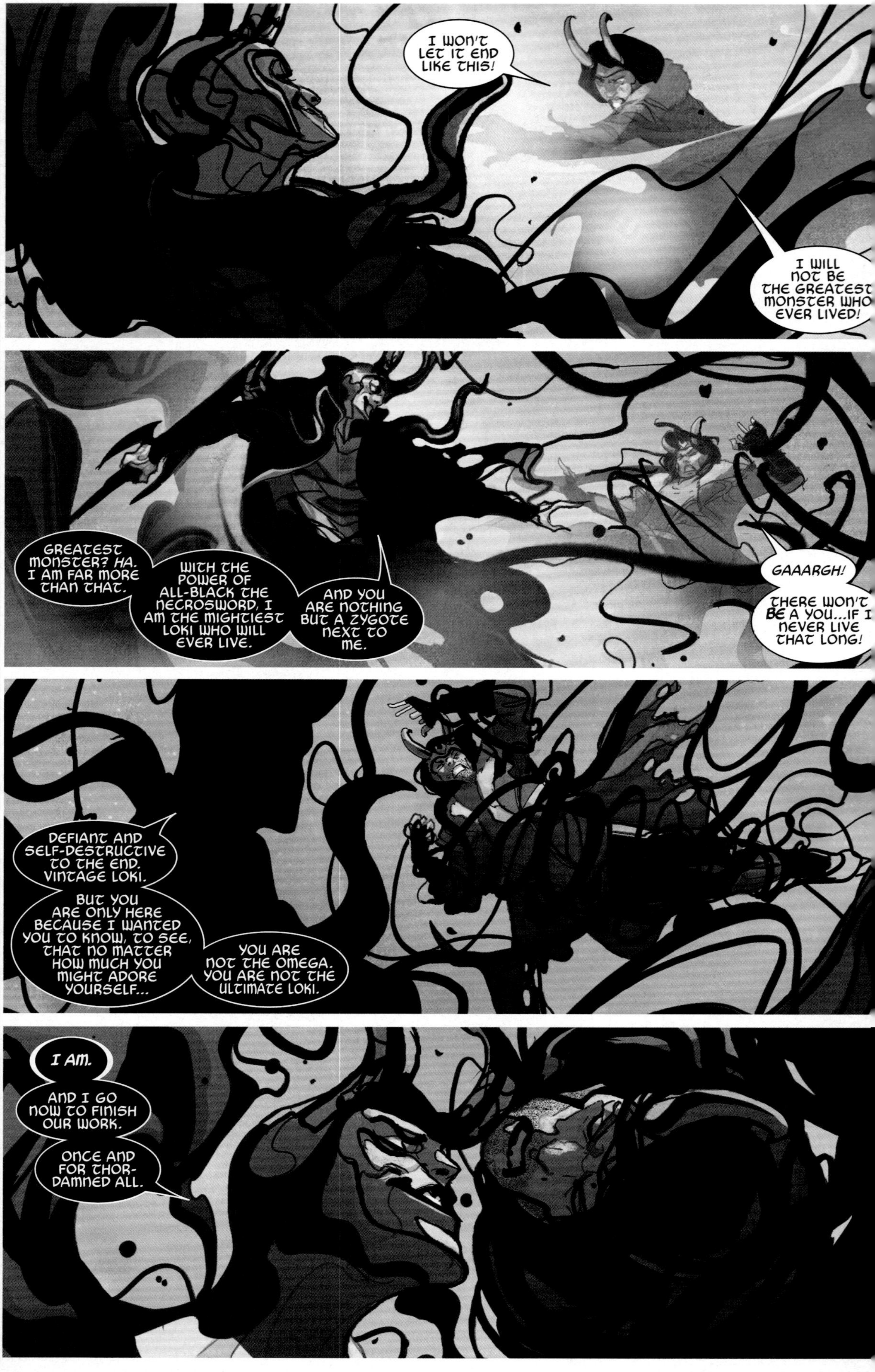
I WON'T LET IT END LIKE THIS!
I WILL NOT BE THE GREATEST MONSTER WHO EVER LIVED!
GREATEST MONSTER? HA. I AM FAR MORE THAN THAT.
WITH THE POWER OF ALL-BLACK THE NECROSWORD, I AM THE MIGHTIEST LOKI WHO WILL EVER LIVE.
AND YOU ARE NOTHING BUT A ZYGOTE NEXT TO ME.
GAAARGH!
THERE WON'T BE A YOU...IF I NEVER LIVE THAT LONG!
DEFIANT AND SELF-DESTRUCTIVE TO THE END. VINTAGE LOKI.
BUT YOU ARE ONLY HERE BECAUSE I WANTED YOU TO KNOW, TO SEE, THAT NO MATTER HOW MUCH YOU MIGHT ADORE YOURSELF...
YOU ARE NOT THE OMEGA. YOU ARE NOT THE ULTIMATE LOKI.
I AM.
AND I GO NOW TO FINISH OUR WORK.
ONCE AND FOR THOR-DAMNED ALL.

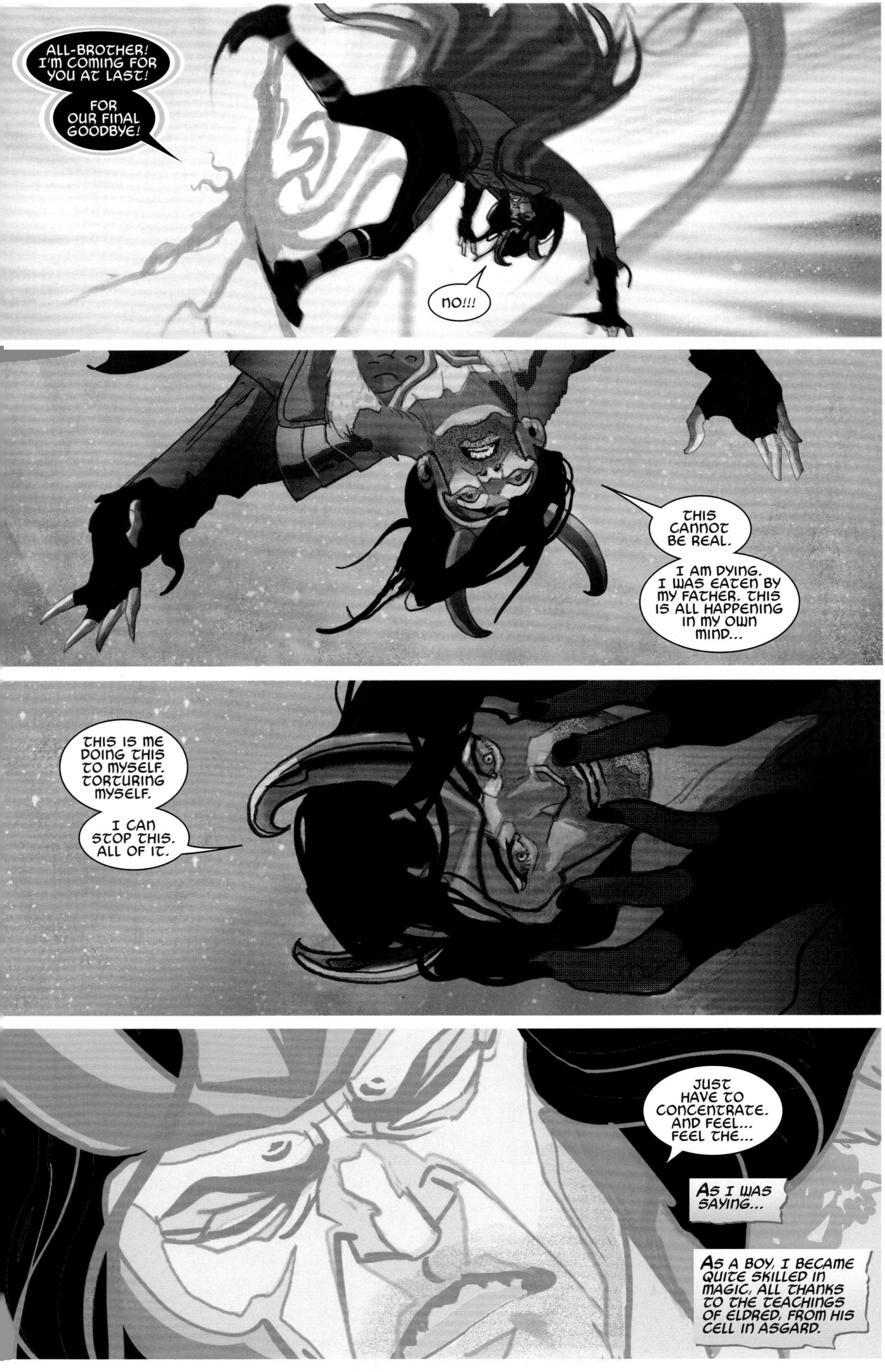
ALL-BROTHER! I'M COMING FOR YOU AT LAST!
FOR OUR FINAL GOODBYE!
NO!!!
THIS CANNOT BE REAL.
I AM DYING. I WAS EATEN BY MY FATHER. THIS IS ALL HAPPENING IN MY OWN MIND...
THIS IS ME DOING THIS TO MYSELF. TORTURING MYSELF.
I CAN STOP THIS. ALL OF IT.
JUST HAVE TO CONCENTRATE. AND FEEL... FEEL THE...
AS I WAS SAYING...
AS A BOY, I BECAME QUITE SKILLED IN MAGIC, ALL THANKS TO THE TEACHINGS OF ELDRED, FROM HIS CELL IN ASGARD.

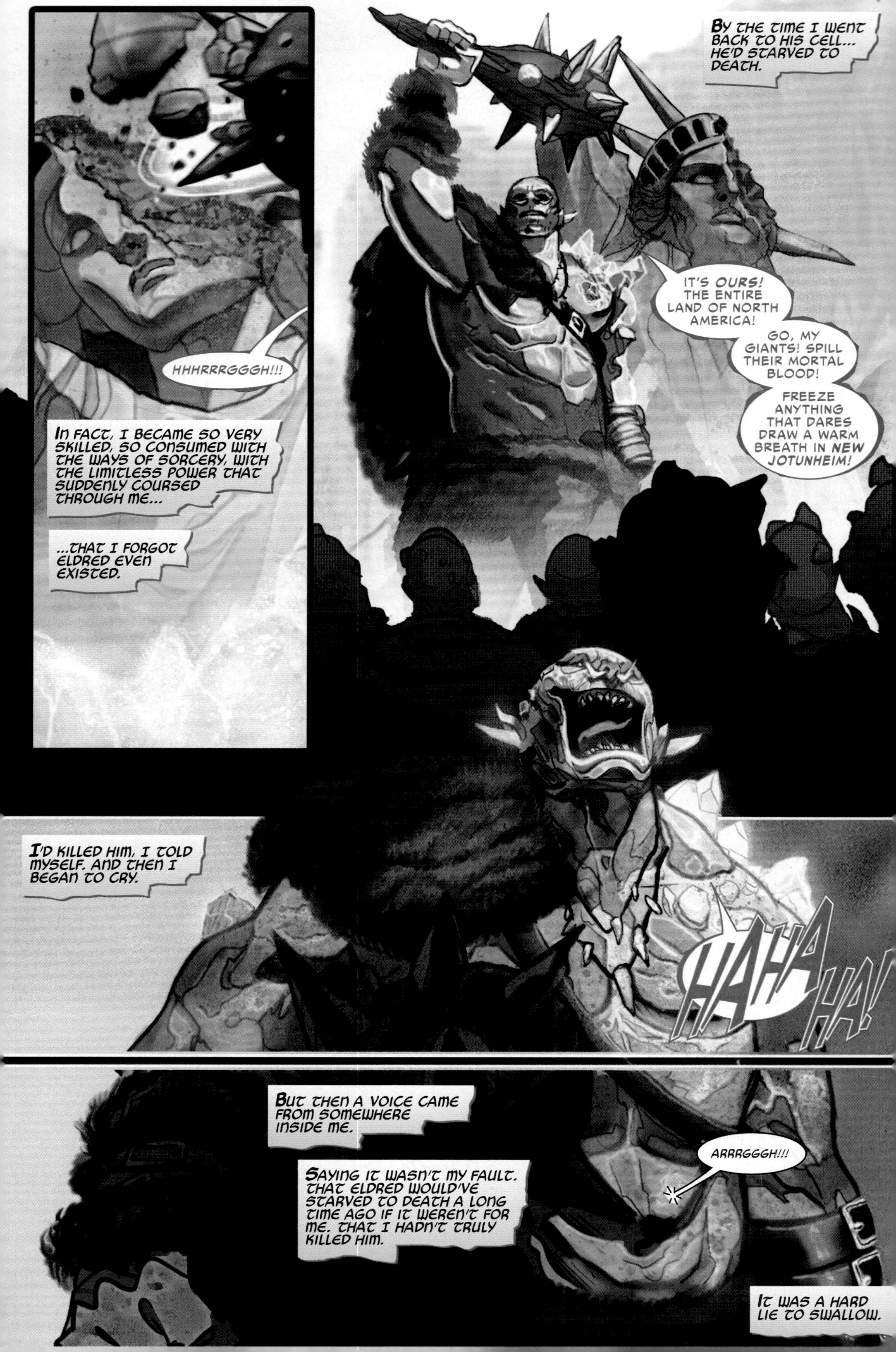
HHHRRRGGGH!!!
In fact, I became so very skilled, so consumed with the ways of sorcery, with the limitless power that suddenly coursed through me...
...that I forgot Eldred even existed.
By the time I went back to his cell... he'd starved to death.
IT'S OURS! THE ENTIRE LAND OF NORTH AMERICA!
GO, MY GIANTS! SPILL THEIR MORTAL BLOOD!
FREEZE ANYTHING THAT DARES DRAW A WARM BREATH IN NEW JOTUNHEIM!
I'd killed him, I told myself. And then I began to cry.
HAHAHA!
But then a voice came from somewhere inside me.
Saying it wasn't my fault. That Eldred would've starved to death a long time ago if it weren't for me. That I hadn't truly killed him.
ARRRGGGH!!!
It was a hard lie to swallow.

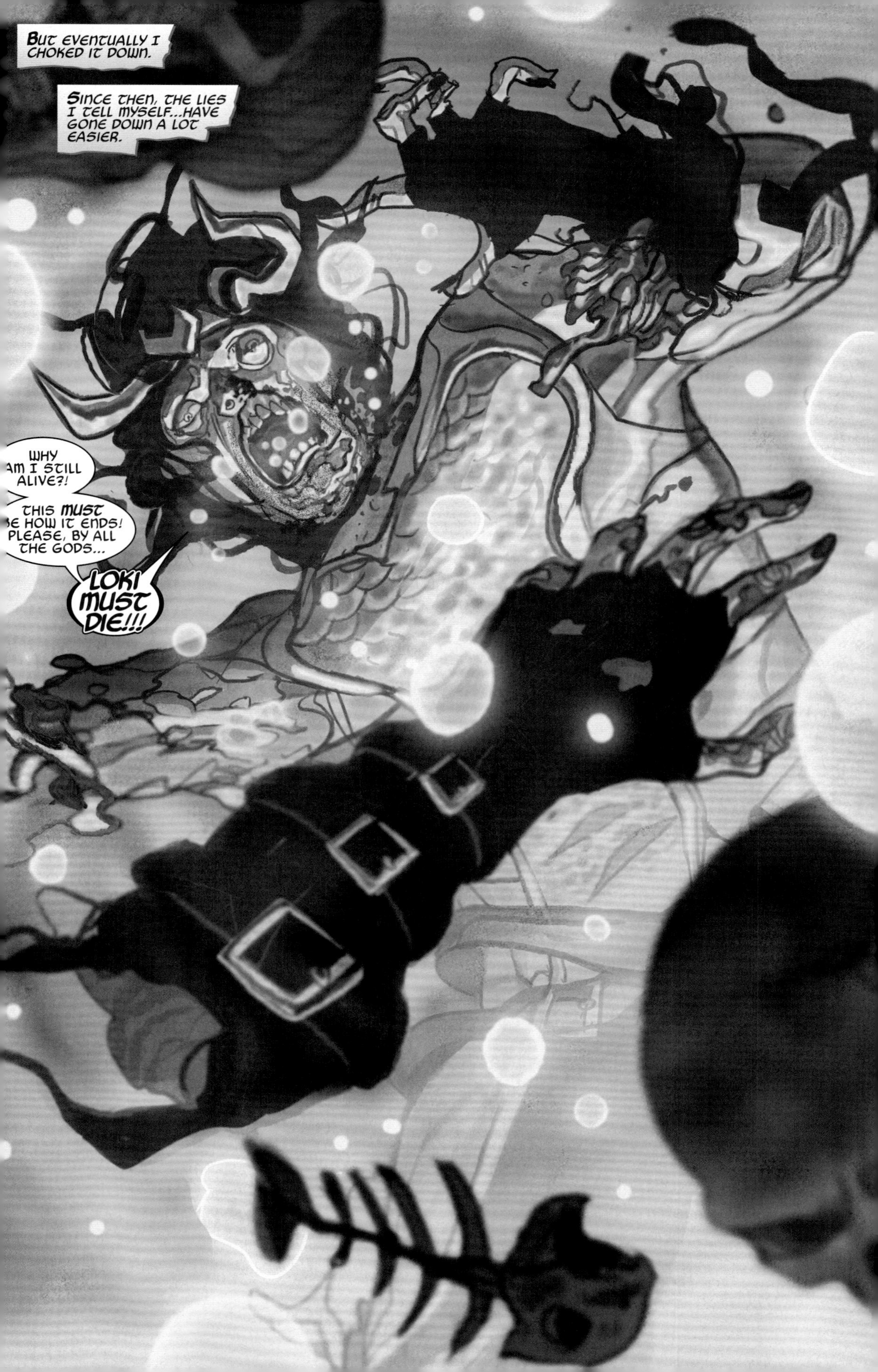
BUT EVENTUALLY I CHOKED IT DOWN.
SINCE THEN, THE LIES I TELL MYSELF...HAVE GONE DOWN A LOT EASIER.
WHY AM I STILL ALIVE?!
THIS MUST BE HOW IT ENDS! PLEASE, BY ALL THE GODS...
LOKI MUST DIE!!!

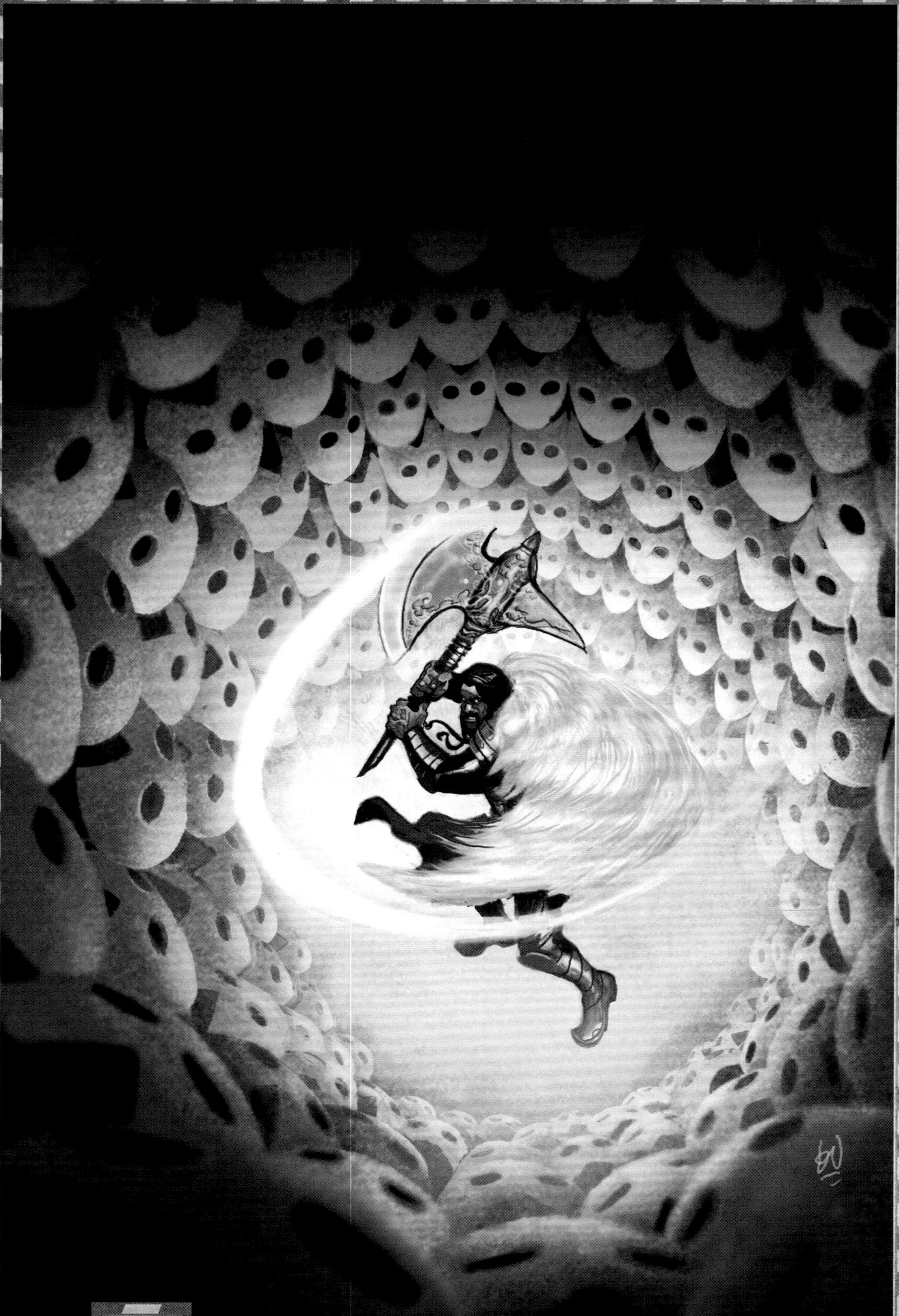

13

"THE BALLAD OF CUL BORSON, GOD OF FEAR"

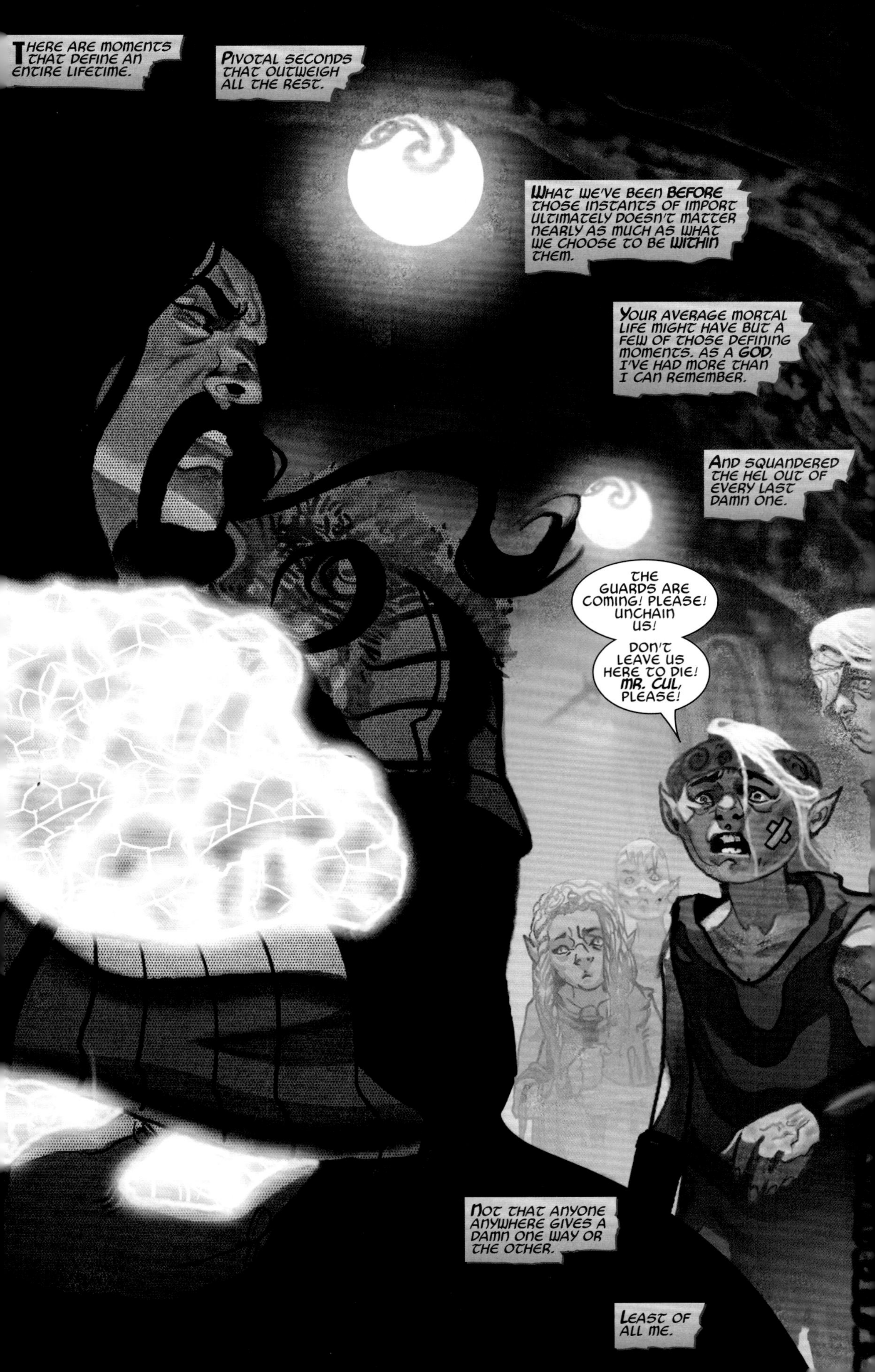
THERE ARE MOMENTS THAT DEFINE AN ENTIRE LIFETIME.
PIVOTAL SECONDS THAT OUTWEIGH ALL THE REST.
WHAT WE'VE BEEN BEFORE THOSE INSTANTS OF IMPORT ULTIMATELY DOESN'T MATTER NEARLY AS MUCH AS WHAT WE CHOOSE TO BE WITHIN THEM.
YOUR AVERAGE MORTAL LIFE MIGHT HAVE BUT A FEW OF THOSE DEFINING MOMENTS. AS A GOD, I'VE HAD MORE THAN I CAN REMEMBER.
AND SQUANDERED THE HEL OUT OF EVERY LAST DAMN ONE.
THE GUARDS ARE COMING! PLEASE! UNCHAIN US!
DON'T LEAVE US HERE TO DIE! MR. CUL, PLEASE!
NOT THAT ANYONE ANYWHERE GIVES A DAMN ONE WAY OR THE OTHER.
LEAST OF ALL ME.

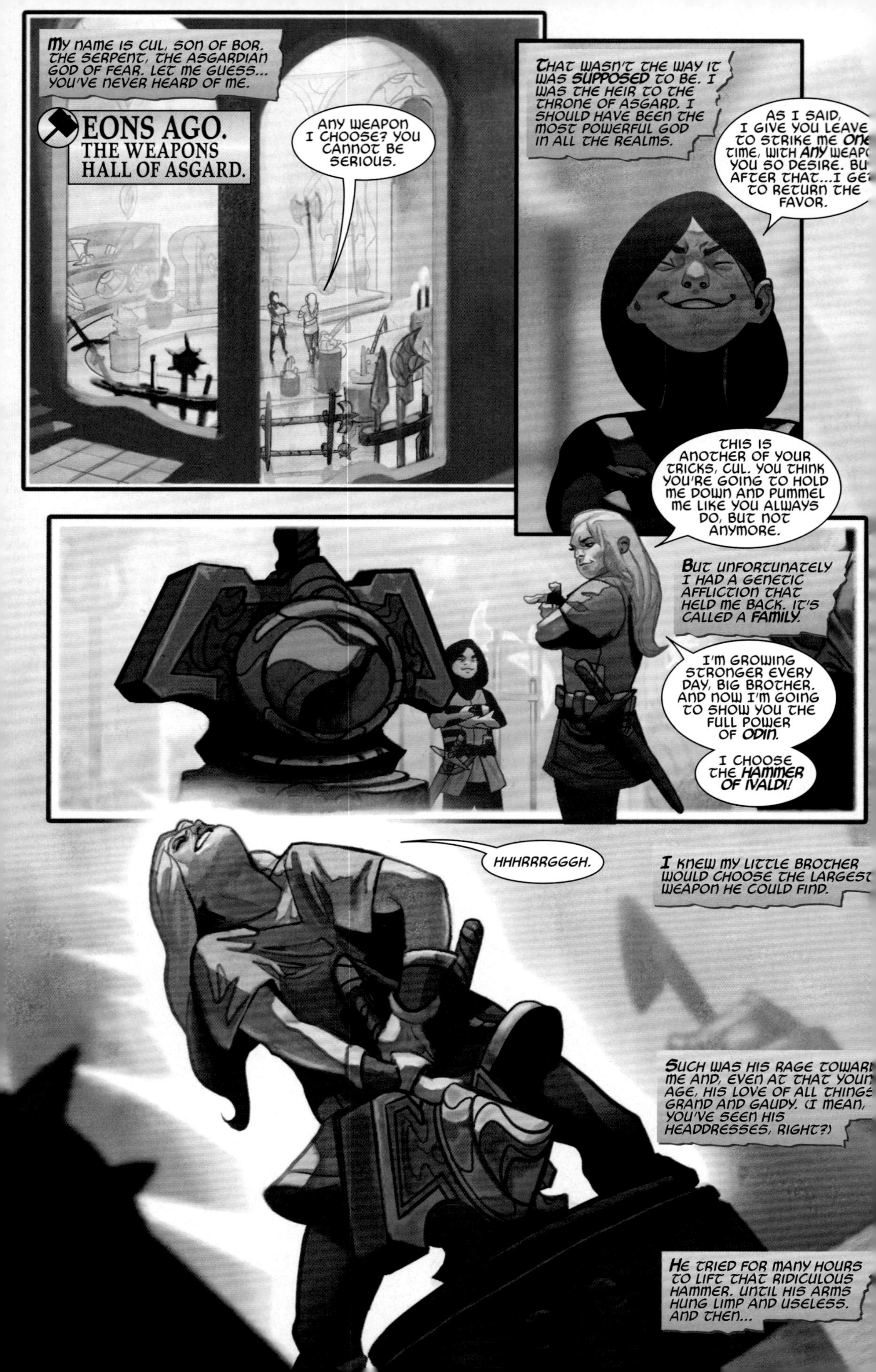

MY NAME IS CUL, SON OF BOR. THE SERPENT, THE ASGARDIAN GOD OF FEAR. LET ME GUESS... YOU'VE NEVER HEARD OF ME.
EONS AGO. THE WEAPONS HALL OF ASGARD.
ANY WEAPON I CHOOSE? YOU CANNOT BE SERIOUS.
THAT WASN'T THE WAY IT WAS SUPPOSED TO BE. I WAS THE HEIR TO THE THRONE OF ASGARD. I SHOULD HAVE BEEN THE MOST POWERFUL GOD IN ALL THE REALMS.
AS I SAID, I GIVE YOU LEAVE TO STRIKE ME ONE TIME, WITH ANY WEAPON YOU SO DESIRE. BUT AFTER THAT...I GET TO RETURN THE FAVOR.
THIS IS ANOTHER OF YOUR TRICKS, CUL. YOU THINK YOU'RE GOING TO HOLD ME DOWN AND PUMMEL ME LIKE YOU ALWAYS DO, BUT NOT ANYMORE.
BUT UNFORTUNATELY I HAD A GENETIC AFFLICTION THAT HELD ME BACK. IT'S CALLED A FAMILY.
I'M GROWING STRONGER EVERY DAY, BIG BROTHER. AND NOW I'M GOING TO SHOW YOU THE FULL POWER OF ODIN.
I CHOOSE THE HAMMER OF IVALDI!
HHHRRRGGGH.
I KNEW MY LITTLE BROTHER WOULD CHOOSE THE LARGEST WEAPON HE COULD FIND.
SUCH WAS HIS RAGE TOWARD ME AND, EVEN AT THAT YOUNG AGE, HIS LOVE OF ALL THINGS GRAND AND GAUDY. (I MEAN, YOU'VE SEEN HIS HEADDRESSES, RIGHT?)
HE TRIED FOR MANY HOURS TO LIFT THAT RIDICULOUS HAMMER. UNTIL HIS ARMS HUNG LIMP AND USELESS. AND THEN...

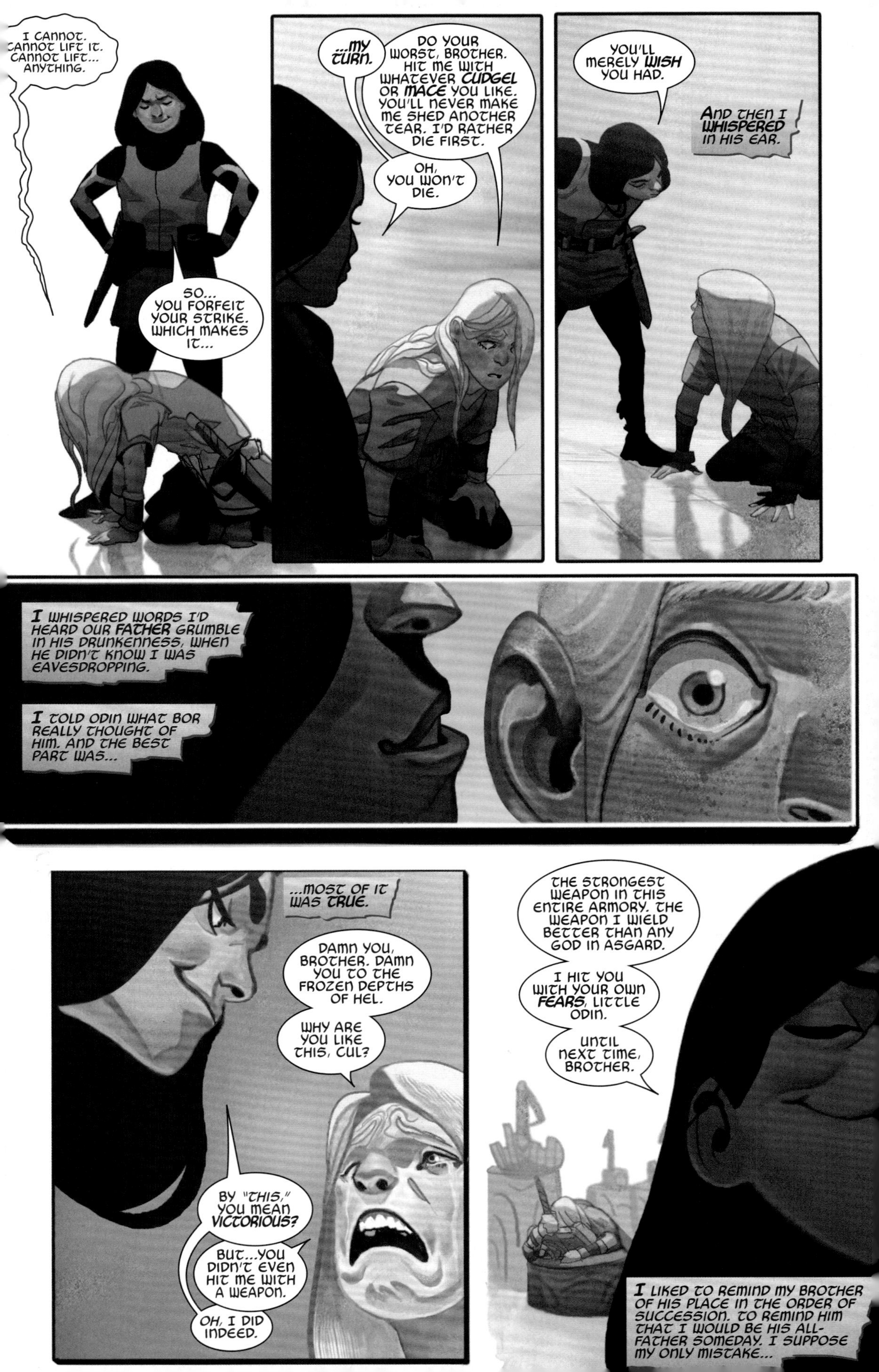
I CANNOT. CANNOT LIFT IT. CANNOT LIFT... ANYTHING.
SO... YOU FORFEIT YOUR STRIKE. WHICH MAKES IT...
...MY TURN.
DO YOUR WORST, BROTHER. HIT ME WITH WHATEVER CUDGEL OR MACE YOU LIKE. YOU'LL NEVER MAKE ME SHED ANOTHER TEAR. I'D RATHER DIE FIRST.
OH, YOU WON'T DIE.
YOU'LL MERELY WISH YOU HAD.
AND THEN I WHISPERED IN HIS EAR.
I WHISPERED WORDS I'D HEARD OUR FATHER GRUMBLE IN HIS DRUNKENNESS, WHEN HE DIDN'T KNOW I WAS EAVESDROPPING.
I TOLD ODIN WHAT BOR REALLY THOUGHT OF HIM. AND THE BEST PART WAS...
...MOST OF IT WAS TRUE.
DAMN YOU, BROTHER. DAMN YOU TO THE FROZEN DEPTHS OF HEL.
WHY ARE YOU LIKE THIS, CUL?
BY "THIS," YOU MEAN VICTORIOUS?
BUT...YOU DIDN'T EVEN HIT ME WITH A WEAPON.
OH, I DID INDEED.
THE STRONGEST WEAPON IN THIS ENTIRE ARMORY. THE WEAPON I WIELD BETTER THAN ANY GOD IN ASGARD.
I HIT YOU WITH YOUR OWN FEARS, LITTLE ODIN.
UNTIL NEXT TIME, BROTHER.
I LIKED TO REMIND MY BROTHER OF HIS PLACE IN THE ORDER OF SUCCESSION. TO REMIND HIM THAT I WOULD BE HIS ALL-FATHER SOMEDAY. I SUPPOSE MY ONLY MISTAKE...

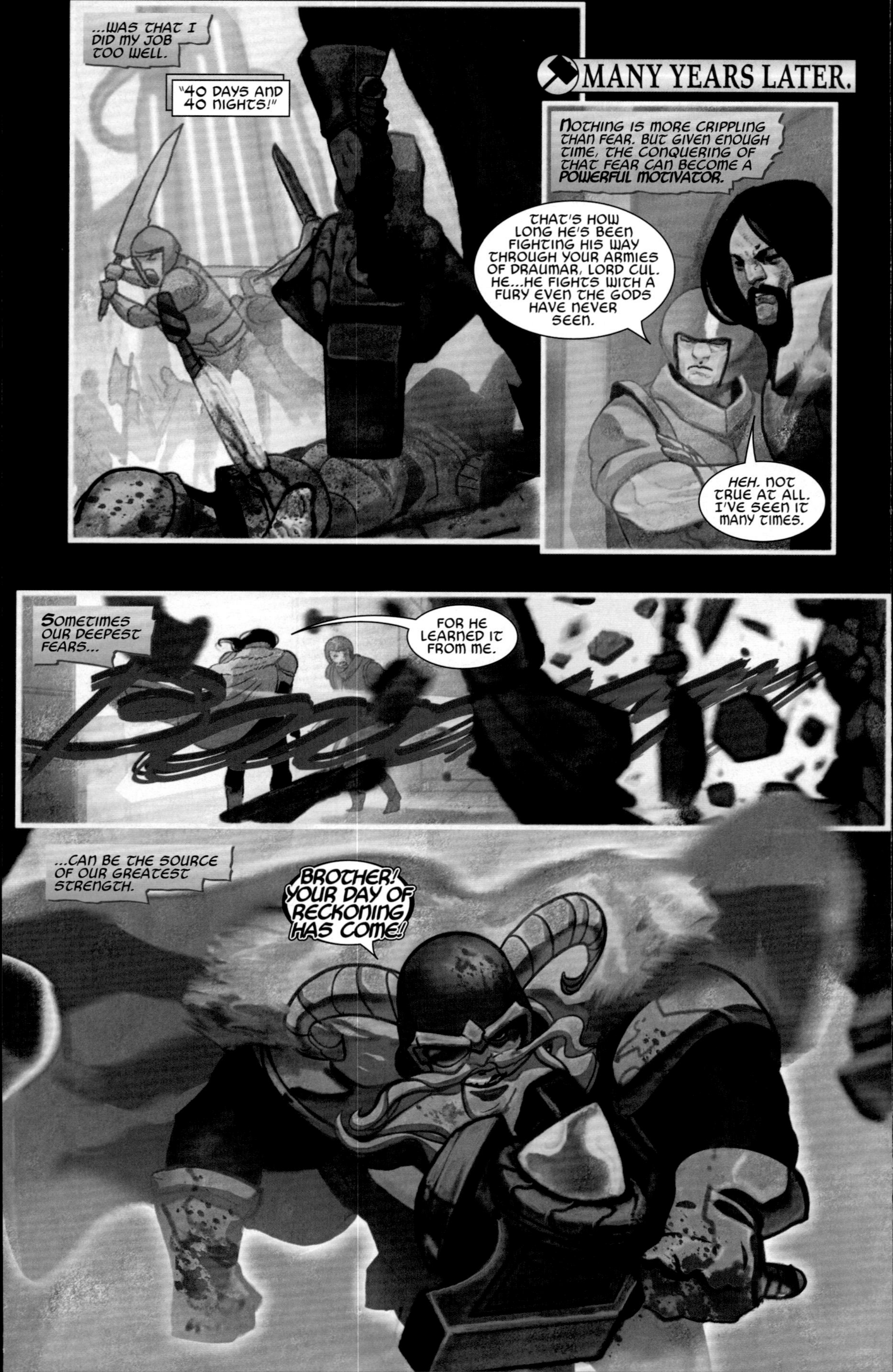
...WAS THAT I DID MY JOB TOO WELL.
"40 DAYS AND 40 NIGHTS!"
MANY YEARS LATER.
NOTHING IS MORE CRIPPLING THAN FEAR. BUT GIVEN ENOUGH TIME, THE CONQUERING OF THAT FEAR CAN BECOME A POWERFUL MOTIVATOR.
THAT'S HOW LONG HE'S BEEN FIGHTING HIS WAY THROUGH YOUR ARMIES OF DRAUMAR, LORD CUL. HE...HE FIGHTS WITH A FURY EVEN THE GODS HAVE NEVER SEEN.
HEH. NOT TRUE AT ALL. I'VE SEEN IT MANY TIMES.
SOMETIMES OUR DEEPEST FEARS...
FOR HE LEARNED IT FROM ME.
...CAN BE THE SOURCE OF OUR GREATEST STRENGTH.
BROTHER! YOUR DAY OF RECKONING HAS COME!

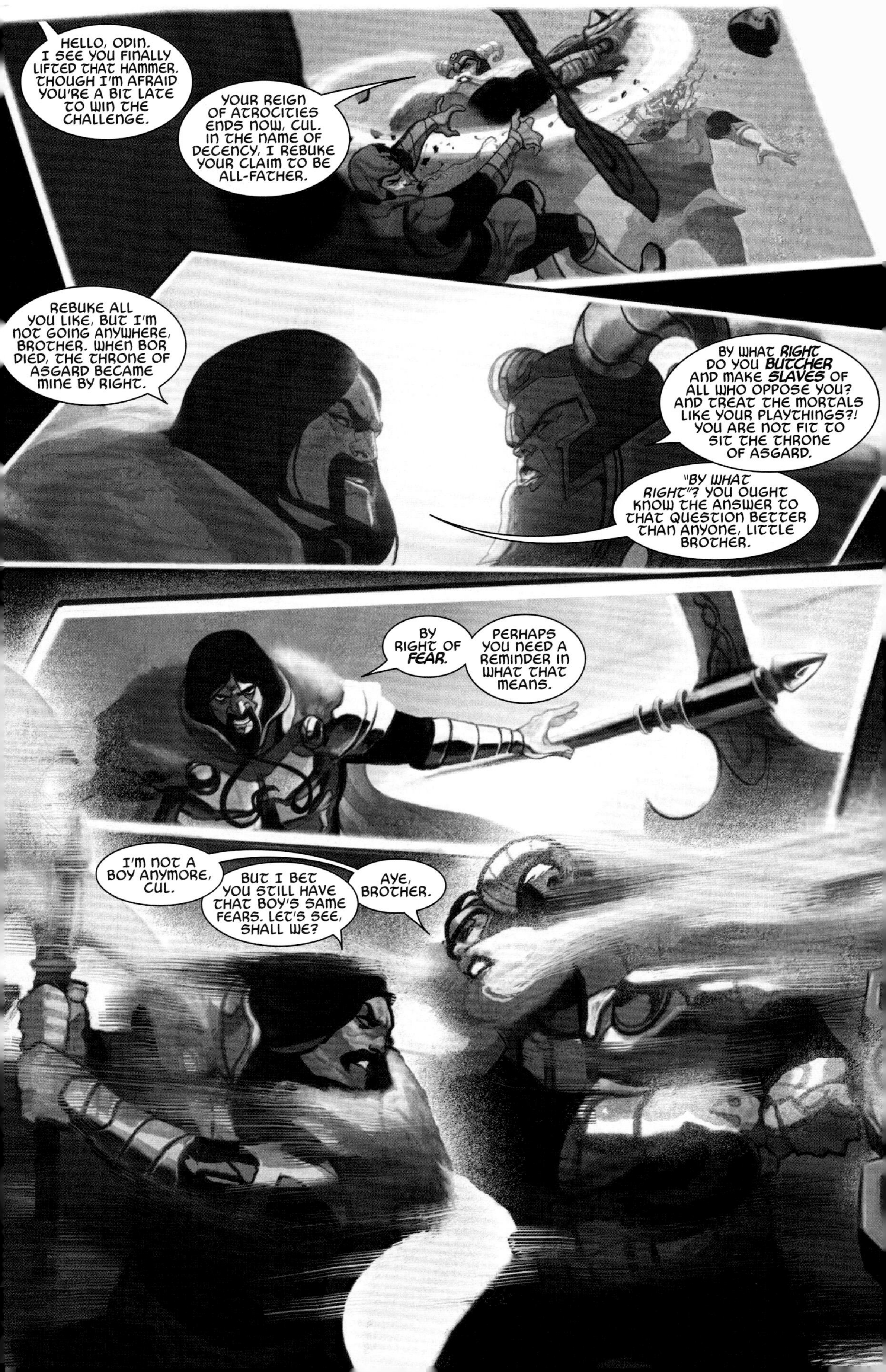
HELLO, ODIN. I SEE YOU FINALLY LIFTED THAT HAMMER. THOUGH I'M AFRAID YOU'RE A BIT LATE TO WIN THE CHALLENGE.
YOUR REIGN OF ATROCITIES ENDS NOW, CUL. IN THE NAME OF DECENCY, I REBUKE YOUR CLAIM TO BE ALL-FATHER.
REBUKE ALL YOU LIKE, BUT I'M NOT GOING ANYWHERE, BROTHER. WHEN BOR DIED, THE THRONE OF ASGARD BECAME MINE BY RIGHT.
BY WHAT RIGHT DO YOU BUTCHER AND MAKE SLAVES OF ALL WHO OPPOSE YOU? AND TREAT THE MORTALS LIKE YOUR PLAYTHINGS?! YOU ARE NOT FIT TO SIT THE THRONE OF ASGARD.
"BY WHAT RIGHT"? YOU OUGHT KNOW THE ANSWER TO THAT QUESTION BETTER THAN ANYONE, LITTLE BROTHER.
BY RIGHT OF FEAR.
PERHAPS YOU NEED A REMINDER IN WHAT THAT MEANS.
I'M NOT A BOY ANYMORE, CUL.
AYE, BROTHER.
BUT I BET YOU STILL HAVE THAT BOY'S SAME FEARS. LET'S SEE, SHALL WE?

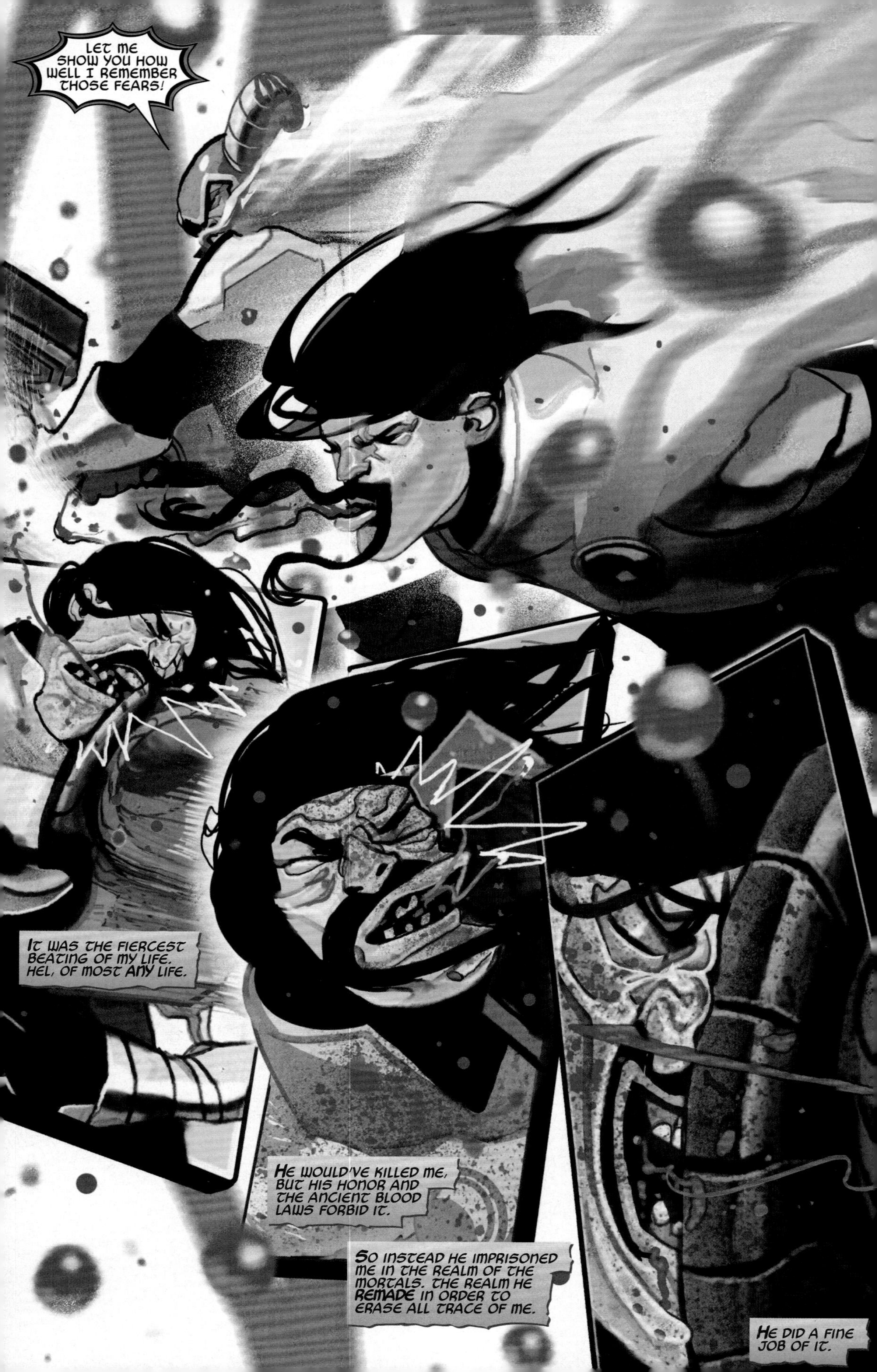
LET ME SHOW YOU HOW WELL I REMEMBER THOSE FEARS!
IT WAS THE FIERCEST BEATING OF MY LIFE. HEL, OF MOST ANY LIFE.
HE WOULD'VE KILLED ME, BUT HIS HONOR AND THE ANCIENT BLOOD LAWS FORBID IT.
SO INSTEAD HE IMPRISONED ME IN THE REALM OF THE MORTALS. THE REALM HE REMADE IN ORDER TO ERASE ALL TRACE OF ME.
HE DID A FINE JOB OF IT.

ASGARDIA. MONTHS AGO.

IT WASN'T JUST YOUR **BIRTHRIGHT** THAT WAS STOLEN, BOY.

APPARENTLY YOUR **SENSES** WERE TAKEN AS WELL!

HOW CAN YOU STAND BY AND LET THIS MASKED WOMAN STEAL NOT JUST YOUR **HAMMER** BUT YOUR VERY **NAME!**

I'VE TOLD YOU, I **GAVE** HER THE NAME! SHE'S EARNED IT. SHE'S MORE WORTHY OF IT THAN I AM RIGHT NOW.

BUT ULTIMATELY I RECURRED AND TRIED ONCE MORE TO DROWN ALL OF MIDGARD IN FEAR. DIDN'T WORK WELL FOR ME THAT TIME EITHER.

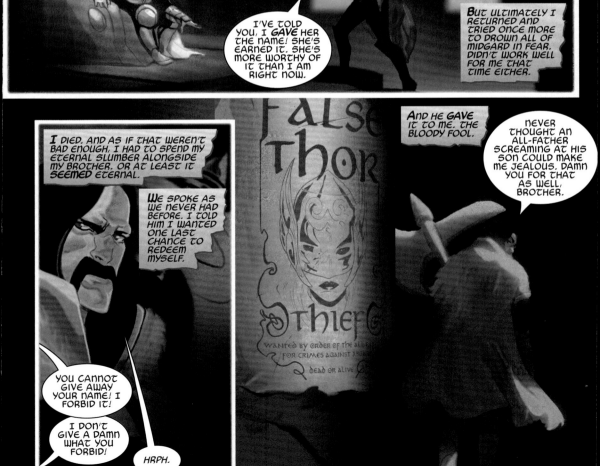

I DIED. AND AS IF THAT WEREN'T BAD ENOUGH, I HAD TO SPEND MY ETERNAL SLUMBER ALONGSIDE MY BROTHER. OR AT LEAST IT **SEEMED** ETERNAL.

WE SPOKE AS WE NEVER HAD BEFORE. I TOLD HIM I WANTED ONE LAST CHANCE TO REDEEM MYSELF.

FALSE Thor Thief

WANTED BY ORDER OF THE ALL...
FOR CRIMES AGAINST ASGA...
DEAD OR ALIVE

AND HE GAVE IT TO ME. THE BLOODY FOOL.

NEVER THOUGHT AN ALL-FATHER SCREAMING AT HIS SON COULD MAKE ME JEALOUS. DAMN YOU FOR THAT AS WELL, BROTHER.

YOU CANNOT GIVE AWAY YOUR NAME! I FORBID IT!

I DON'T GIVE A DAMN WHAT YOU FORBID!

HRPH.

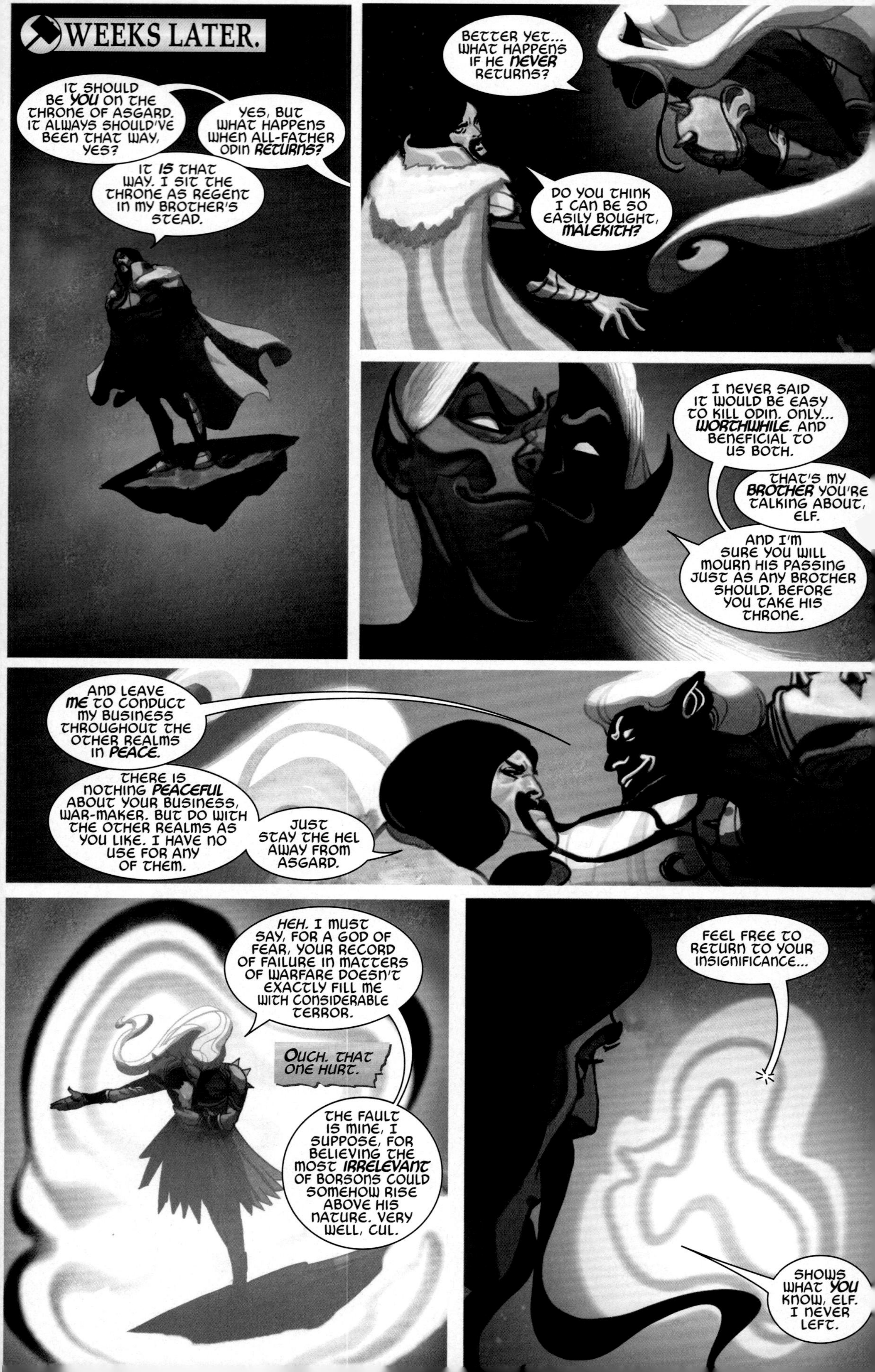
WEEKS LATER.
IT SHOULD BE YOU ON THE THRONE OF ASGARD. IT ALWAYS SHOULD'VE BEEN THAT WAY, YES?
YES, BUT WHAT HAPPENS WHEN ALL-FATHER ODIN RETURNS?
IT IS THAT WAY. I SIT THE THRONE AS REGENT IN MY BROTHER'S STEAD.
BETTER YET... WHAT HAPPENS IF HE NEVER RETURNS?
DO YOU THINK I CAN BE SO EASILY BOUGHT, MALEKITH?
I NEVER SAID IT WOULD BE EASY TO KILL ODIN. ONLY... WORTHWHILE. AND BENEFICIAL TO US BOTH.
THAT'S MY BROTHER YOU'RE TALKING ABOUT, ELF.
AND I'M SURE YOU WILL MOURN HIS PASSING JUST AS ANY BROTHER SHOULD. BEFORE YOU TAKE HIS THRONE.
AND LEAVE ME TO CONDUCT MY BUSINESS THROUGHOUT THE OTHER REALMS IN PEACE.
THERE IS NOTHING PEACEFUL ABOUT YOUR BUSINESS, WAR-MAKER. BUT DO WITH THE OTHER REALMS AS YOU LIKE. I HAVE NO USE FOR ANY OF THEM.
JUST STAY THE HEL AWAY FROM ASGARD.
HEH. I MUST SAY, FOR A GOD OF FEAR, YOUR RECORD OF FAILURE IN MATTERS OF WARFARE DOESN'T EXACTLY FILL ME WITH CONSIDERABLE TERROR.
OUCH. THAT ONE HURT.
THE FAULT IS MINE, I SUPPOSE, FOR BELIEVING THE MOST IRRELEVANT OF BORSONS COULD SOMEHOW RISE ABOVE HIS NATURE. VERY WELL, CUL.
FEEL FREE TO RETURN TO YOUR INSIGNIFICANCE...
SHOWS WHAT YOU KNOW, ELF. I NEVER LEFT.

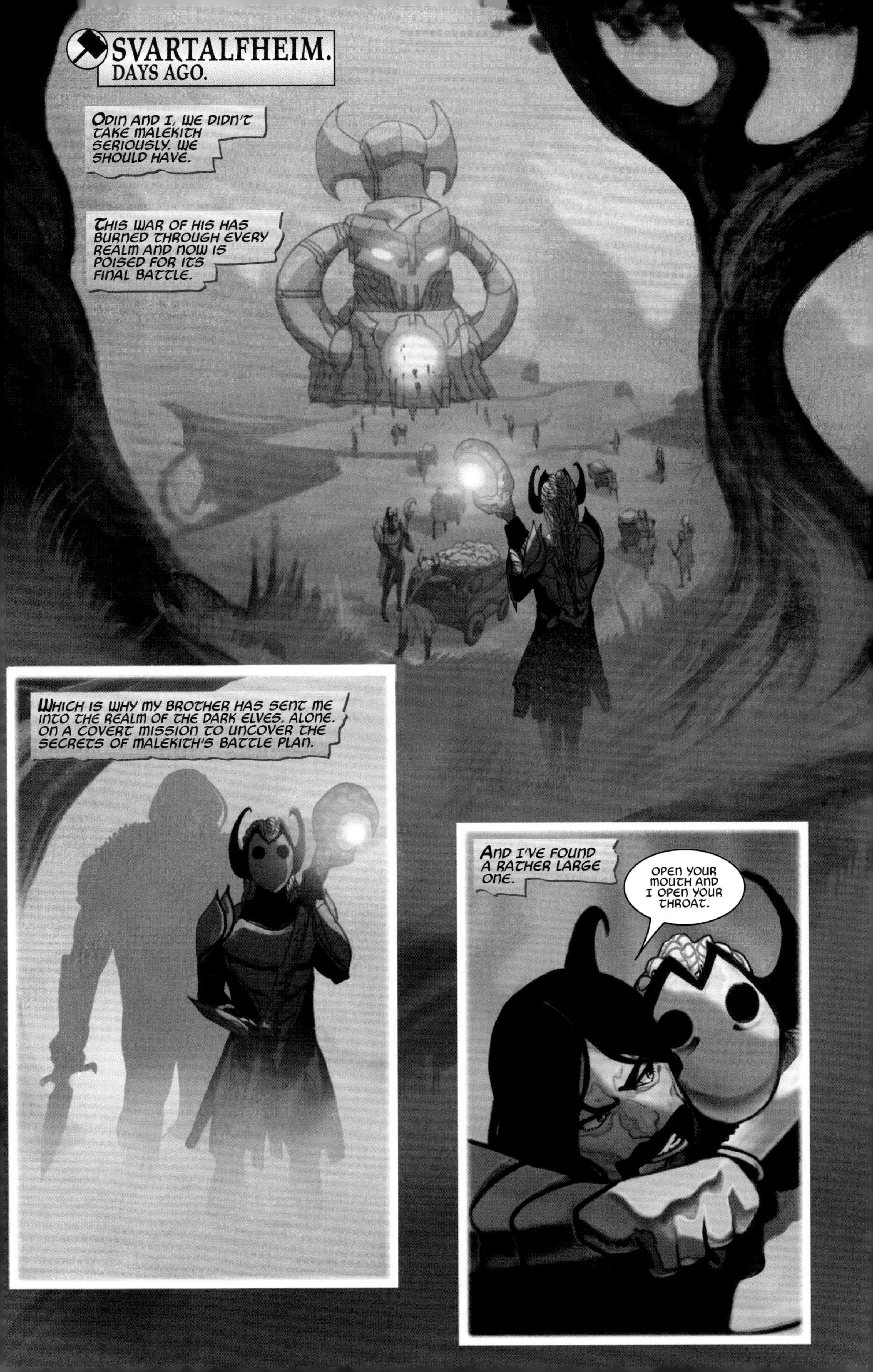
SVARTALFHEIM. DAYS AGO.
ODIN AND I, WE DIDN'T TAKE MALEKITH SERIOUSLY. WE SHOULD HAVE.
THIS WAR OF HIS HAS BURNED THROUGH EVERY REALM AND NOW IS POISED FOR ITS FINAL BATTLE.
WHICH IS WHY MY BROTHER HAS SENT ME INTO THE REALM OF THE DARK ELVES. ALONE. ON A COVERT MISSION TO UNCOVER THE SECRETS OF MALEKITH'S BATTLE PLAN.
AND I'VE FOUND A RATHER LARGE ONE.
OPEN YOUR MOUTH AND I OPEN YOUR THROAT.

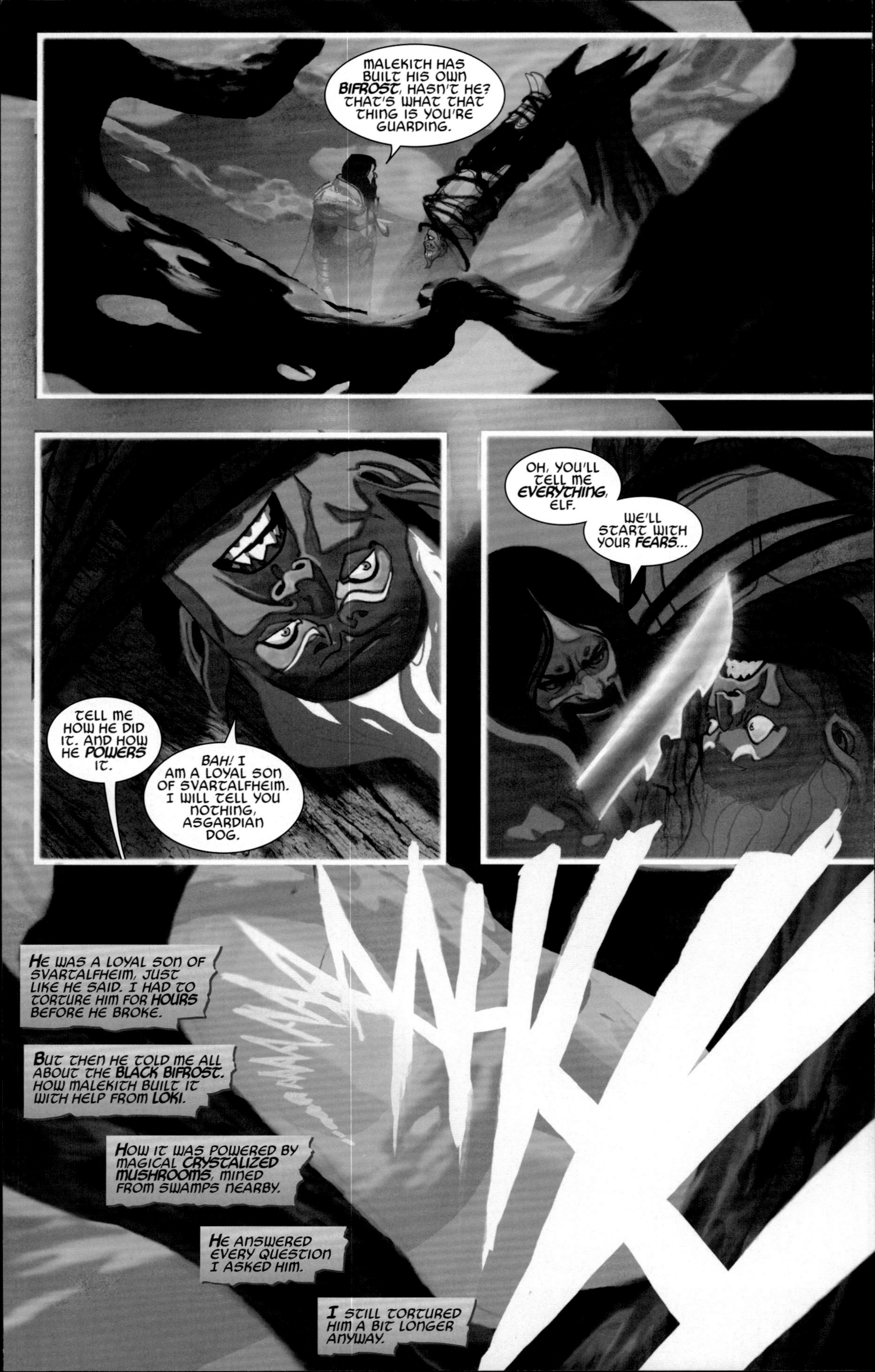
MALEKITH HAS BUILT HIS OWN BIFROST, HASN'T HE? THAT'S WHAT THAT THING IS YOU'RE GUARDING.
TELL ME HOW HE DID IT. AND HOW HE POWERS IT.
BAH! I AM A LOYAL SON OF SVARTALFHEIM. I WILL TELL YOU NOTHING, ASGARDIAN DOG.
OH, YOU'LL TELL ME EVERYTHING, ELF.
WE'LL START WITH YOUR FEARS...
HE WAS A LOYAL SON OF SVARTALFHEIM, JUST LIKE HE SAID. I HAD TO TORTURE HIM FOR HOURS BEFORE HE BROKE.
BUT THEN HE TOLD ME ALL ABOUT THE BLACK BIFROST. HOW MALEKITH BUILT IT WITH HELP FROM LOKI.
HOW IT WAS POWERED BY MAGICAL CRYSTALIZED MUSHROOMS, MINED FROM SWAMPS NEARBY.
HE ANSWERED EVERY QUESTION I ASKED HIM.
I STILL TORTURED HIM A BIT LONGER ANYWAY.

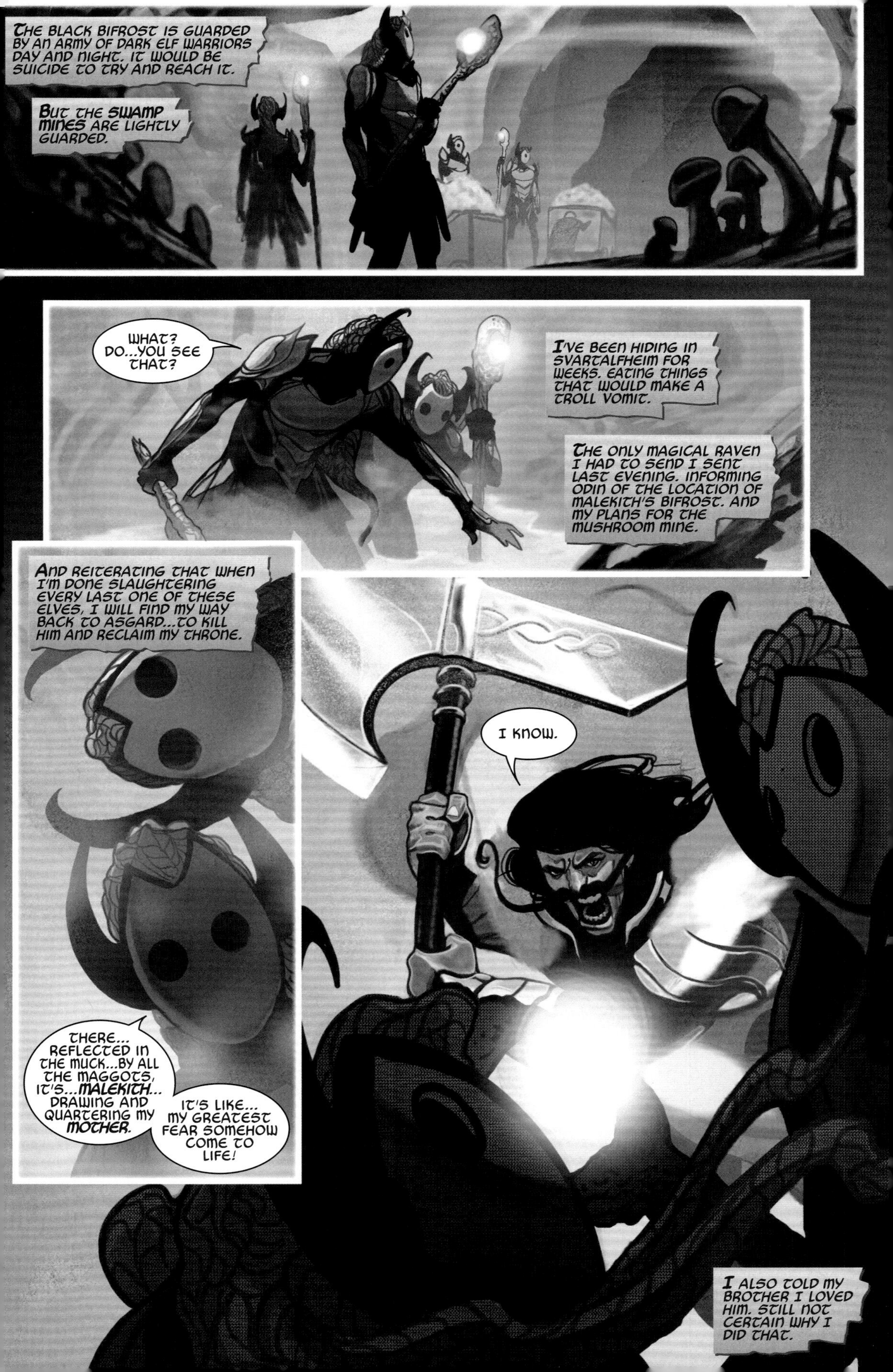

THE BLACK BIFROST IS GUARDED BY AN ARMY OF DARK ELF WARRIORS DAY AND NIGHT. IT WOULD BE SUICIDE TO TRY AND REACH IT.
BUT THE SWAMP MINES ARE LIGHTLY GUARDED.
WHAT? DO...YOU SEE THAT?
I'VE BEEN HIDING IN SVARTALFHEIM FOR WEEKS. EATING THINGS THAT WOULD MAKE A TROLL VOMIT.
THE ONLY MAGICAL RAVEN I HAD TO SEND I SENT LAST EVENING. INFORMING ODIN OF THE LOCATION OF MALEKITH'S BIFROST. AND MY PLANS FOR THE MUSHROOM MINE.
AND REITERATING THAT WHEN I'M DONE SLAUGHTERING EVERY LAST ONE OF THESE ELVES, I WILL FIND MY WAY BACK TO ASGARD...TO KILL HIM AND RECLAIM MY THRONE.
THERE... REFLECTED IN THE MUCK...BY ALL THE MAGGOTS, IT'S...MALEKITH... DRAWING AND QUARTERING MY MOTHER.
IT'S LIKE... MY GREATEST FEAR SOMEHOW COME TO LIFE!
I KNOW.
I ALSO TOLD MY BROTHER I LOVED HIM. STILL NOT CERTAIN WHY I DID THAT.

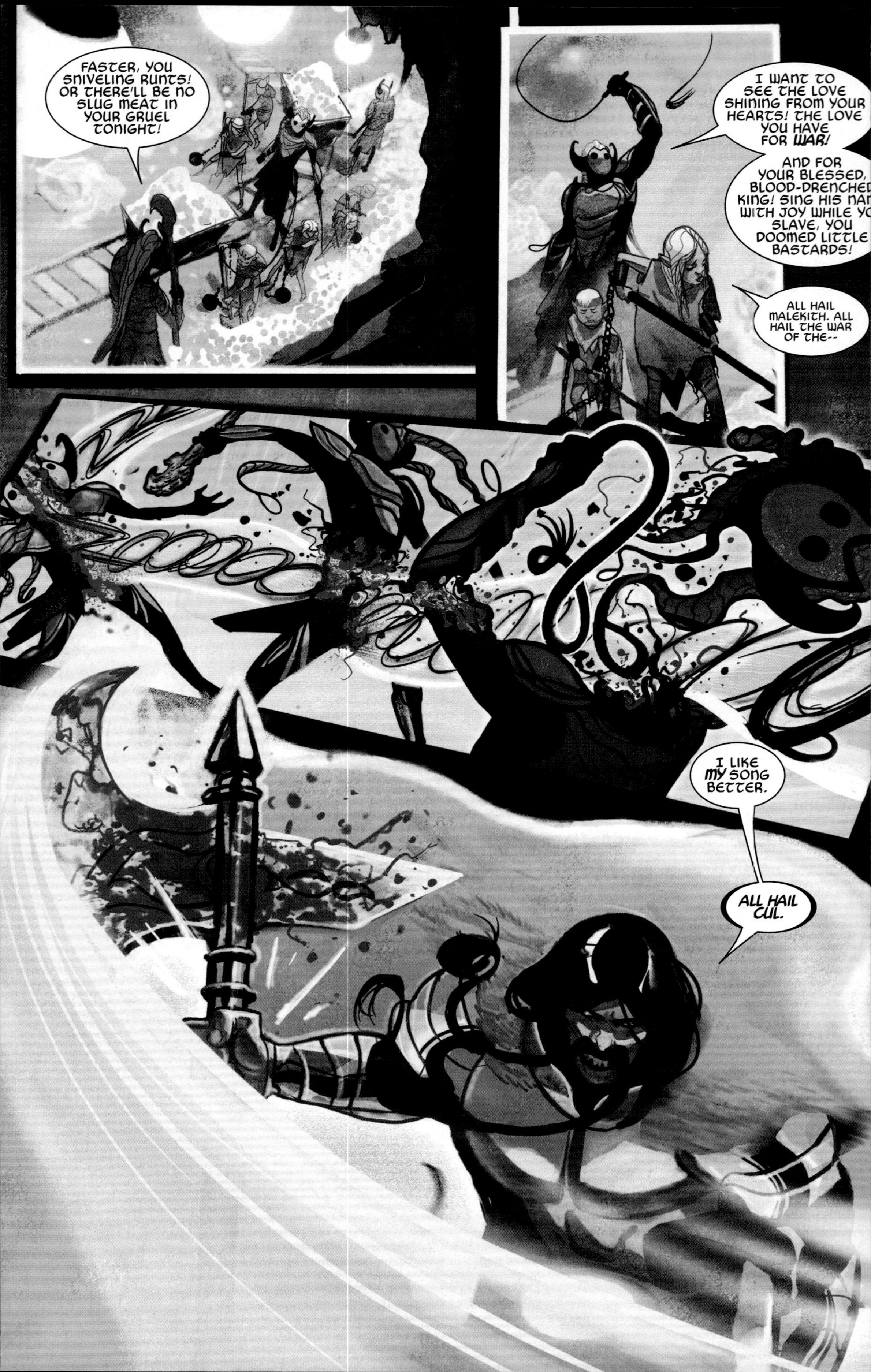
FASTER, YOU SNIVELING RUNTS! OR THERE'LL BE NO SLUG MEAT IN YOUR GRUEL TONIGHT!
I WANT TO SEE THE LOVE SHINING FROM YOUR HEARTS! THE LOVE YOU HAVE FOR WAR!
AND FOR YOUR BLESSED, BLOOD-DRENCHED KING! SING HIS NAM WITH JOY WHILE YO SLAVE, YOU DOOMED LITTLE BASTARDS!
ALL HAIL MALEKITH. ALL HAIL THE WAR OF THE--
I LIKE MY SONG BETTER.
ALL HAIL CUL.

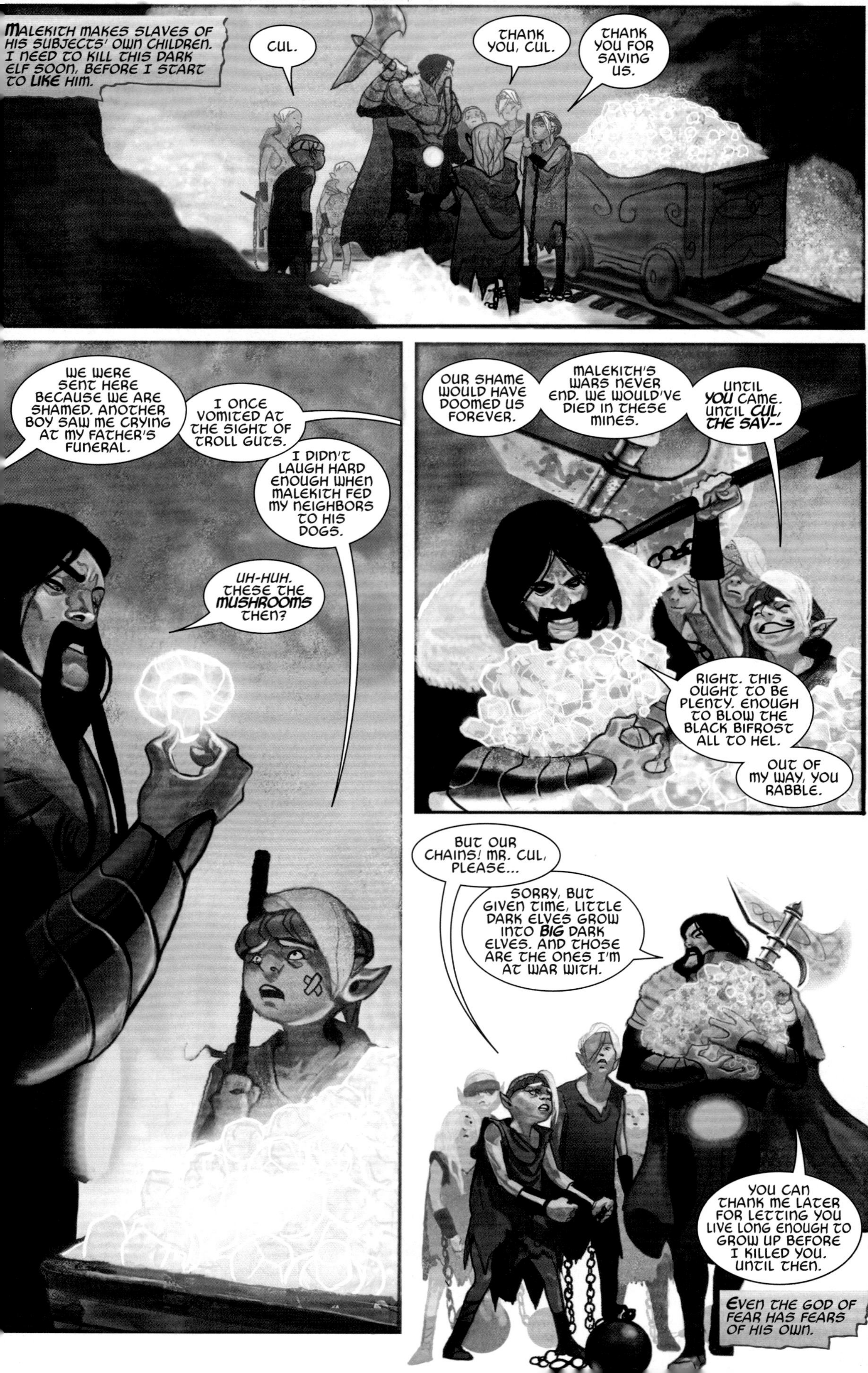
MALEKITH MAKES SLAVES OF HIS SUBJECTS' OWN CHILDREN. I NEED TO KILL THIS DARK ELF SOON, BEFORE I START TO LIKE HIM.
CUL.
THANK YOU, CUL.
THANK YOU FOR SAVING US.
WE WERE SENT HERE BECAUSE WE ARE SHAMED. ANOTHER BOY SAW ME CRYING AT MY FATHER'S FUNERAL.
I ONCE VOMITED AT THE SIGHT OF TROLL GUTS.
I DIDN'T LAUGH HARD ENOUGH WHEN MALEKITH FED MY NEIGHBORS TO HIS DOGS.
UH-HUH. THESE THE MUSHROOMS THEN?
OUR SHAME WOULD HAVE DOOMED US FOREVER.
MALEKITH'S WARS NEVER END. WE WOULD'VE DIED IN THESE MINES.
UNTIL YOU CAME. UNTIL CUL, THE SAV--
RIGHT. THIS OUGHT TO BE PLENTY. ENOUGH TO BLOW THE BLACK BIFROST ALL TO HEL.
OUT OF MY WAY, YOU RABBLE.
BUT OUR CHAINS! MR. CUL, PLEASE...
SORRY, BUT GIVEN TIME, LITTLE DARK ELVES GROW INTO BIG DARK ELVES. AND THOSE ARE THE ONES I'M AT WAR WITH.
YOU CAN THANK ME LATER FOR LETTING YOU LIVE LONG ENOUGH TO GROW UP BEFORE I KILLED YOU. UNTIL THEN.
EVEN THE GOD OF FEAR HAS FEARS OF HIS OWN.

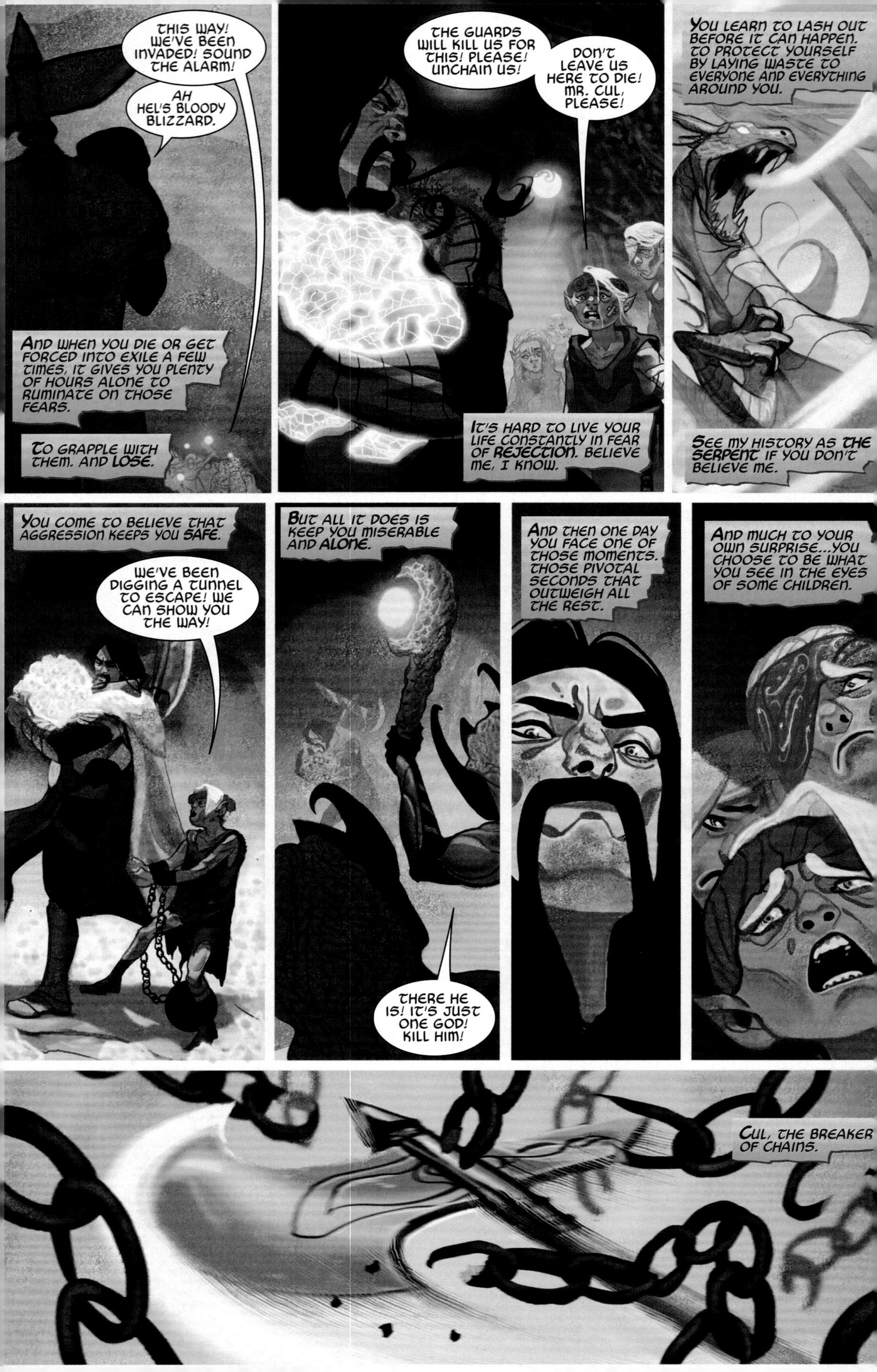

THIS WAY! WE'VE BEEN INVADED! SOUND THE ALARM!
AH HEL'S BLOODY BLIZZARD.
AND WHEN YOU DIE OR GET FORCED INTO EXILE A FEW TIMES, IT GIVES YOU PLENTY OF HOURS ALONE TO RUMINATE ON THOSE FEARS.
TO GRAPPLE WITH THEM. AND LOSE.
THE GUARDS WILL KILL US FOR THIS! PLEASE! UNCHAIN US!
DON'T LEAVE US HERE TO DIE! MR. CUL, PLEASE!
IT'S HARD TO LIVE YOUR LIFE CONSTANTLY IN FEAR OF REJECTION. BELIEVE ME, I KNOW.
YOU LEARN TO LASH OUT BEFORE IT CAN HAPPEN. TO PROTECT YOURSELF BY LAYING WASTE TO EVERYONE AND EVERYTHING AROUND YOU.
SEE MY HISTORY AS THE SERPENT IF YOU DON'T BELIEVE ME.
YOU COME TO BELIEVE THAT AGGRESSION KEEPS YOU SAFE.
WE'VE BEEN DIGGING A TUNNEL TO ESCAPE! WE CAN SHOW YOU THE WAY!
BUT ALL IT DOES IS KEEP YOU MISERABLE AND ALONE.
THERE HE IS! IT'S JUST ONE GOD! KILL HIM!
AND THEN ONE DAY YOU FACE ONE OF THOSE MOMENTS. THOSE PIVOTAL SECONDS THAT OUTWEIGH ALL THE REST.
AND MUCH TO YOUR OWN SURPRISE...YOU CHOOSE TO BE WHAT YOU SEE IN THE EYES OF SOME CHILDREN.
CUL, THE BREAKER OF CHAINS.

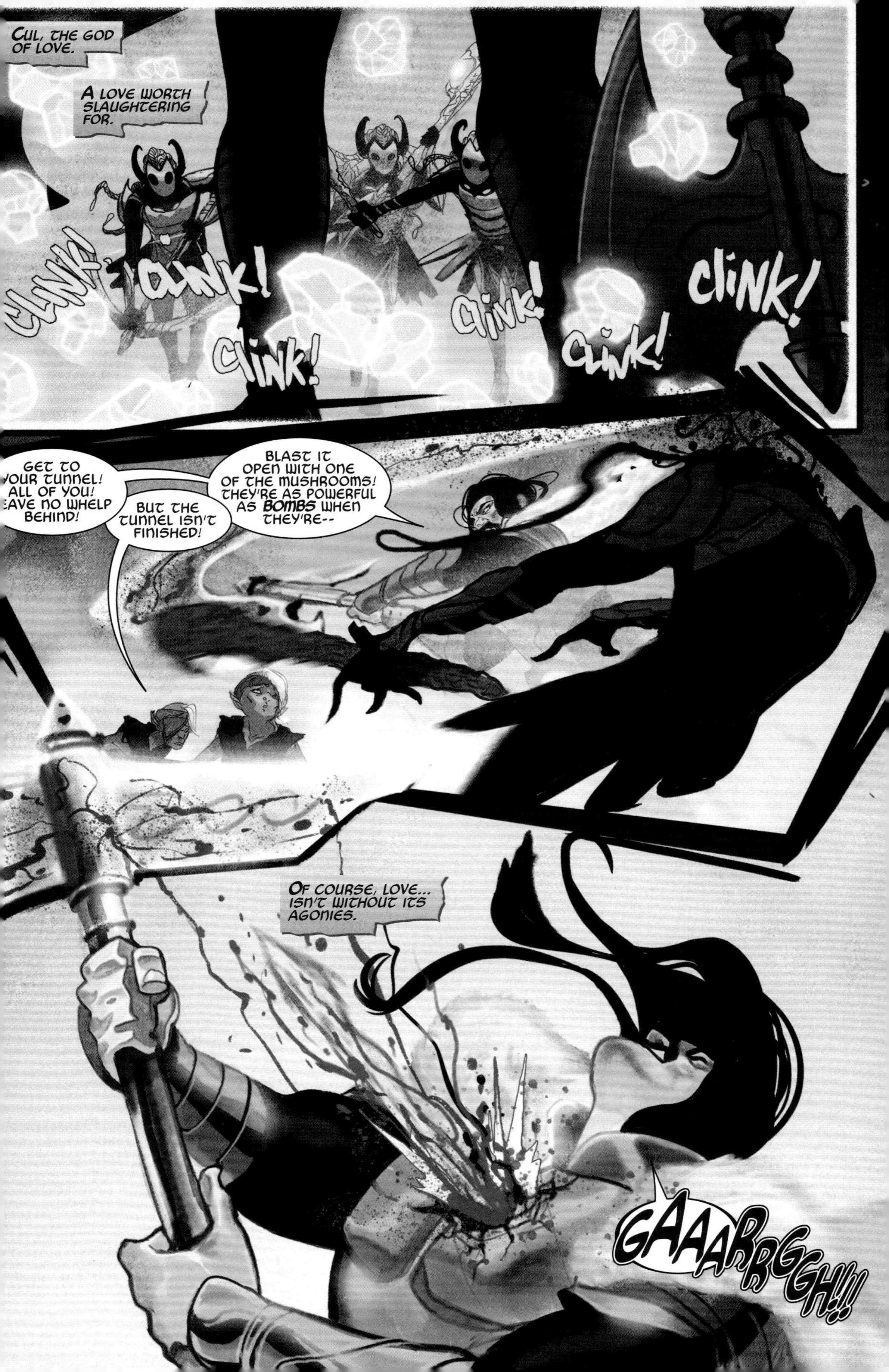
CUL, THE GOD OF LOVE.
A LOVE WORTH SLAUGHTERING FOR.
CLINK!
CLINK!
CLINK!
CLINK!
CLINK!
CLINK!
GET TO YOUR TUNNEL! ALL OF YOU! LEAVE NO WHELP BEHIND!
BLAST IT OPEN WITH ONE OF THE MUSHROOMS! THEY'RE AS POWERFUL AS BOMBS WHEN THEY'RE--
BUT THE TUNNEL ISN'T FINISHED!
OF COURSE, LOVE... ISN'T WITHOUT ITS AGONIES.
GAAARRGGH!!!

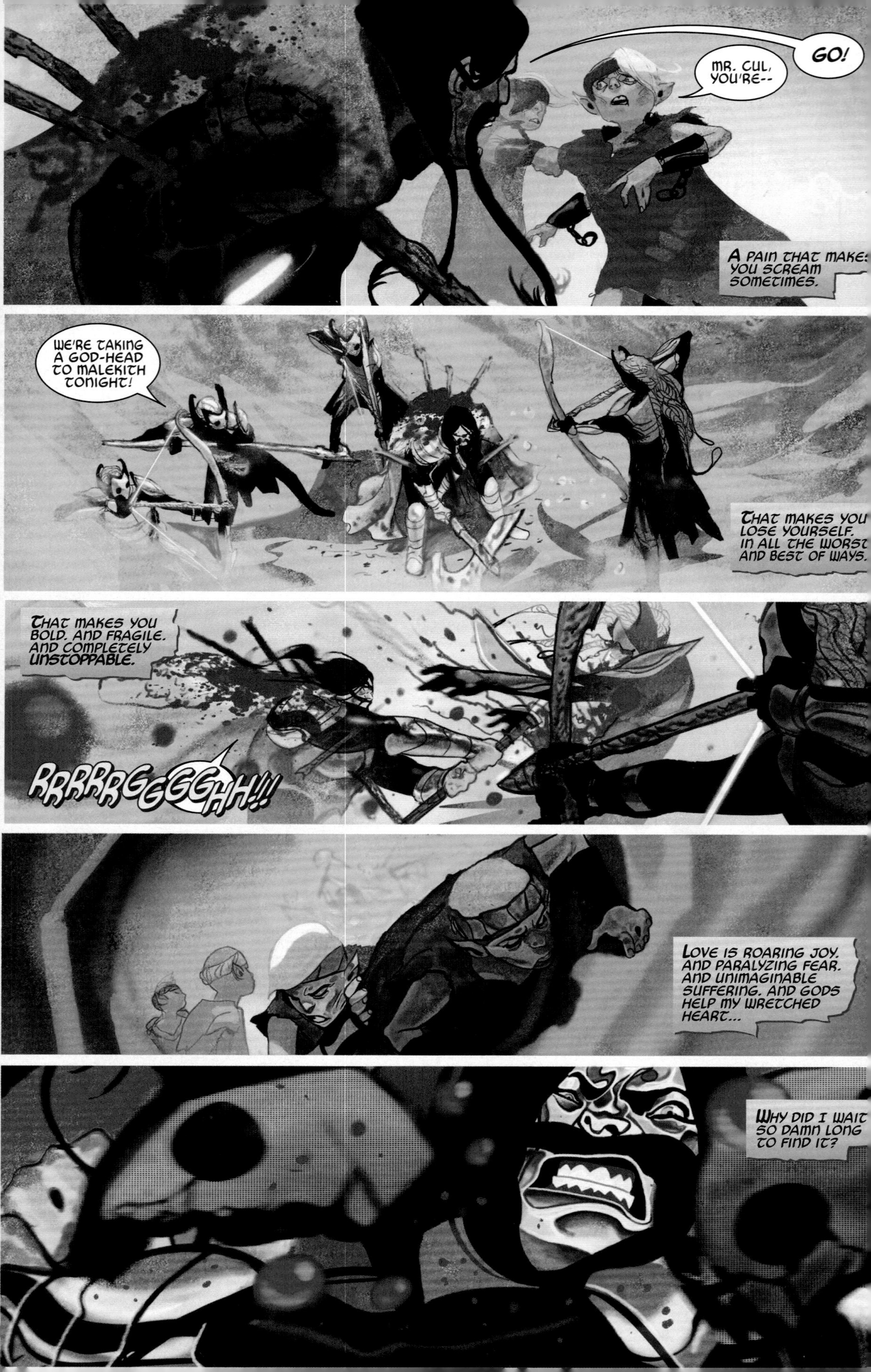
MR. CUL, YOU'RE--
GO!
A PAIN THAT MAKE YOU SCREAM SOMETIMES.
WE'RE TAKING A GOD-HEAD TO MALEKITH TONIGHT!
THAT MAKES YOU LOSE YOURSELF. IN ALL THE WORST AND BEST OF WAYS.
THAT MAKES YOU BOLD. AND FRAGILE. AND COMPLETELY UNSTOPPABLE.
RRRRRGGGGHH!!!
LOVE IS ROARING JOY. AND PARALYZING FEAR. AND UNIMAGINABLE SUFFERING. AND GODS HELP MY WRETCHED HEART...
WHY DID I WAIT SO DAMN LONG TO FIND IT?

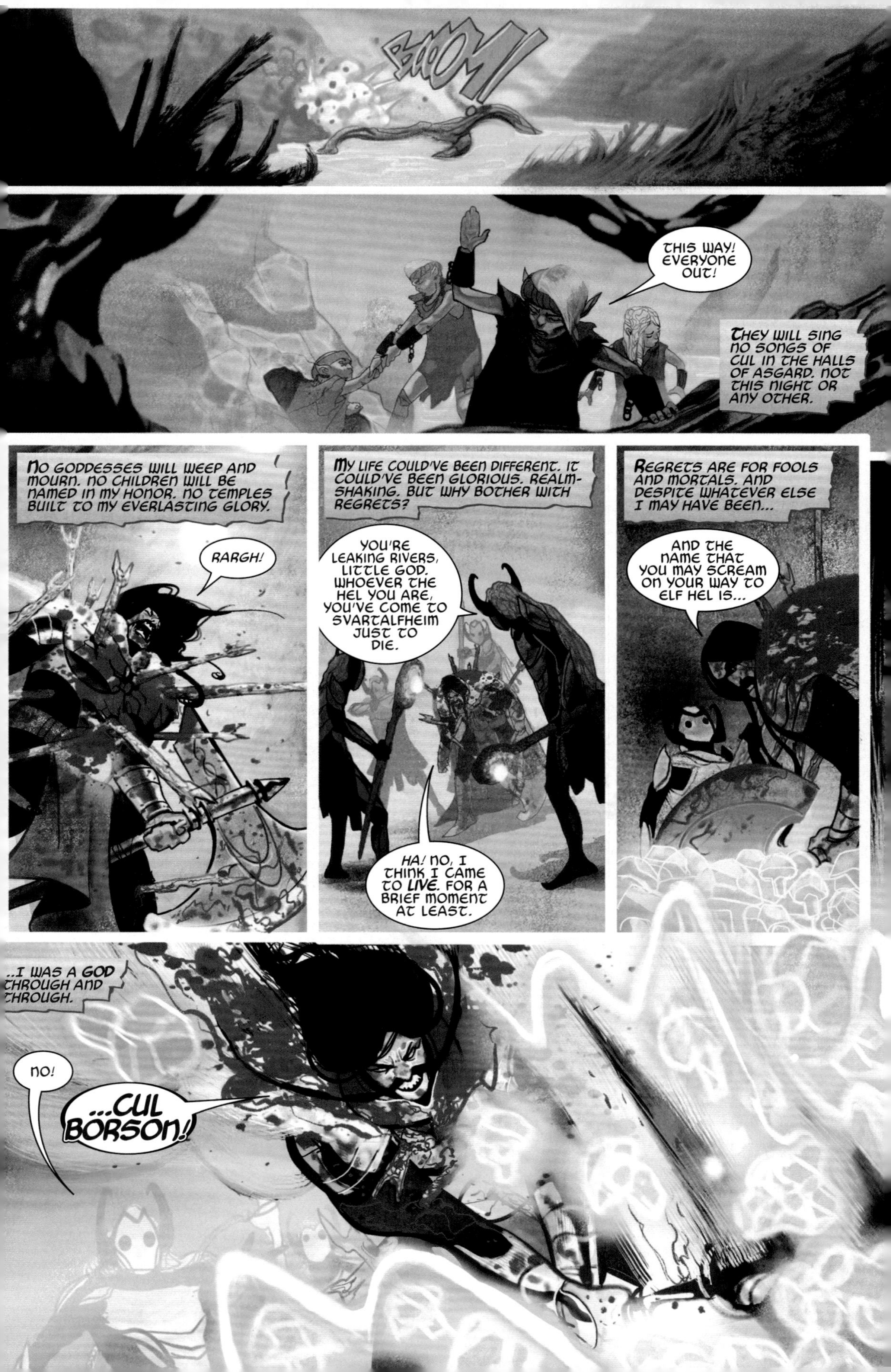
BOOM!
THIS WAY! EVERYONE OUT!
THEY WILL SING NO SONGS OF CUL IN THE HALLS OF ASGARD. NOT THIS NIGHT OR ANY OTHER.
NO GODDESSES WILL WEEP AND MOURN. NO CHILDREN WILL BE NAMED IN MY HONOR. NO TEMPLES BUILT TO MY EVERLASTING GLORY.
RARGH!
MY LIFE COULD'VE BEEN DIFFERENT. IT COULD'VE BEEN GLORIOUS. REALM-SHAKING. BUT WHY BOTHER WITH REGRETS?
YOU'RE LEAKING RIVERS, LITTLE GOD. WHOEVER THE HEL YOU ARE, YOU'VE COME TO SVARTALFHEIM JUST TO DIE.
HA! NO, I THINK I CAME TO LIVE. FOR A BRIEF MOMENT AT LEAST.
REGRETS ARE FOR FOOLS AND MORTALS. AND DESPITE WHATEVER ELSE I MAY HAVE BEEN...
AND THE NAME THAT YOU MAY SCREAM ON YOUR WAY TO ELF HEL IS...
...I WAS A GOD THROUGH AND THROUGH.
NO!
...CUL BÖRSON!

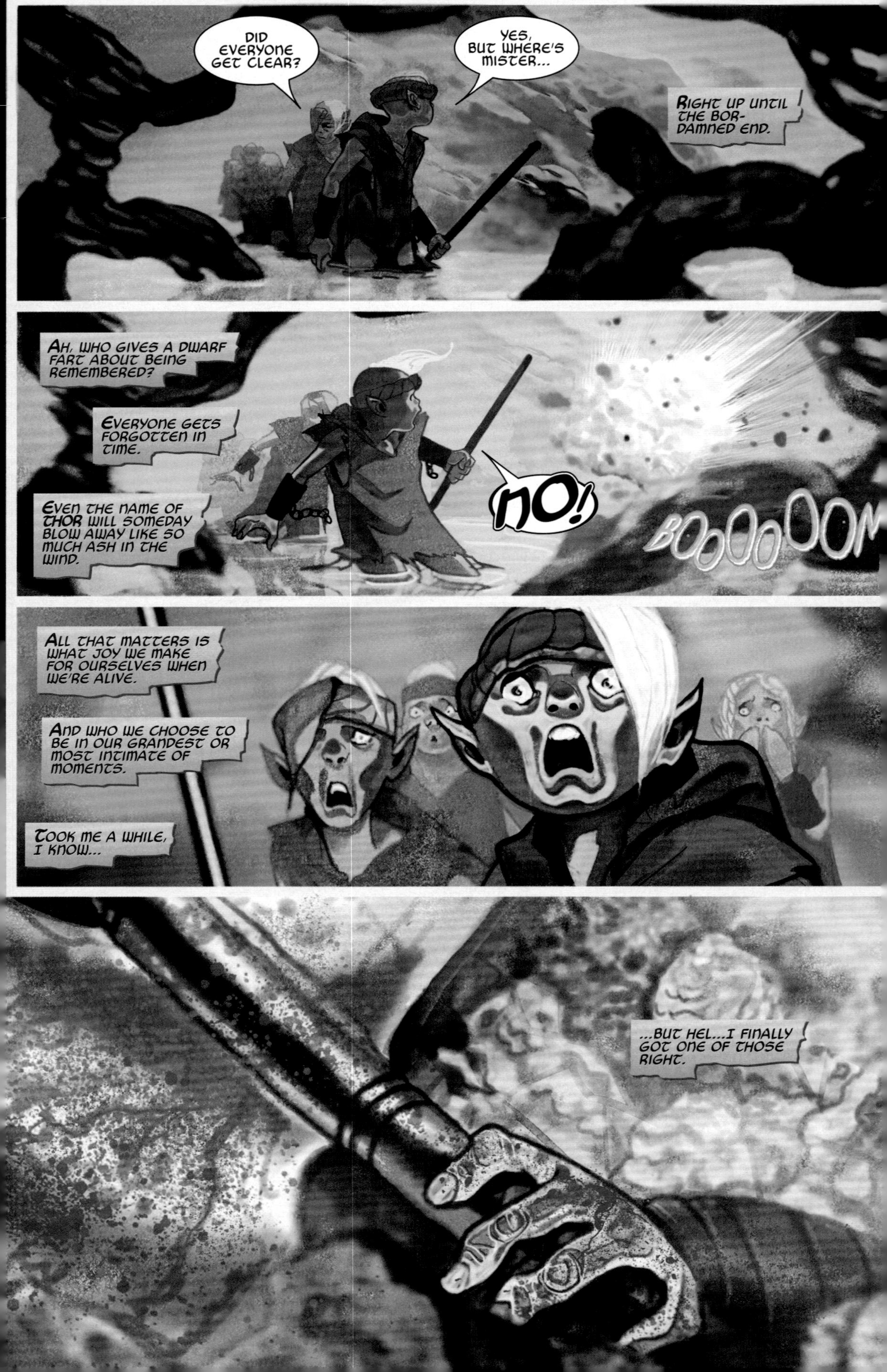
DID EVERYONE GET CLEAR?
YES, BUT WHERE'S MISTER...
RIGHT UP UNTIL THE BOR-DAMNED END.
AH, WHO GIVES A DWARF FART ABOUT BEING REMEMBERED?
EVERYONE GETS FORGOTTEN IN TIME.
EVEN THE NAME OF THOR WILL SOMEDAY BLOW AWAY LIKE SO MUCH ASH IN THE WIND.
NO!
BOOOOOOOM
ALL THAT MATTERS IS WHAT JOY WE MAKE FOR OURSELVES WHEN WE'RE ALIVE.
AND WHO WE CHOOSE TO BE IN OUR GRANDEST OR MOST INTIMATE OF MOMENTS.
TOOK ME A WHILE, I KNOW...
...BUT HEL...I FINALLY GOT ONE OF THOSE RIGHT.

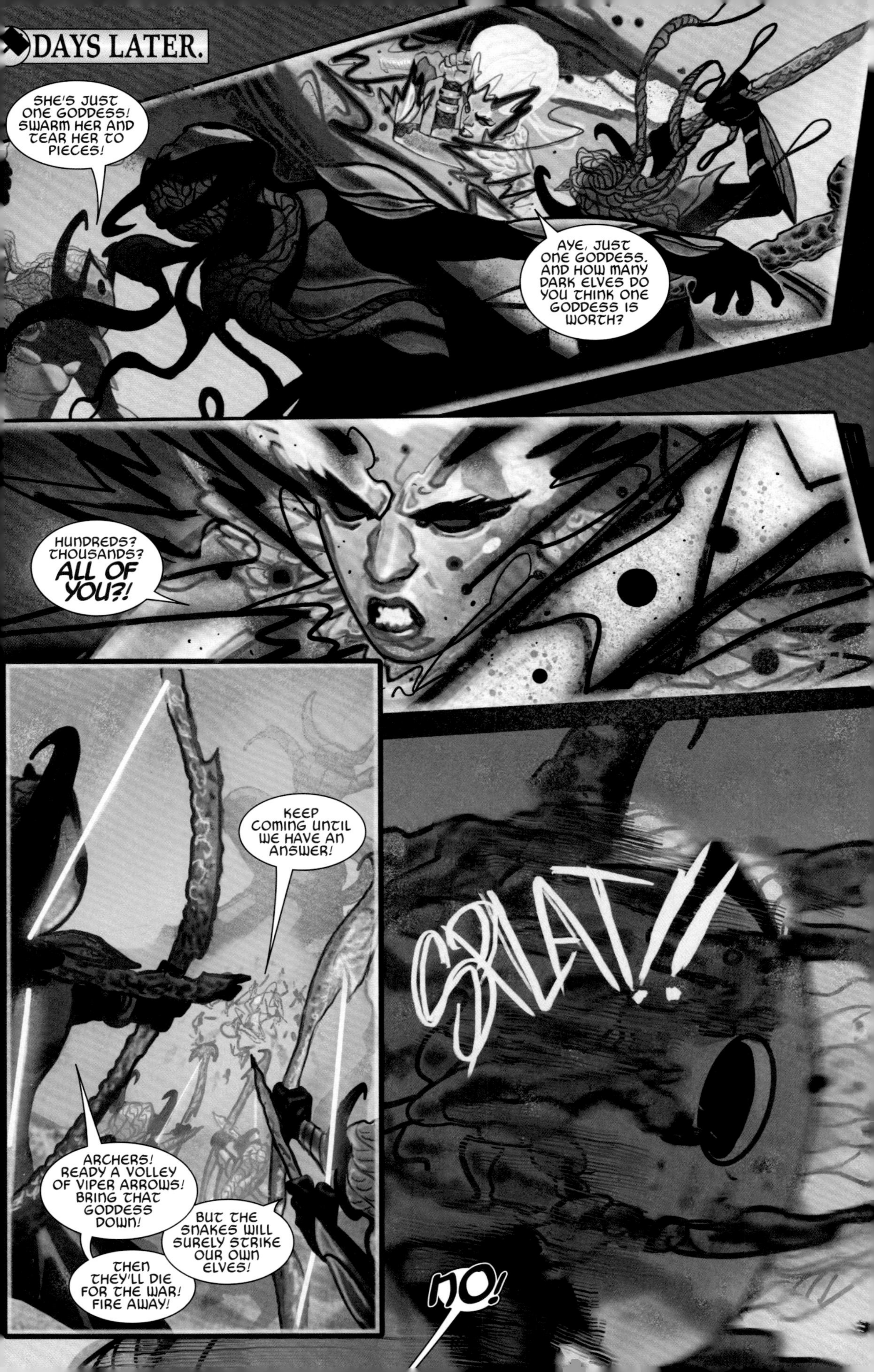
DAYS LATER.
SHE'S JUST ONE GODDESS! SWARM HER AND TEAR HER TO PIECES!
AYE, JUST ONE GODDESS. AND HOW MANY DARK ELVES DO YOU THINK ONE GODDESS IS WORTH?
HUNDREDS? THOUSANDS? ALL OF YOU?!
KEEP COMING UNTIL WE HAVE AN ANSWER!
ARCHERS! READY A VOLLEY OF VIPER ARROWS! BRING THAT GODDESS DOWN!
BUT THE SNAKES WILL SURELY STRIKE OUR OWN ELVES!
THEN THEY'LL DIE FOR THE WAR! FIRE AWAY!
SPLAT!!
NO!

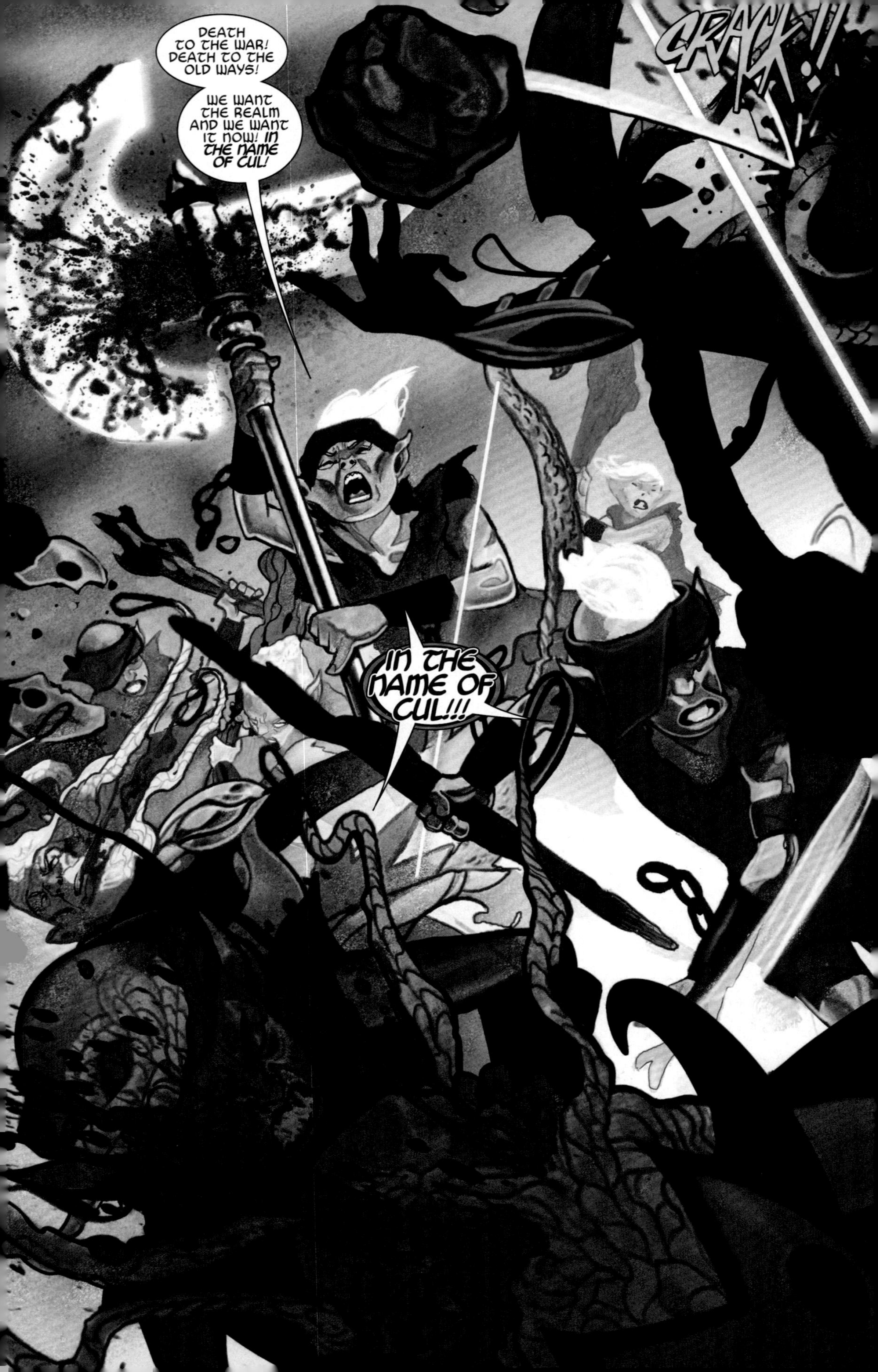
DEATH TO THE WAR! DEATH TO THE OLD WAYS!
WE WANT THE REALM AND WE WANT IT NOW! IN THE NAME OF CUL!
CRACK!!
IN THE NAME OF CUL!!!

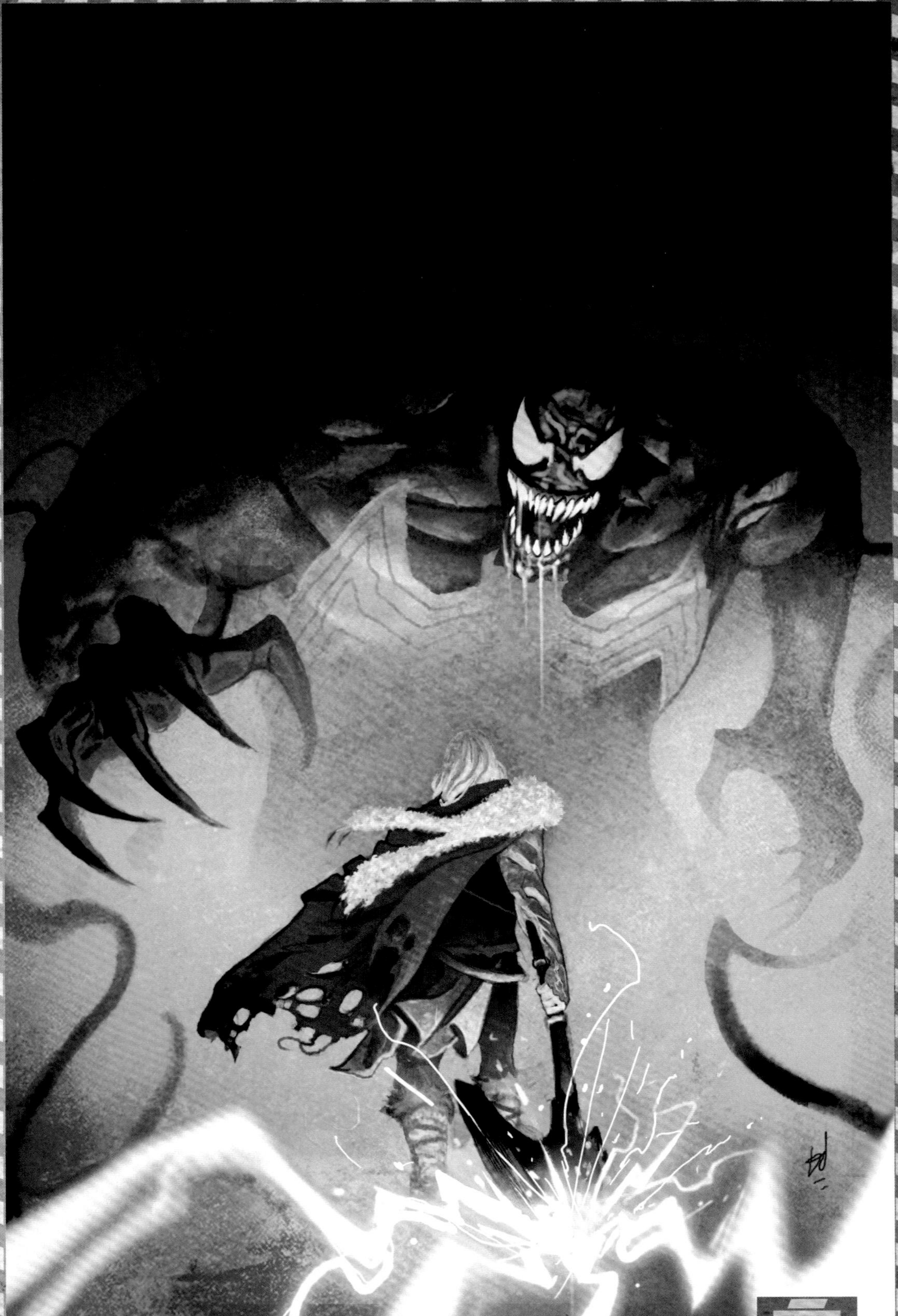

14

"TO HEL WITH HAMMERS"

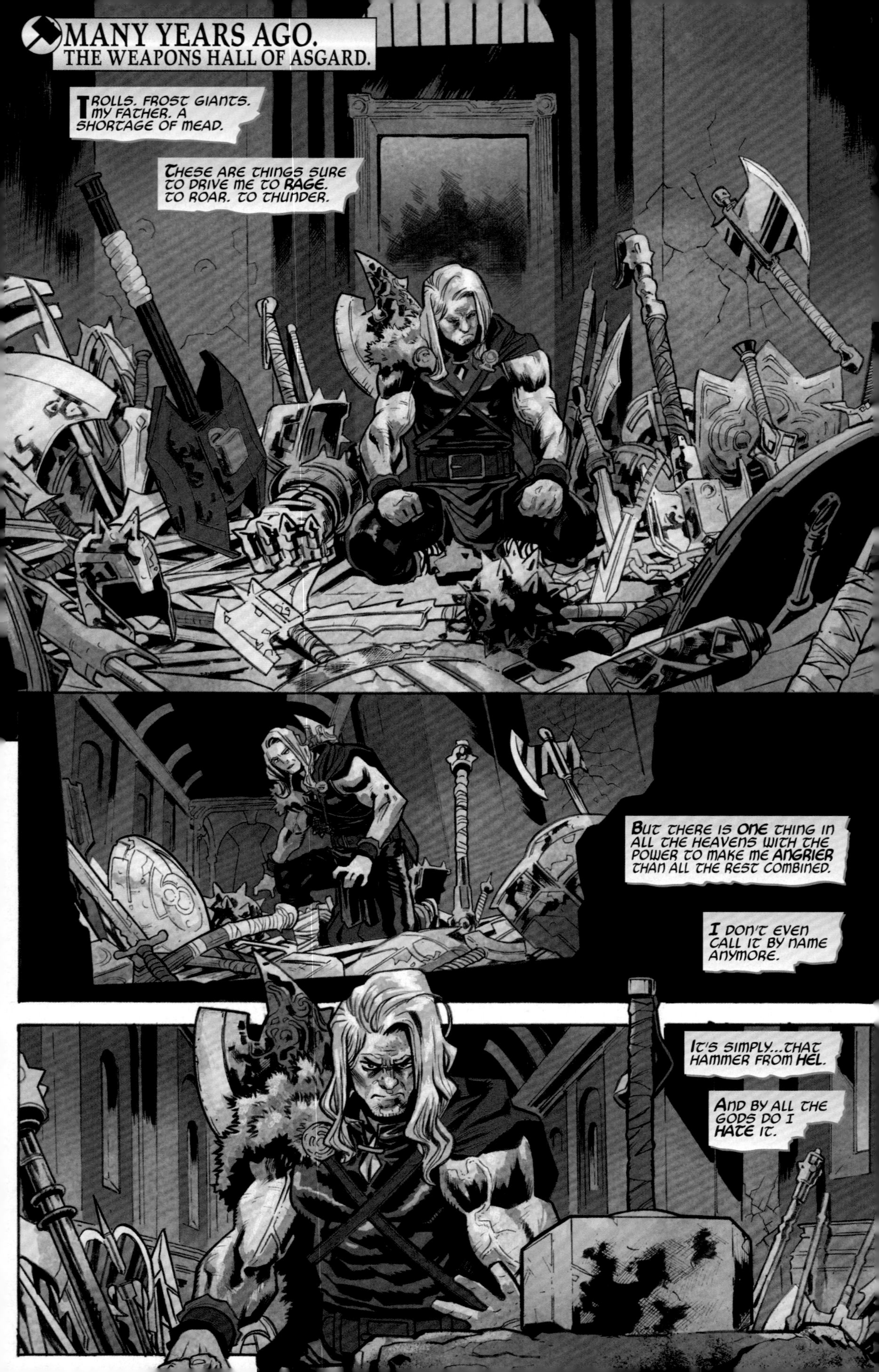
MANY YEARS AGO.
THE WEAPONS HALL OF ASGARD.
TROLLS. FROST GIANTS. MY FATHER. A SHORTAGE OF MEAD.
THESE ARE THINGS SURE TO DRIVE ME TO RAGE. TO ROAR. TO THUNDER.
BUT THERE IS ONE THING IN ALL THE HEAVENS WITH THE POWER TO MAKE ME ANGRIER THAN ALL THE REST COMBINED.
I DON'T EVEN CALL IT BY NAME ANYMORE.
IT'S SIMPLY...THAT HAMMER FROM HEL.
AND BY ALL THE GODS DO I HATE IT.

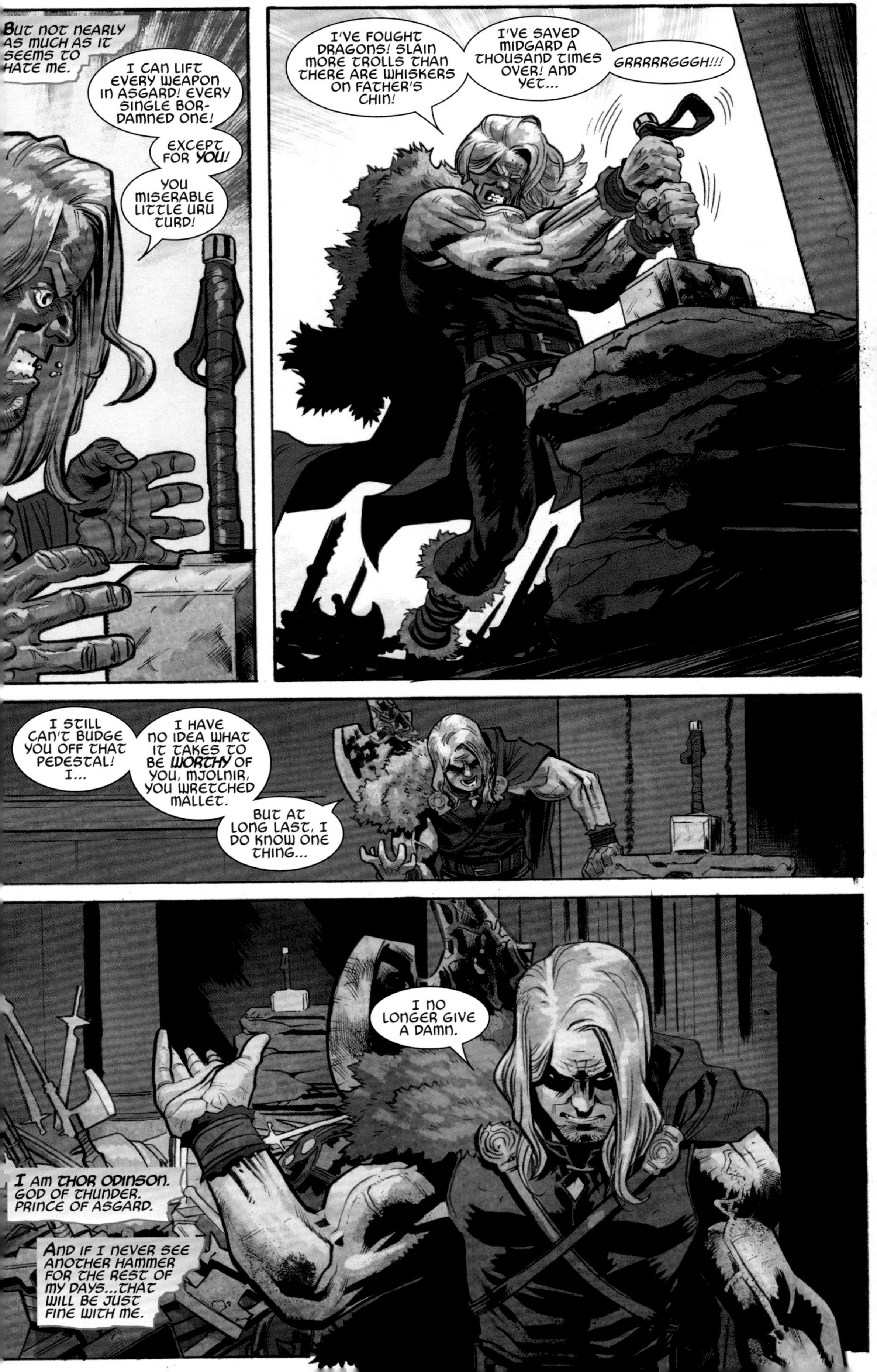
But not nearly as much as it seems to hate me.
I can lift every weapon in Asgard! Every single bor-damned one!
Except for YOU!
You miserable little uru turd!
I've fought dragons! Slain more trolls than there are whiskers on Father's chin!
I've saved Midgard a thousand times over! And yet...
GRRRRRGGGH!!!
I still can't budge you off that pedestal! I...
I have no idea what it takes to be WORTHY of you, Mjolnir, you wretched mallet.
But at long last, I do know one thing...
I no longer give a damn.
I am Thor Odinson. God of Thunder. Prince of Asgard.
And if I never see another hammer for the rest of my days...that will be just fine with me.

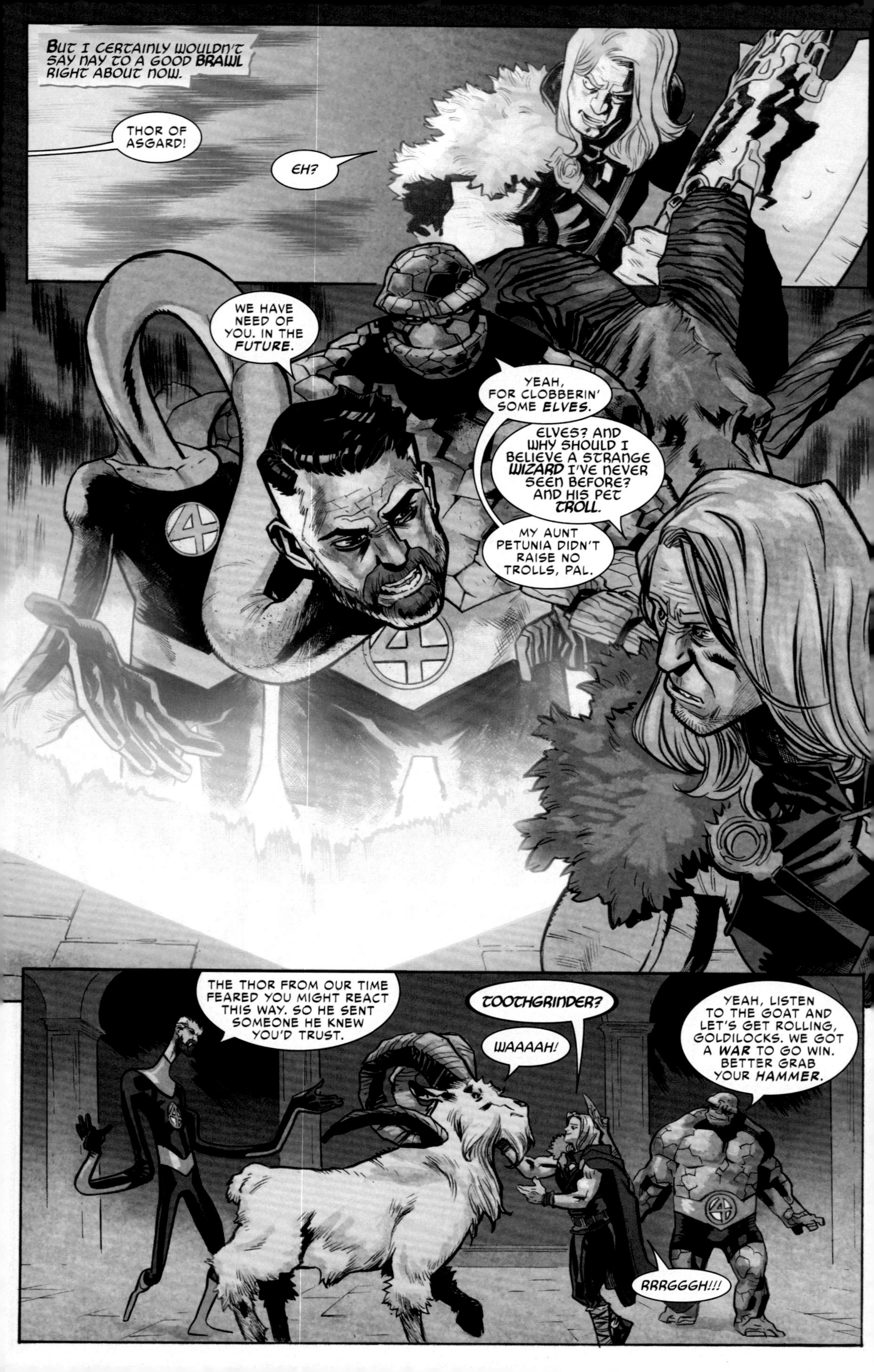
BUT I CERTAINLY WOULDN'T SAY NAY TO A GOOD BRAWL RIGHT ABOUT NOW.
THOR OF ASGARD!
EH?
WE HAVE NEED OF YOU. IN THE FUTURE.
YEAH, FOR CLOBBERIN' SOME ELVES.
ELVES? AND WHY SHOULD I BELIEVE A STRANGE WIZARD I'VE NEVER SEEN BEFORE? AND HIS PET TROLL.
MY AUNT PETUNIA DIDN'T RAISE NO TROLLS, PAL.
THE THOR FROM OUR TIME FEARED YOU MIGHT REACT THIS WAY. SO HE SENT SOMEONE HE KNEW YOU'D TRUST.
TOOTHGRINDER?
WAAAAH!
YEAH, LISTEN TO THE GOAT AND LET'S GET ROLLING, GOLDILOCKS. WE GOT A WAR TO GO WIN. BETTER GRAB YOUR HAMMER.
RRRGGGH!!!

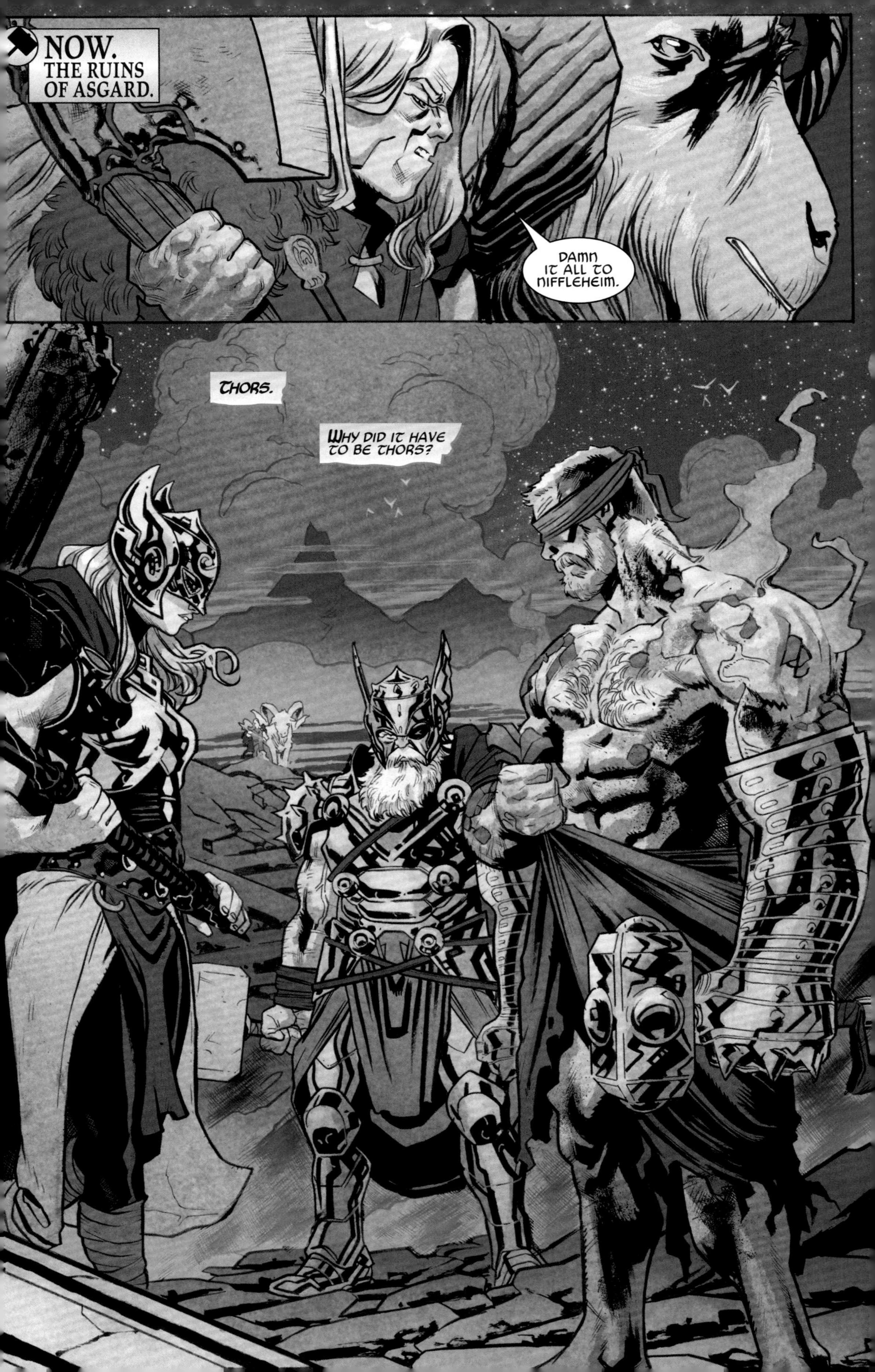
NOW.
THE RUINS OF ASGARD.
DAMN IT ALL TO NIFFLEHEIM.
THORS.
WHY DID IT HAVE TO BE THORS?

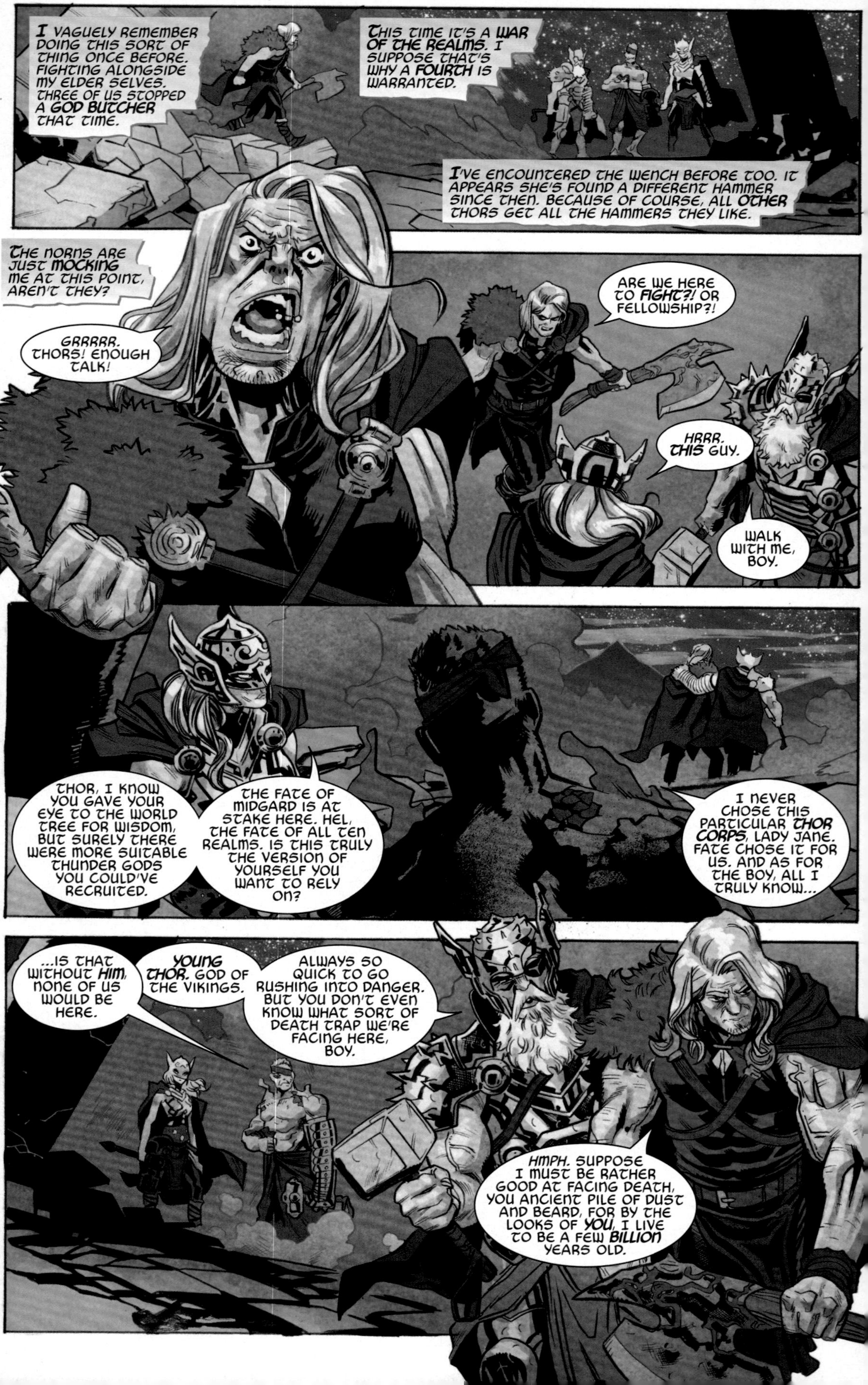
I VAGUELY REMEMBER DOING THIS SORT OF THING ONCE BEFORE. FIGHTING ALONGSIDE MY ELDER SELVES. THREE OF US STOPPED A GOD BUTCHER THAT TIME.
THIS TIME IT'S A WAR OF THE REALMS. I SUPPOSE THAT'S WHY A FOURTH IS WARRANTED.
I'VE ENCOUNTERED THE WENCH BEFORE TOO. IT APPEARS SHE'S FOUND A DIFFERENT HAMMER SINCE THEN. BECAUSE OF COURSE, ALL OTHER THORS GET ALL THE HAMMERS THEY LIKE.
THE NORNS ARE JUST MOCKING ME AT THIS POINT, AREN'T THEY?
GRRRRR. THORS! ENOUGH TALK!
ARE WE HERE TO FIGHT?! OR FELLOWSHIP?!
HRRR. THIS GUY.
WALK WITH ME, BOY.
THOR, I KNOW YOU GAVE YOUR EYE TO THE WORLD TREE FOR WISDOM, BUT SURELY THERE WERE MORE SUITABLE THUNDER GODS YOU COULD'VE RECRUITED.
THE FATE OF MIDGARD IS AT STAKE HERE. HEL, THE FATE OF ALL TEN REALMS. IS THIS TRULY THE VERSION OF YOURSELF YOU WANT TO RELY ON?
I NEVER CHOSE THIS PARTICULAR THOR CORPS, LADY JANE. FATE CHOSE IT FOR US. AND AS FOR THE BOY, ALL I TRULY KNOW...
...IS THAT WITHOUT HIM, NONE OF US WOULD BE HERE.
YOUNG THOR. GOD OF THE VIKINGS.
ALWAYS SO QUICK TO GO RUSHING INTO DANGER. BUT YOU DON'T EVEN KNOW WHAT SORT OF DEATH TRAP WE'RE FACING HERE, BOY.
HMPH. SUPPOSE I MUST BE RATHER GOOD AT FACING DEATH, YOU ANCIENT PILE OF DUST AND BEARD, FOR BY THE LOOKS OF YOU, I LIVE TO BE A FEW BILLION YEARS OLD.

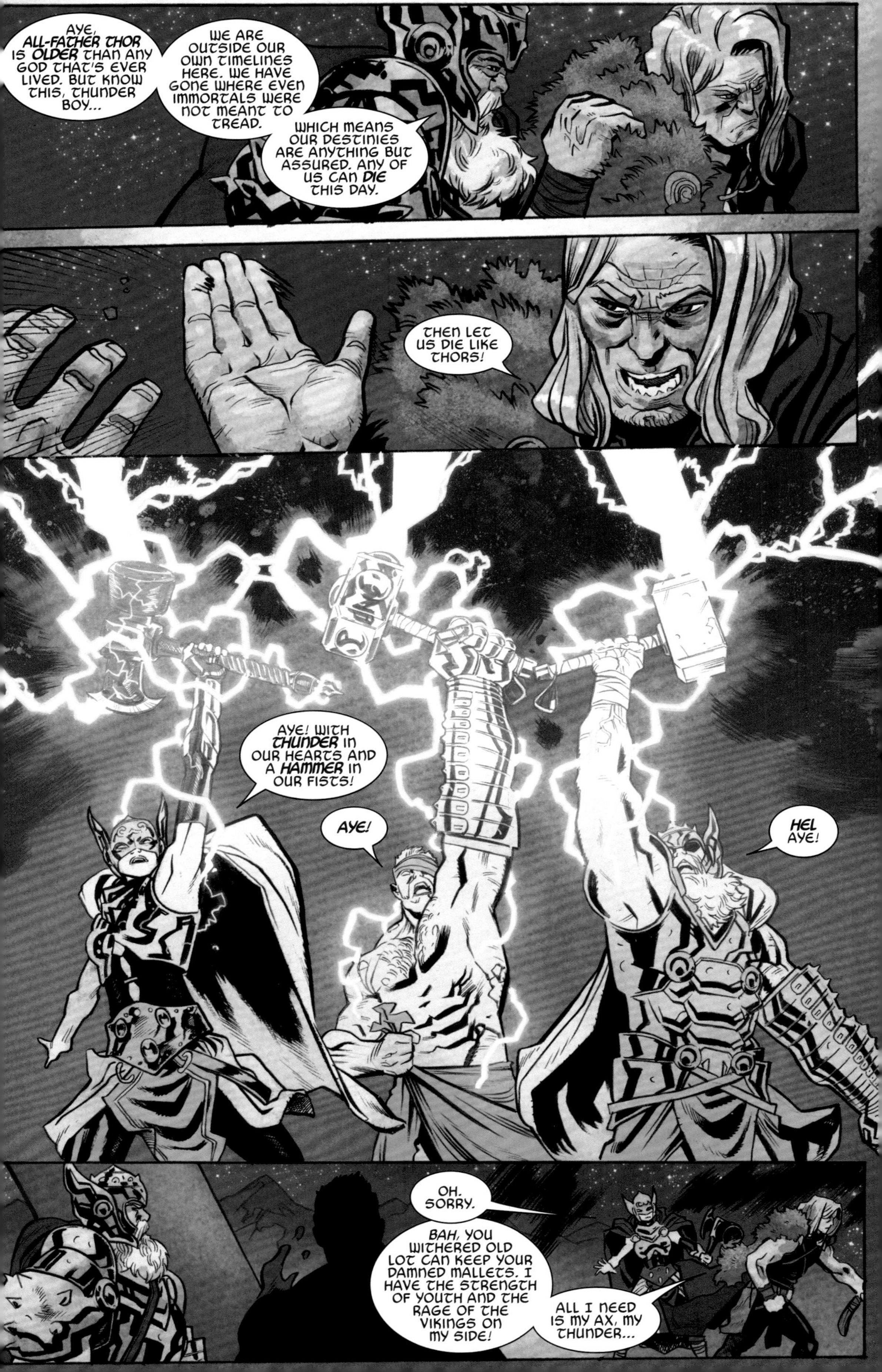
AYE, ALL-FATHER THOR IS OLDER THAN ANY GOD THAT'S EVER LIVED. BUT KNOW THIS, THUNDER BOY...
WE ARE OUTSIDE OUR OWN TIMELINES HERE. WE HAVE GONE WHERE EVEN IMMORTALS WERE NOT MEANT TO TREAD.
WHICH MEANS OUR DESTINIES ARE ANYTHING BUT ASSURED. ANY OF US CAN DIE THIS DAY.
THEN LET US DIE LIKE THORS!
AYE! WITH THUNDER IN OUR HEARTS AND A HAMMER IN OUR FISTS!
AYE!
HEL AYE!
OH. SORRY.
BAH, YOU WITHERED OLD LOT CAN KEEP YOUR DAMNED MALLETS. I HAVE THE STRENGTH OF YOUTH AND THE RAGE OF THE VIKINGS ON MY SIDE!
ALL I NEED IS MY AX, MY THUNDER...

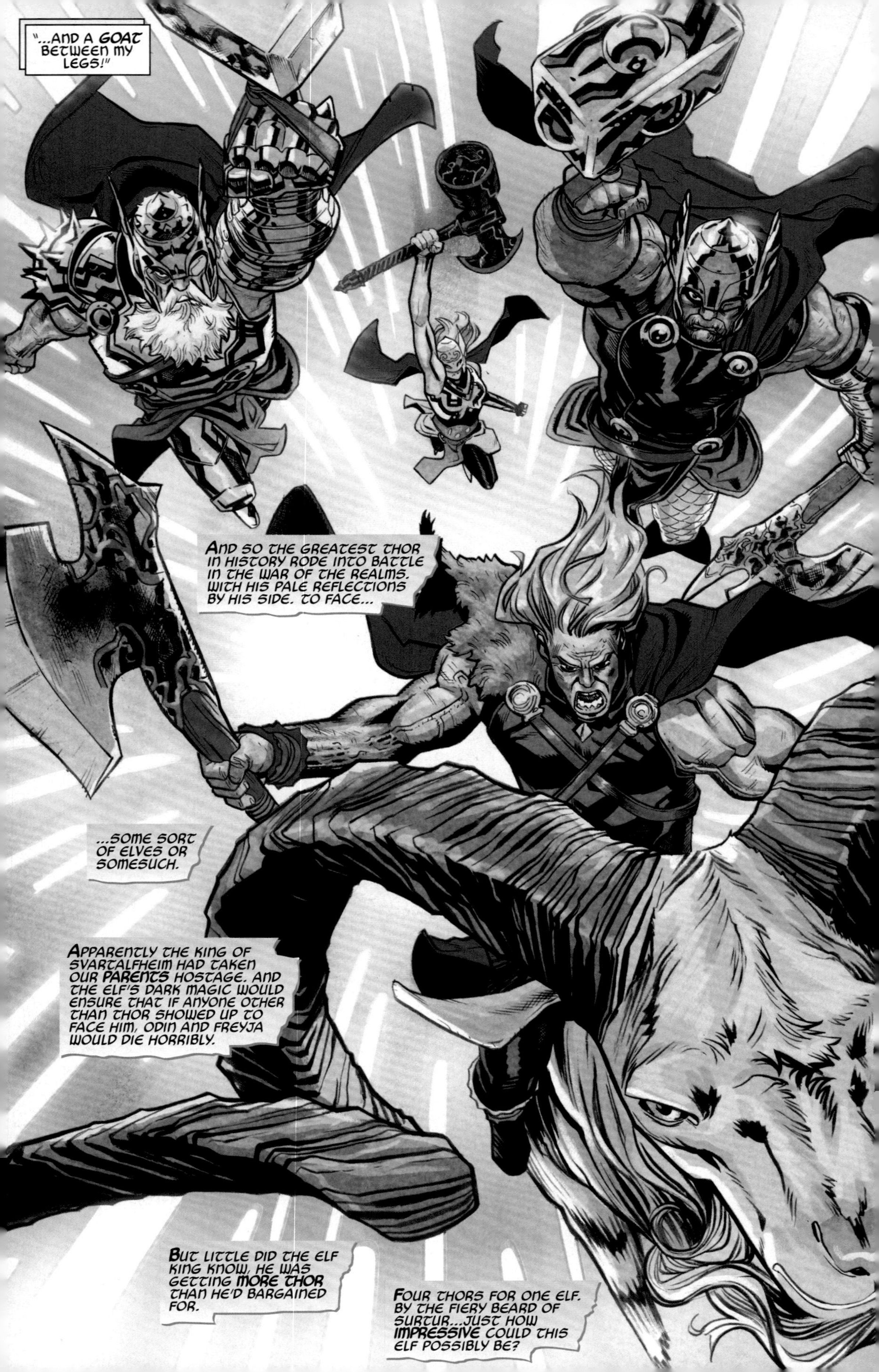
"...AND A GOAT BETWEEN MY LEGS!"
AND SO THE GREATEST THOR IN HISTORY RODE INTO BATTLE IN THE WAR OF THE REALMS. WITH HIS PALE REFLECTIONS BY HIS SIDE. TO FACE...
...SOME SORT OF ELVES OR SOMESUCH.
APPARENTLY THE KING OF SVARTALFHEIM HAD TAKEN OUR PARENTS HOSTAGE. AND THE ELF'S DARK MAGIC WOULD ENSURE THAT IF ANYONE OTHER THAN THOR SHOWED UP TO FACE HIM, ODIN AND FREYJA WOULD DIE HORRIBLY.
BUT LITTLE DID THE ELF KING KNOW, HE WAS GETTING MORE THOR THAN HE'D BARGAINED FOR.
FOUR THORS FOR ONE ELF. BY THE FIERY BEARD OF SURTUR...JUST HOW IMPRESSIVE COULD THIS ELF POSSIBLY BE?

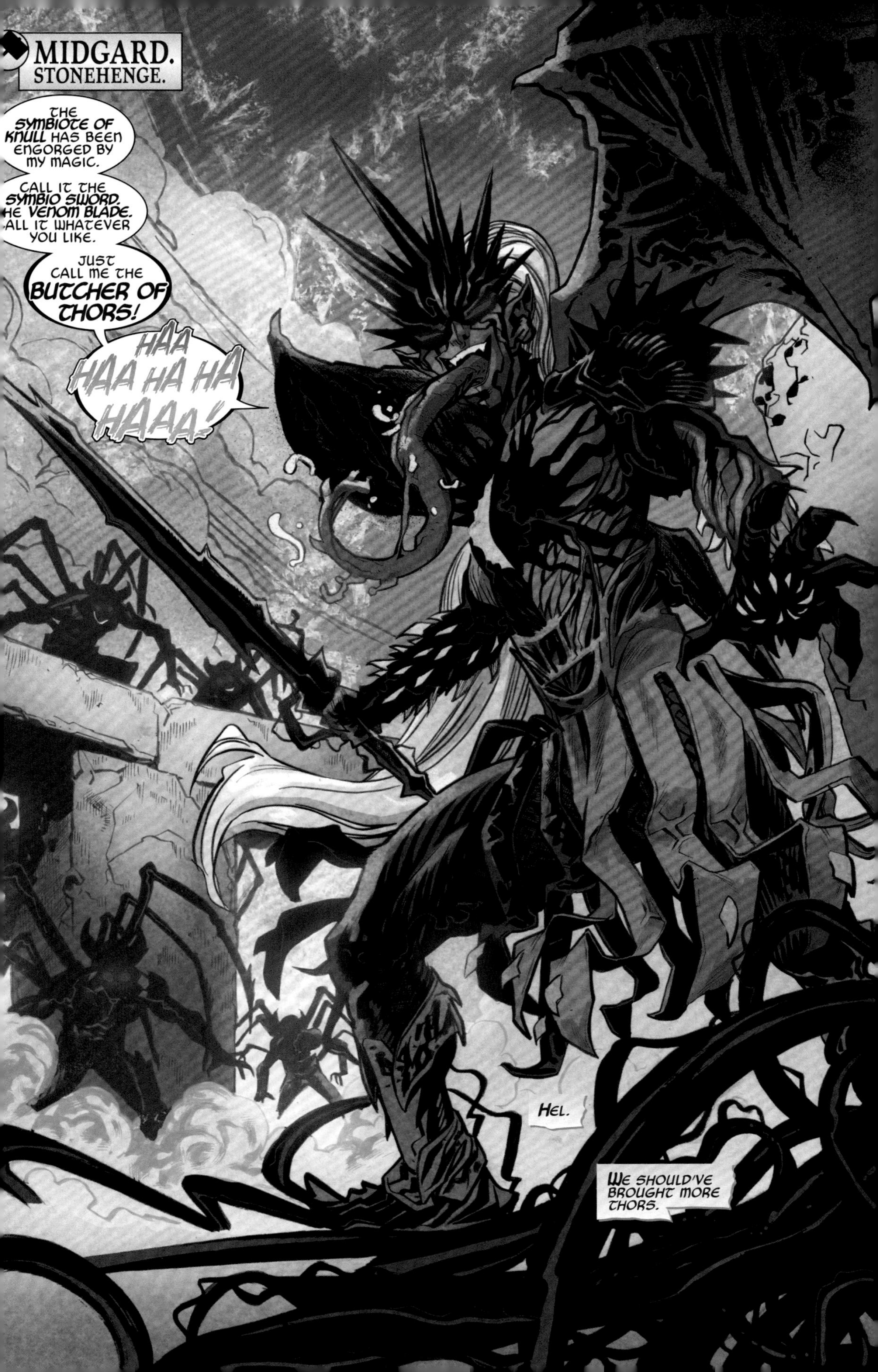
MIDGARD. STONEHENGE.
THE SYMBIOTE OF KNULL HAS BEEN ENGORGED BY MY MAGIC.
CALL IT THE SYMBIO SWORD. THE VENOM BLADE. CALL IT WHATEVER YOU LIKE.
JUST CALL ME THE BUTCHER OF THORS!
HAA HAA HA HA HAAA!
HEL.
WE SHOULD'VE BROUGHT MORE THORS.

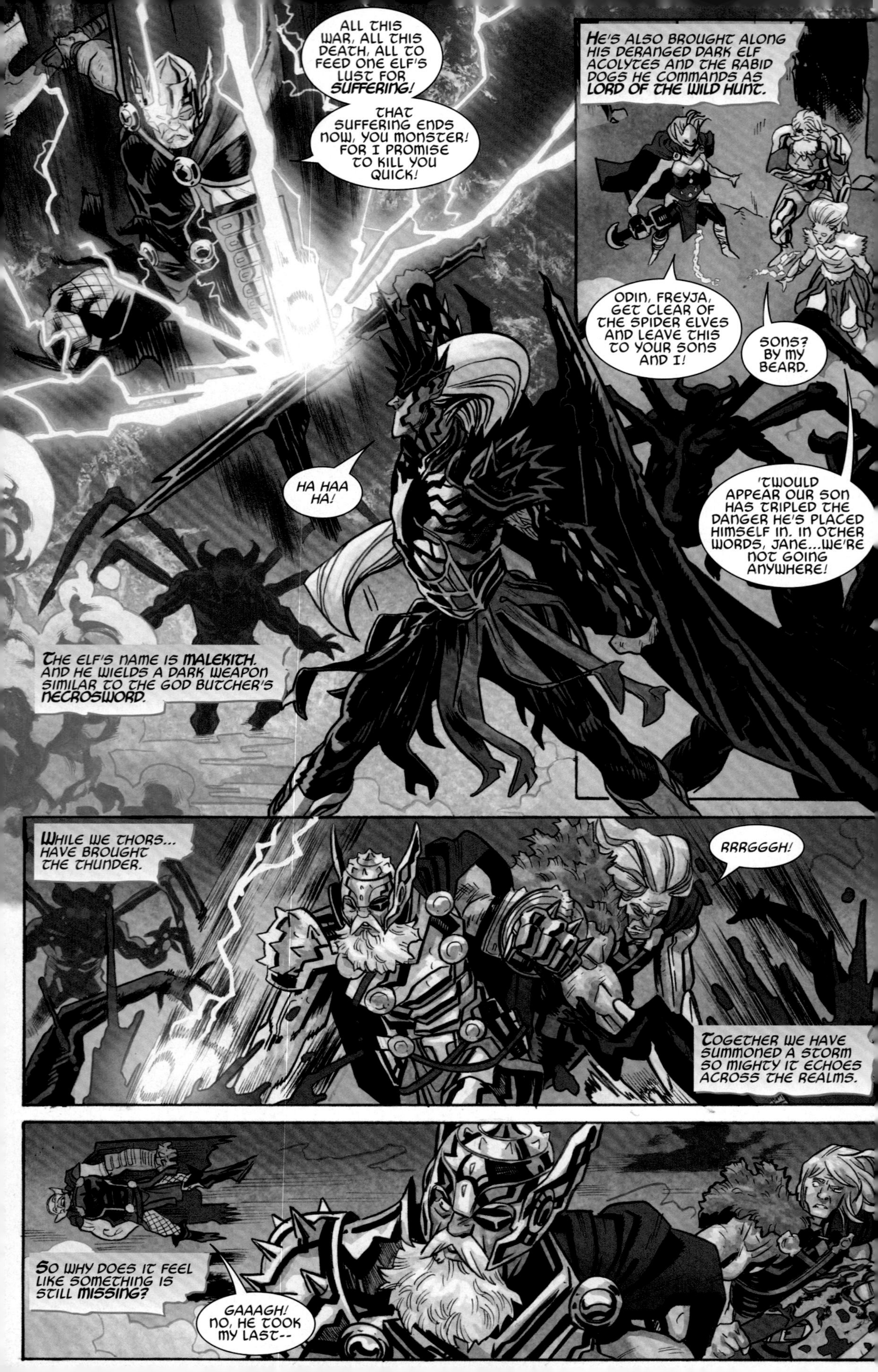
ALL THIS WAR, ALL THIS DEATH, ALL TO FEED ONE ELF'S LUST FOR SUFFERING!
THAT SUFFERING ENDS NOW, YOU MONSTER! FOR I PROMISE TO KILL YOU QUICK!
HE'S ALSO BROUGHT ALONG HIS DERANGED DARK ELF ACOLYTES AND THE RABID DOGS HE COMMANDS AS LORD OF THE WILD HUNT.
ODIN, FREYJA, GET CLEAR OF THE SPIDER ELVES AND LEAVE THIS TO YOUR SONS AND I!
SONS? BY MY BEARD.
HA HAA HA!
'TWOULD APPEAR OUR SON HAS TRIPLED THE DANGER HE'S PLACED HIMSELF IN. IN OTHER WORDS, JANE...WE'RE NOT GOING ANYWHERE!
THE ELF'S NAME IS MALEKITH. AND HE WIELDS A DARK WEAPON SIMILAR TO THE GOD BUTCHER'S NECROSWORD.
WHILE WE THORS... HAVE BROUGHT THE THUNDER.
RRRGGGH!
TOGETHER WE HAVE SUMMONED A STORM SO MIGHTY IT ECHOES ACROSS THE REALMS.
SO WHY DOES IT FEEL LIKE SOMETHING IS STILL MISSING?
GAAAGH! NO, HE TOOK MY LAST--

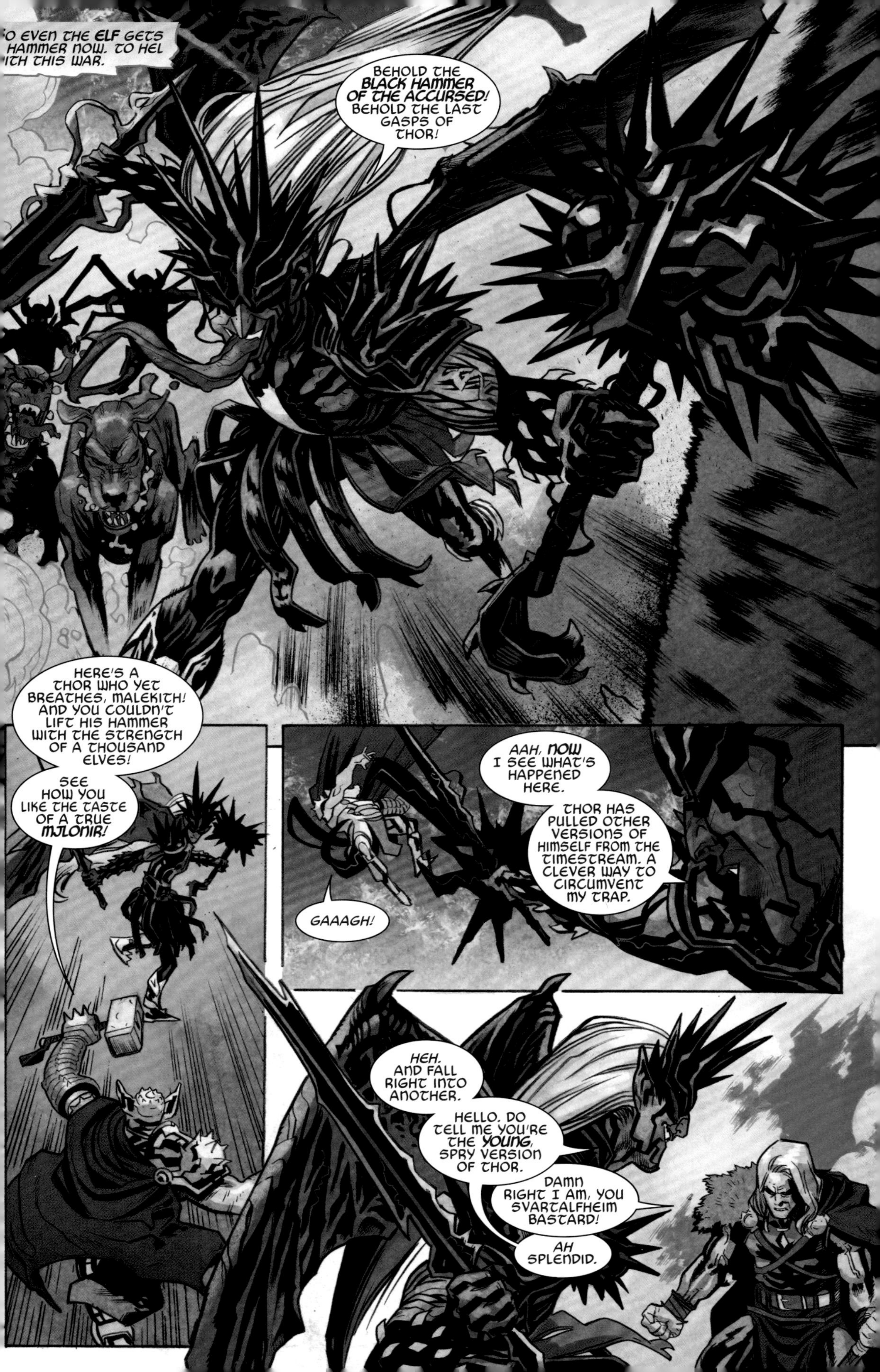

O EVEN THE ELF GETS HAMMER NOW. TO HEL ITH THIS WAR.
BEHOLD THE BLACK HAMMER OF THE ACCURSED! BEHOLD THE LAST GASPS OF THOR!
HERE'S A THOR WHO YET BREATHES, MALEKITH! AND YOU COULDN'T LIFT HIS HAMMER WITH THE STRENGTH OF A THOUSAND ELVES!
SEE HOW YOU LIKE THE TASTE OF A TRUE MJOLNIR!
AAH, NOW I SEE WHAT'S HAPPENED HERE.
THOR HAS PULLED OTHER VERSIONS OF HIMSELF FROM THE TIMESTREAM. A CLEVER WAY TO CIRCUMVENT MY TRAP.
GAAAGH!
HEH. AND FALL RIGHT INTO ANOTHER.
HELLO. DO TELL ME YOU'RE THE YOUNG, SPRY VERSION OF THOR.
DAMN RIGHT I AM, YOU SVARTALFHEIM BASTARD!
AH SPLENDID.

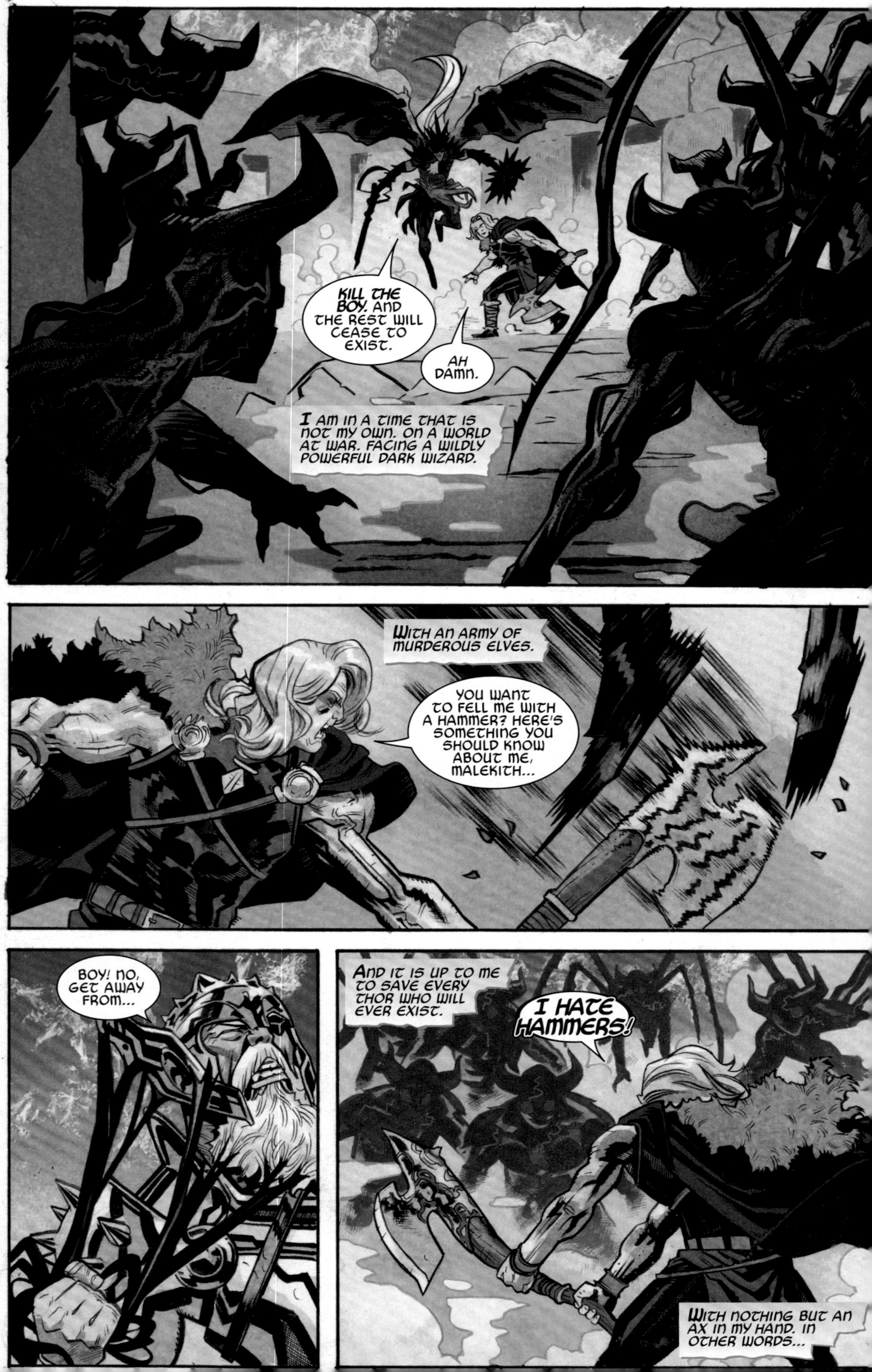

KILL THE BOY. AND THE REST WILL CEASE TO EXIST.
AH DAMN.
I AM IN A TIME THAT IS NOT MY OWN. ON A WORLD AT WAR. FACING A WILDLY POWERFUL DARK WIZARD.
WITH AN ARMY OF MURDEROUS ELVES.
YOU WANT TO FELL ME WITH A HAMMER? HERE'S SOMETHING YOU SHOULD KNOW ABOUT ME, MALEKITH...
BOY! NO, GET AWAY FROM...
AND IT IS UP TO ME TO SAVE EVERY THOR WHO WILL EVER EXIST.
I HATE HAMMERS!
WITH NOTHING BUT AN AX IN MY HAND. IN OTHER WORDS...

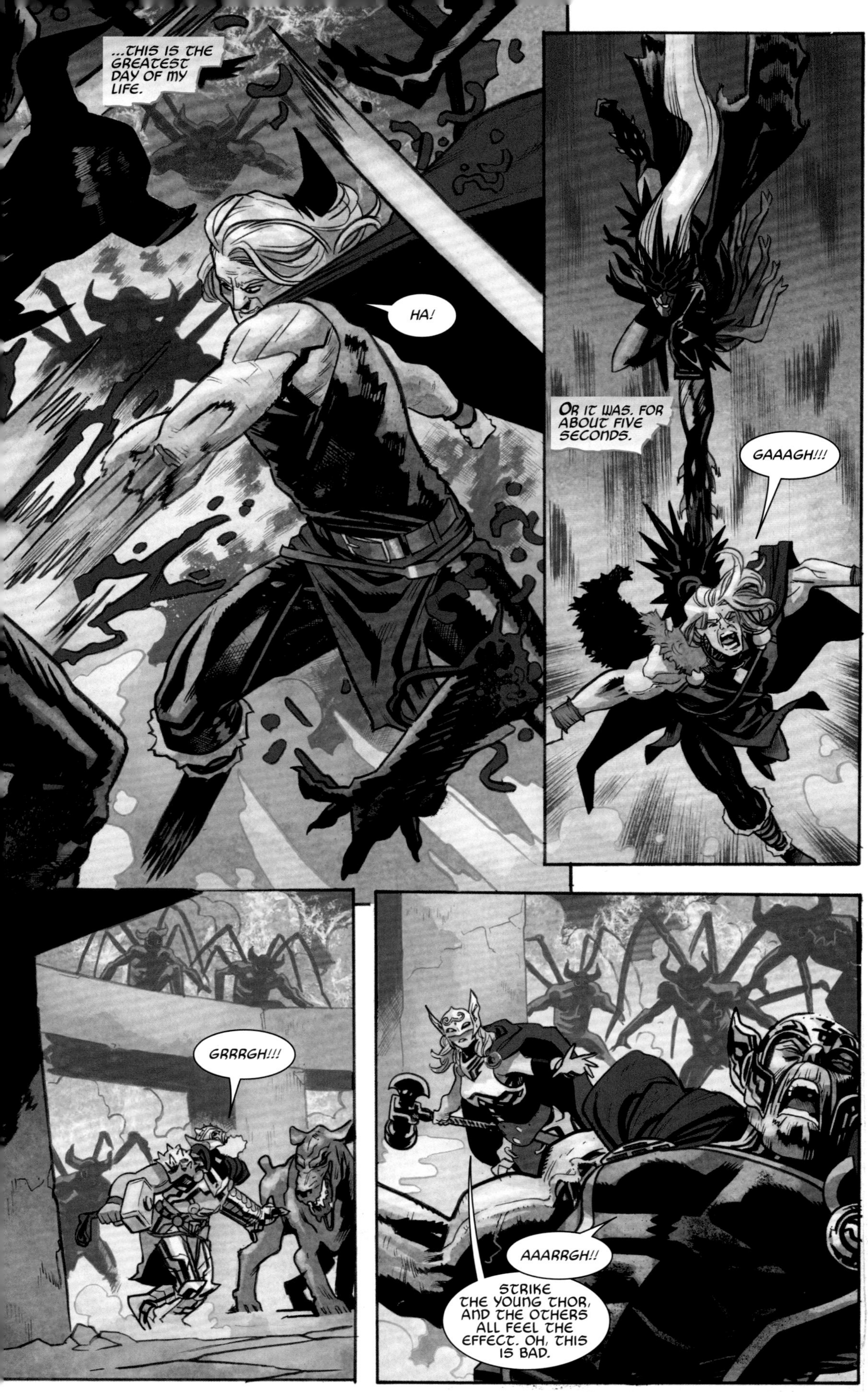
...THIS IS THE GREATEST DAY OF MY LIFE.
HA!
OR IT WAS. FOR ABOUT FIVE SECONDS.
GAAAGH!!!
GRRRGH!!!
AAARRGH!!
STRIKE THE YOUNG THOR, AND THE OTHERS ALL FEEL THE EFFECT. OH, THIS IS BAD.

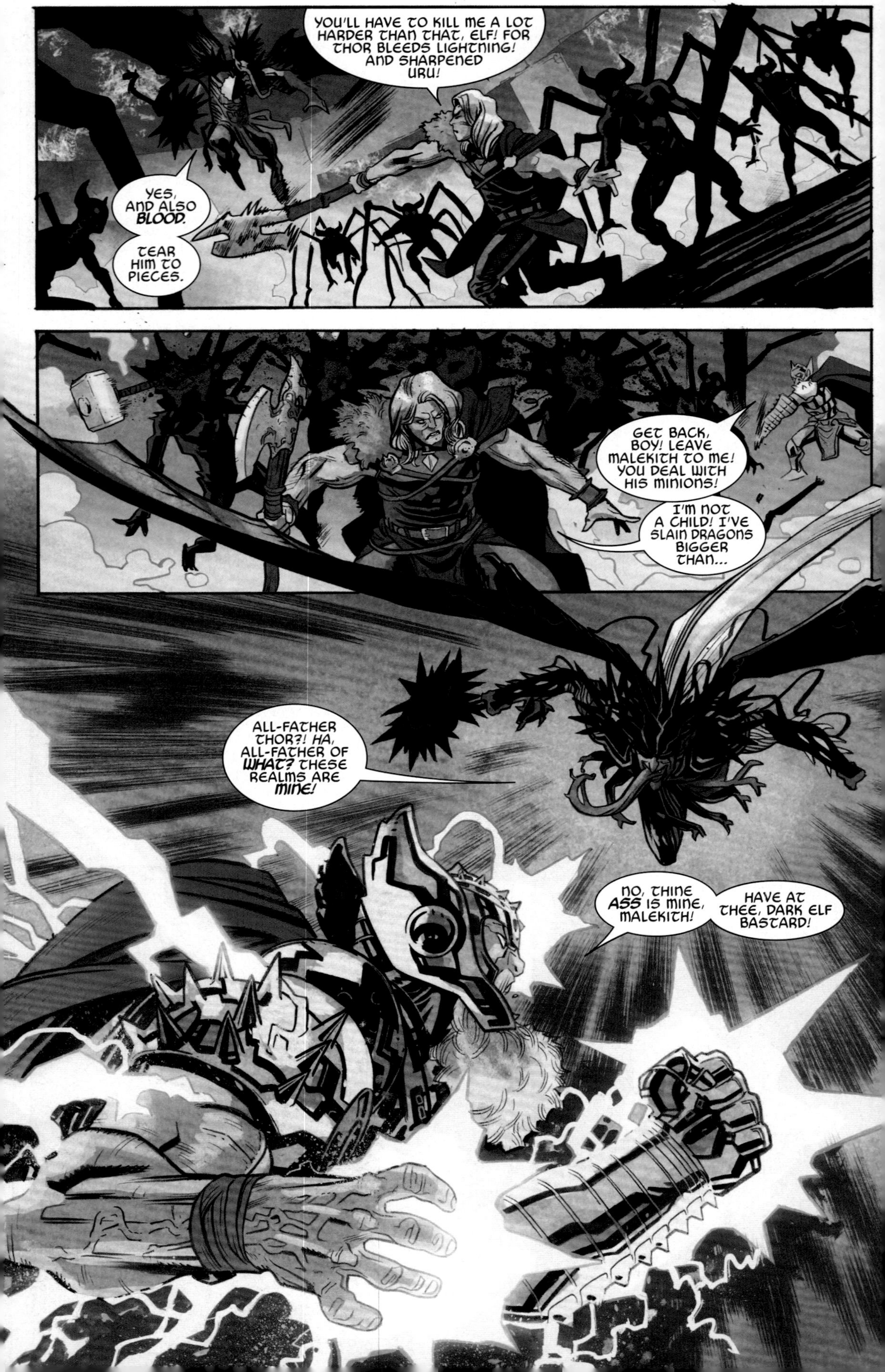
YOU'LL HAVE TO KILL ME A LOT HARDER THAN THAT, ELF! FOR THOR BLEEDS LIGHTNING! AND SHARPENED URU!
YES, AND ALSO BLOOD.
TEAR HIM TO PIECES.
GET BACK, BOY! LEAVE MALEKITH TO ME! YOU DEAL WITH HIS MINIONS!
I'M NOT A CHILD! I'VE SLAIN DRAGONS BIGGER THAN...
ALL-FATHER THOR?! HA, ALL-FATHER OF WHAT? THESE REALMS ARE MINE!
NO, THINE ASS IS MINE, MALEKITH!
HAVE AT THEE, DARK ELF BASTARD!

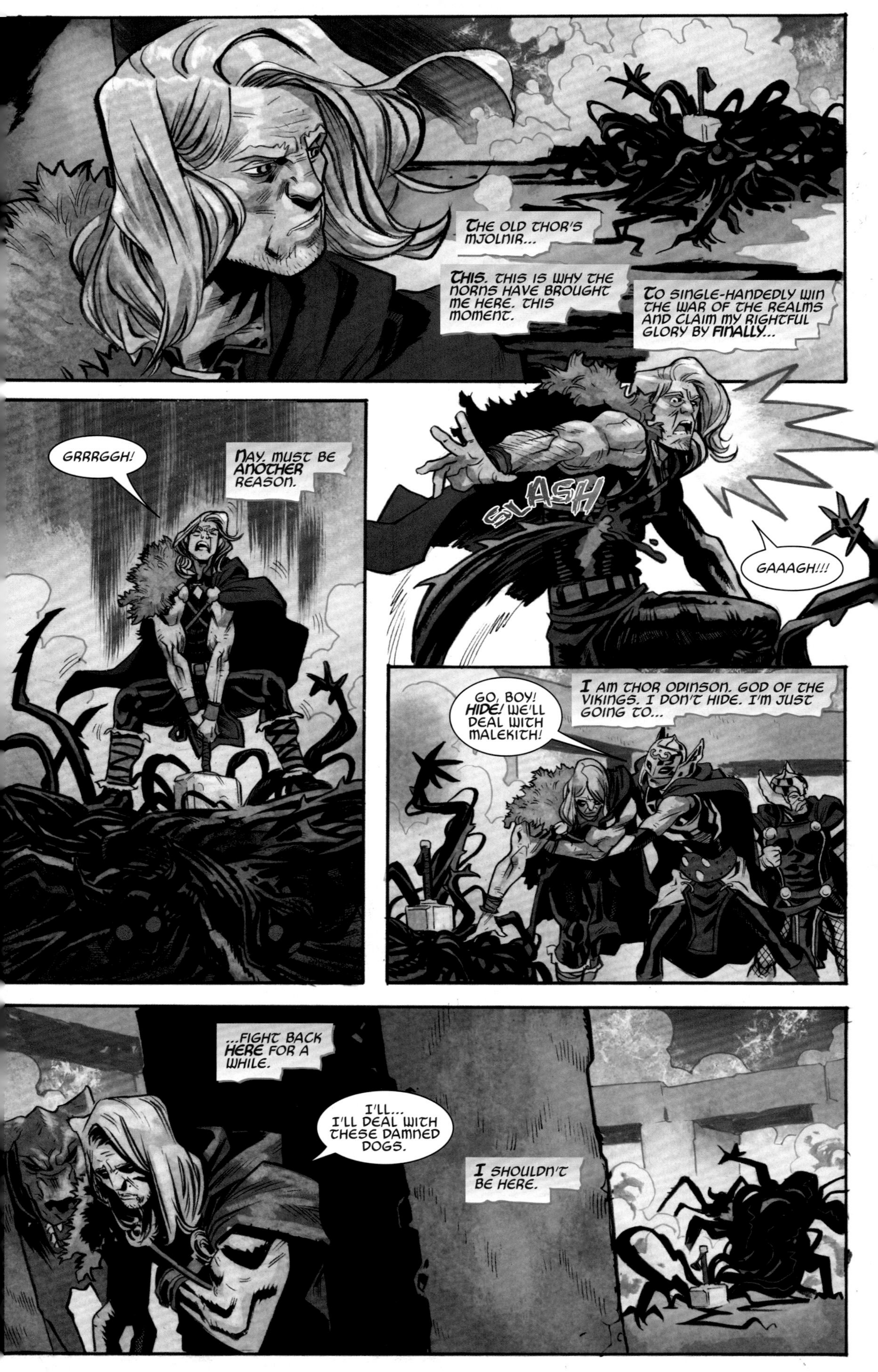

THE OLD THOR'S MJOLNIR...
THIS. THIS IS WHY THE NORNS HAVE BROUGHT ME HERE. THIS MOMENT.
TO SINGLE-HANDEDLY WIN THE WAR OF THE REALMS AND CLAIM MY RIGHTFUL GLORY BY FINALLY...
GRRRGGH!
NAY. MUST BE ANOTHER REASON.
SLASH
GAAAGH!!!
I AM THOR ODINSON. GOD OF THE VIKINGS. I DON'T HIDE. I'M JUST GOING TO...
GO, BOY! HIDE! WE'LL DEAL WITH MALEKITH!
...FIGHT BACK HERE FOR A WHILE.
I'LL... I'LL DEAL WITH THESE DAMNED DOGS.
I SHOULDN'T BE HERE.

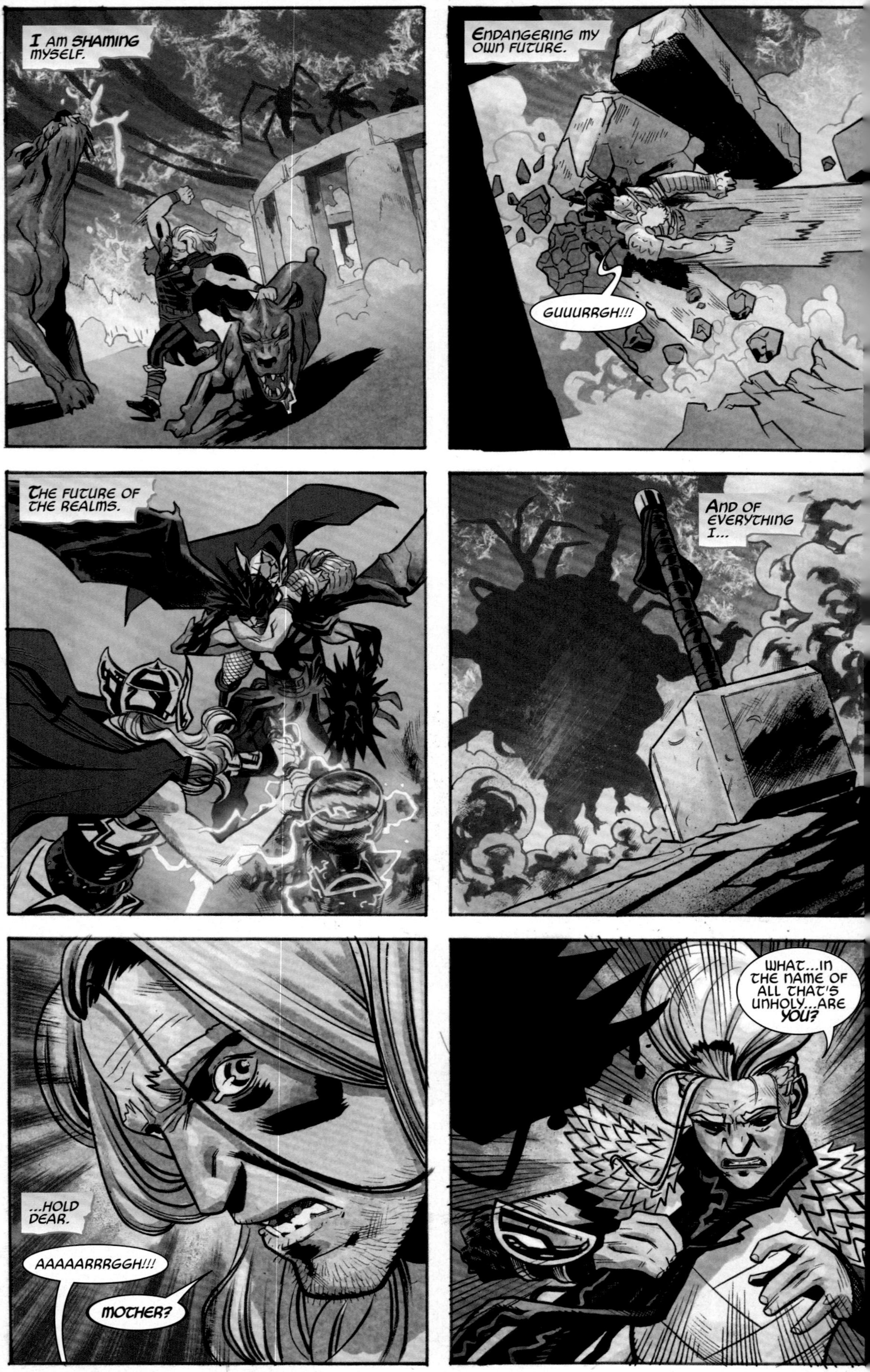
I AM SHAMING MYSELF.
ENDANGERING MY OWN FUTURE.
GUUURRGH!!!
THE FUTURE OF THE REALMS.
AND OF EVERYTHING I...
...HOLD DEAR.
AAAAARRRGGH!!!
MOTHER?
WHAT...IN THE NAME OF ALL THAT'S UNHOLY...ARE YOU?

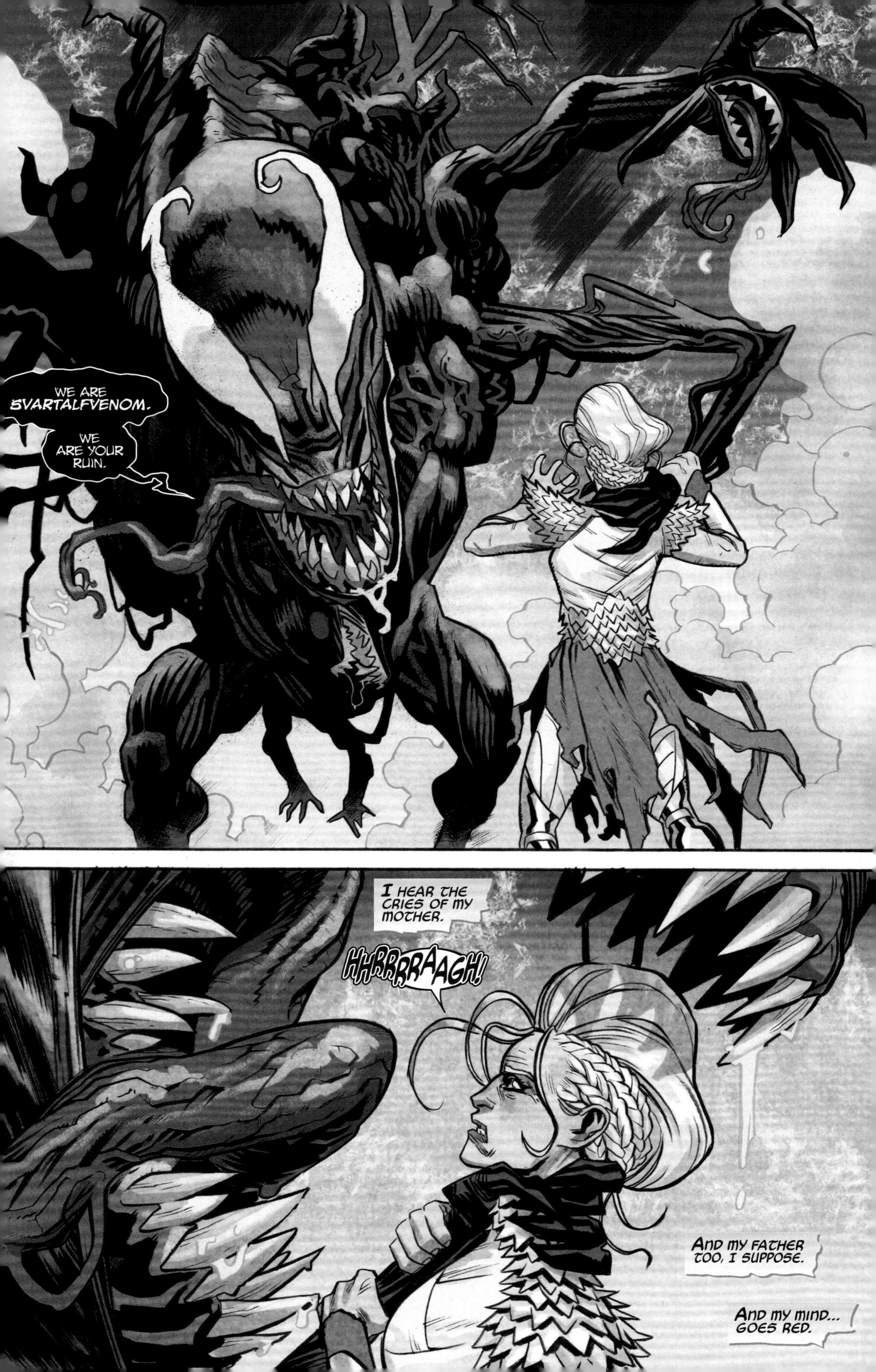
WE ARE SVARTALFVENOM.
WE ARE YOUR RUIN.
I HEAR THE CRIES OF MY MOTHER.
HHRRRRAAGH!
AND MY FATHER TOO, I SUPPOSE.
AND MY MIND... GOES RED.

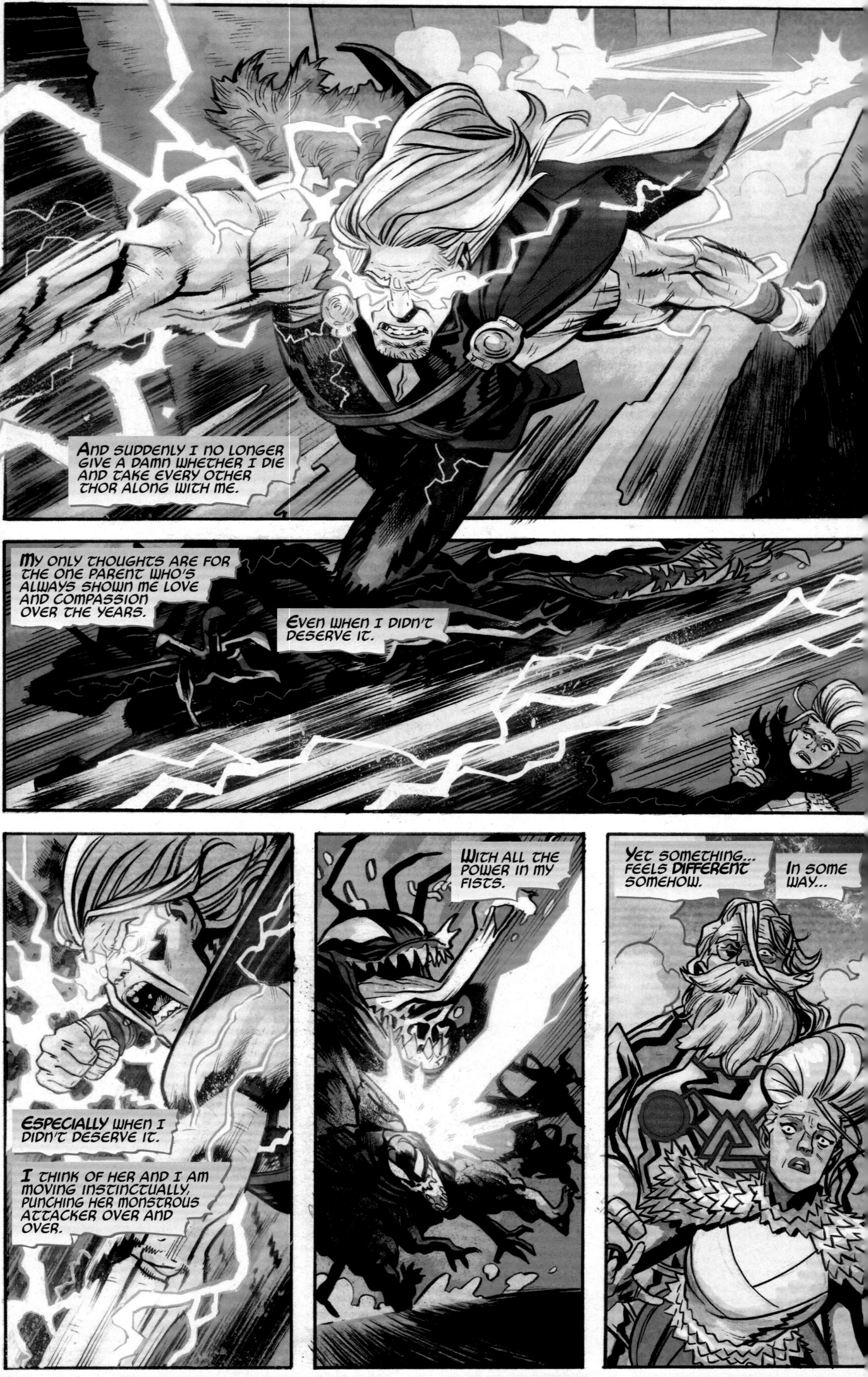
And suddenly I no longer give a damn whether I die and take every other Thor along with me.
My only thoughts are for the one parent who's always shown me love and compassion over the years.
Even when I didn't deserve it.
Especially when I didn't deserve it.
I think of her and I am moving instinctually, punching her monstrous attacker over and over.
With all the power in my fists.
Yet something... feels different somehow.
In some way...

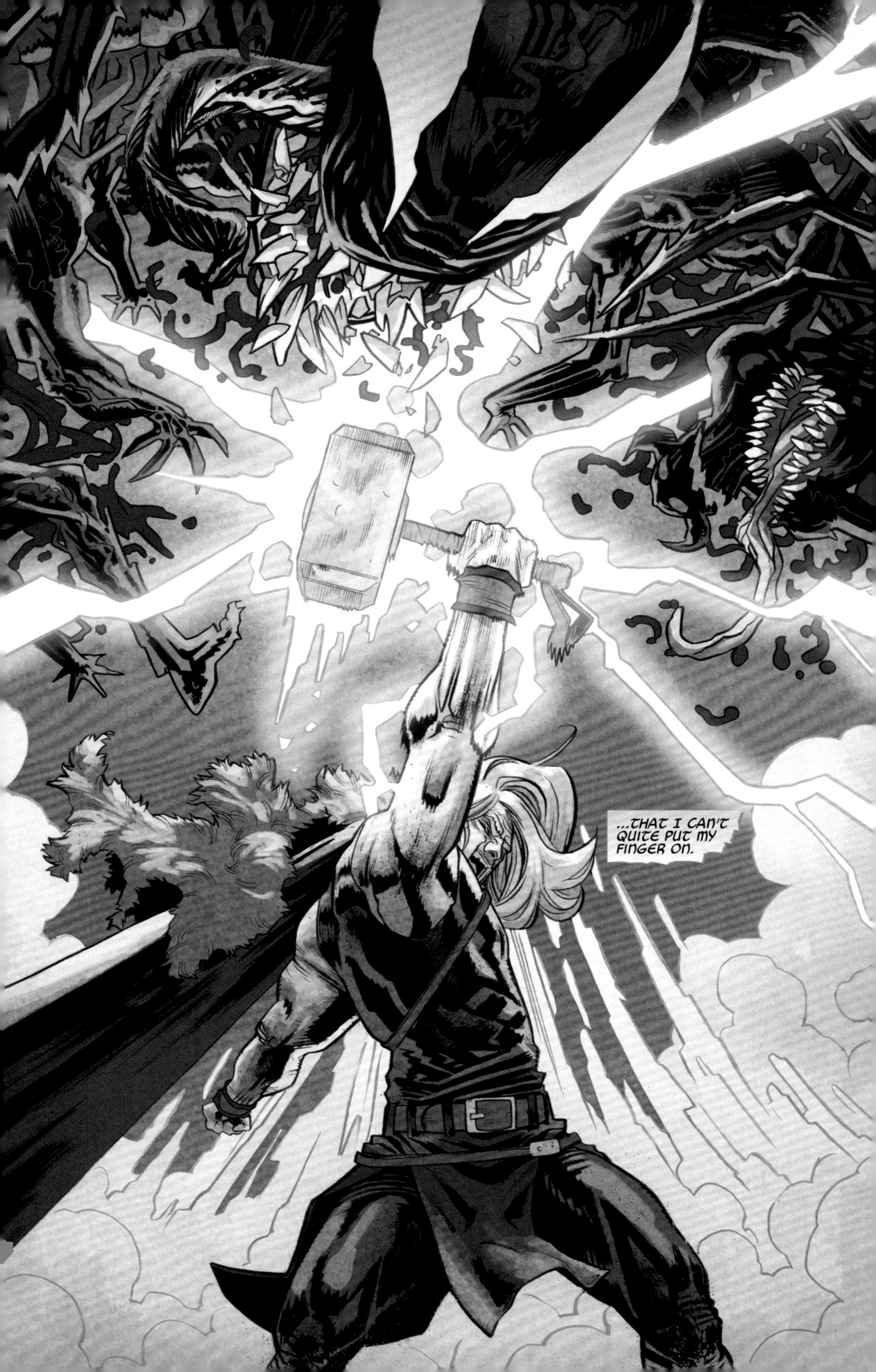
...THAT I CAN'T QUITE PUT MY FINGER ON.

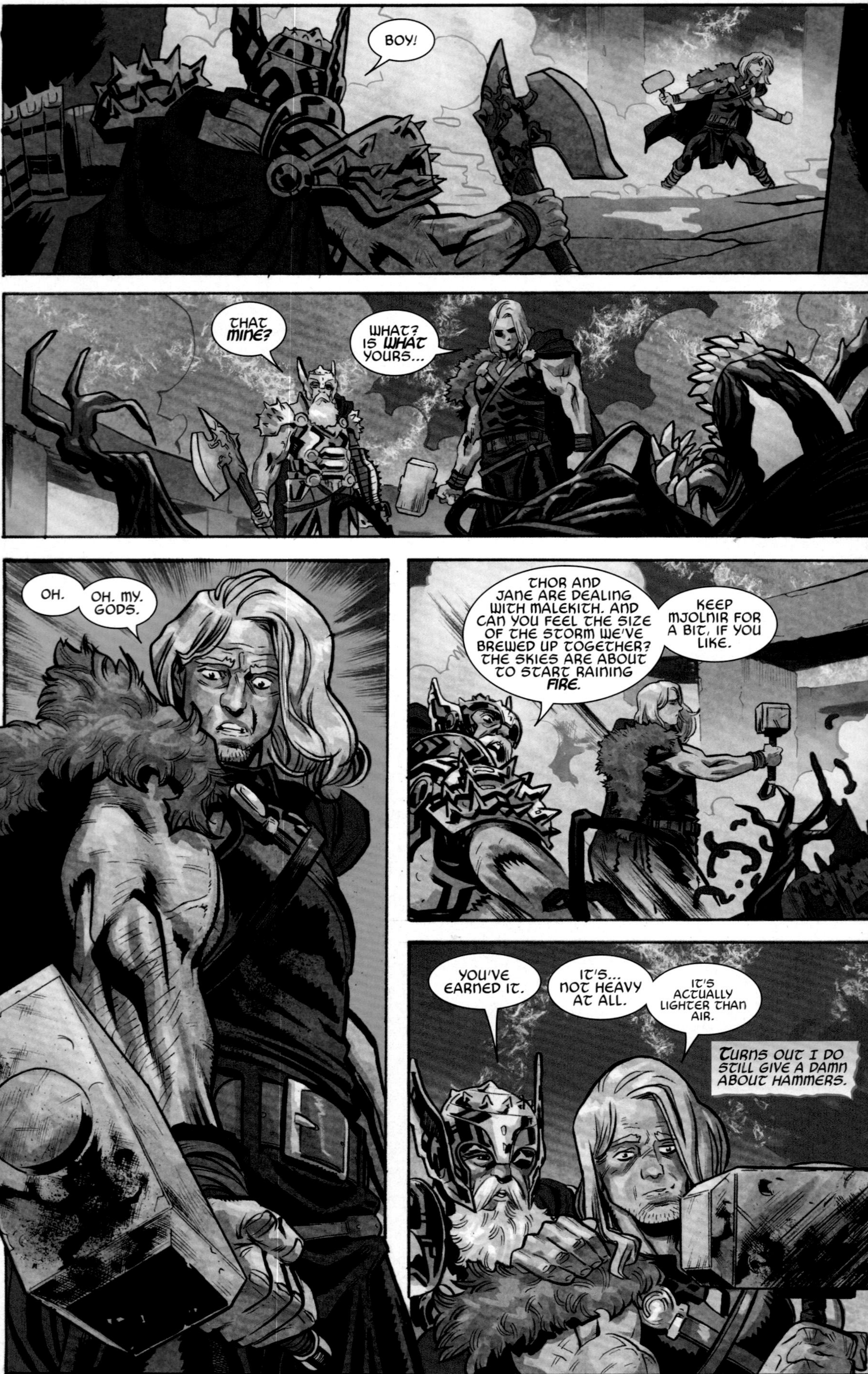
BOY!
THAT MINE?
WHAT? IS WHAT YOURS...
OH.
OH. MY. GODS.
THOR AND JANE ARE DEALING WITH MALEKITH. AND CAN YOU FEEL THE SIZE OF THE STORM WE'VE BREWED UP TOGETHER? THE SKIES ARE ABOUT TO START RAINING FIRE.
KEEP MJOLNIR FOR A BIT, IF YOU LIKE.
YOU'VE EARNED IT.
IT'S... NOT HEAVY AT ALL.
IT'S ACTUALLY LIGHTER THAN AIR.
TURNS OUT I DO STILL GIVE A DAMN ABOUT HAMMERS.

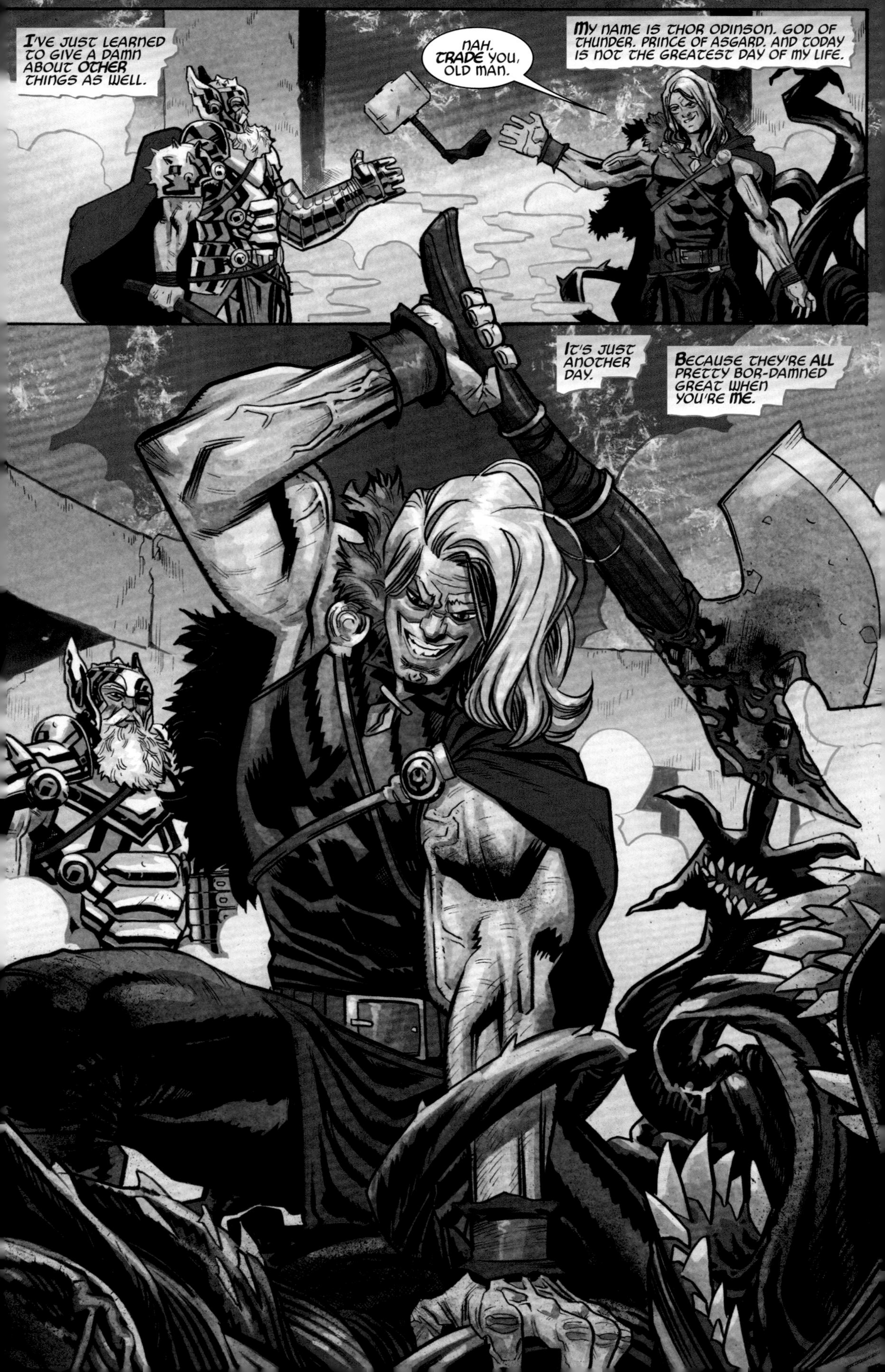
I'VE JUST LEARNED TO GIVE A DAMN ABOUT OTHER THINGS AS WELL.
NAH. TRADE YOU, OLD MAN.
MY NAME IS THOR ODINSON. GOD OF THUNDER. PRINCE OF ASGARD. AND TODAY IS NOT THE GREATEST DAY OF MY LIFE.
IT'S JUST ANOTHER DAY.
BECAUSE THEY'RE ALL PRETTY BOR-DAMNED GREAT WHEN YOU'RE ME.

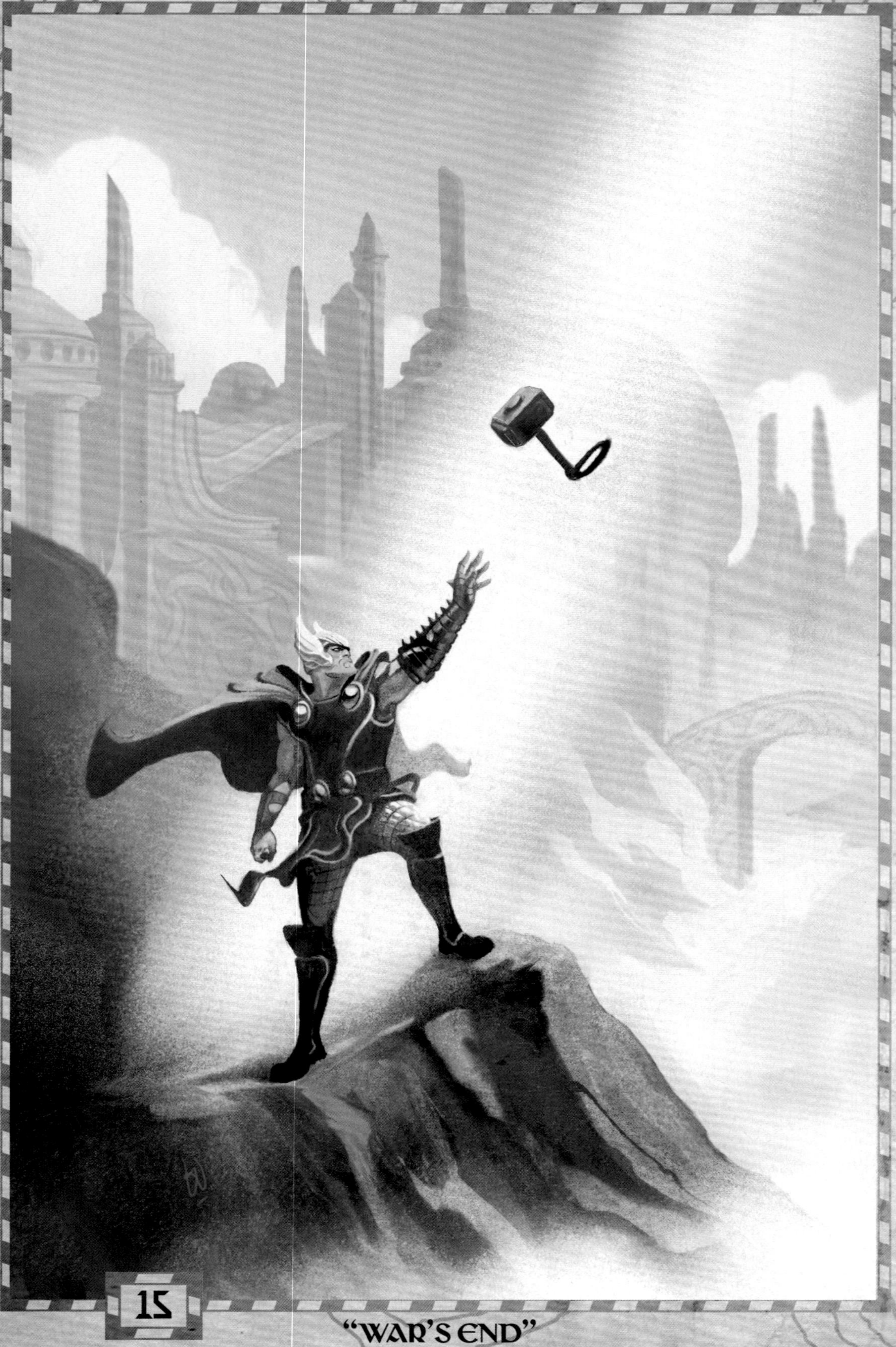

15

"WAR'S END"

The War of the Realms is over!

When the Dark Elf King Malekith gave Thor an ultimatum to face him alone or witness the death of his parents, Thor sought out the World Tree, now growing from the sun, for answers.

And he found them.

Gathering Thors from across space and time—including Jane Foster as the War Thor—the God of Thunder confronted Malekith and, with the wisdom of the World Tree and the energy of the Mother Storm, reforged the lost hammer Mjolnir.

Now Malekith is defeated. Loki is resurrected after bursting through the stomach of his father, King Laufey. Jane Foster is on the verge of a new transformation after the War Thor's hammer broke apart. And Odin just declared his son the new All-Father of Asgard.

Things are changing in the Ten Realms. What happens next?

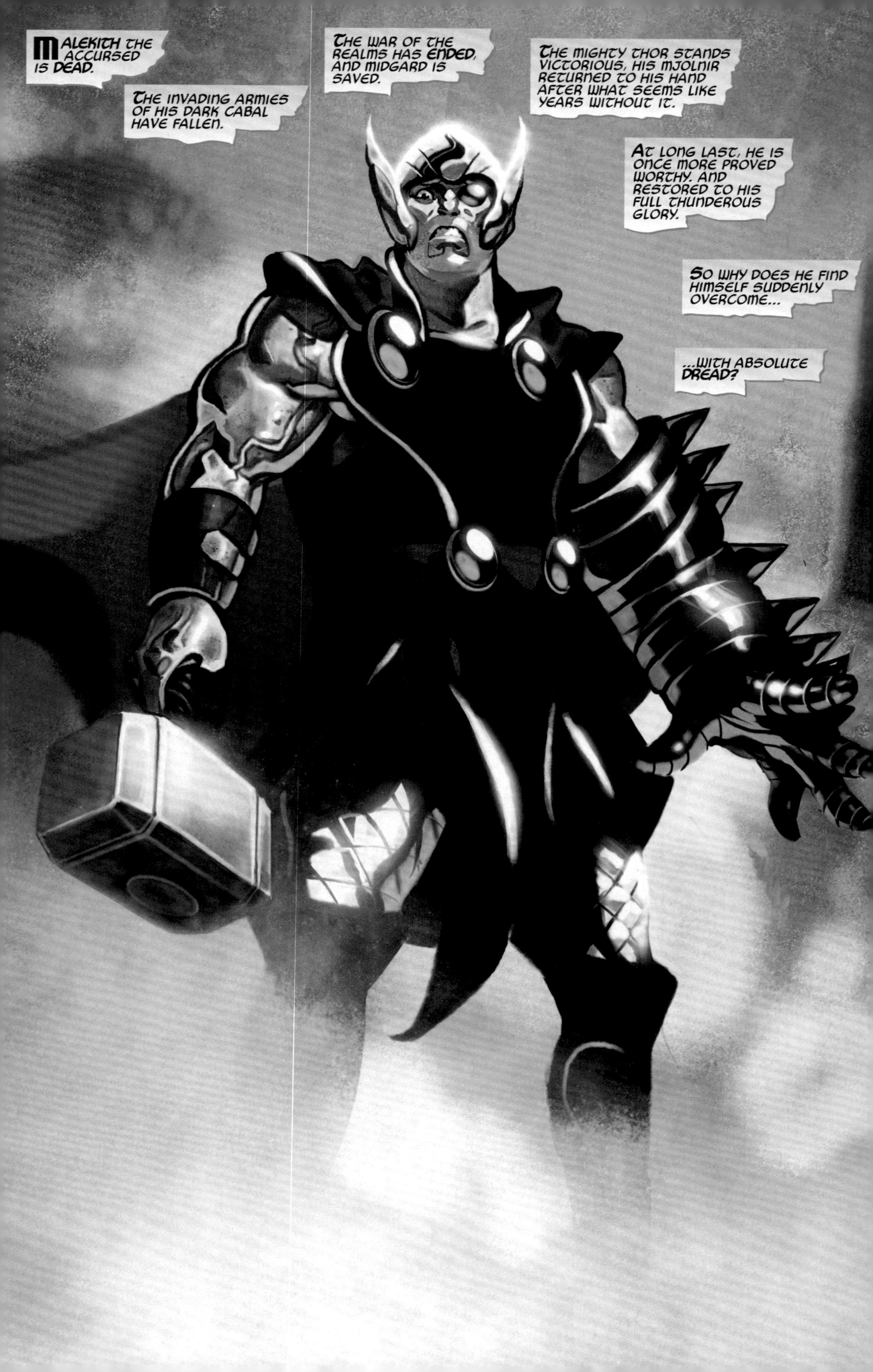
MALEKITH THE ACCURSED IS DEAD.
THE INVADING ARMIES OF HIS DARK CABAL HAVE FALLEN.
THE WAR OF THE REALMS HAS ENDED, AND MIDGARD IS SAVED.
THE MIGHTY THOR STANDS VICTORIOUS, HIS MJOLNIR RETURNED TO HIS HAND AFTER WHAT SEEMS LIKE YEARS WITHOUT IT.
AT LONG LAST, HE IS ONCE MORE PROVED WORTHY. AND RESTORED TO HIS FULL THUNDEROUS GLORY.
SO WHY DOES HE FIND HIMSELF SUDDENLY OVERCOME...
...WITH ABSOLUTE DREAD?

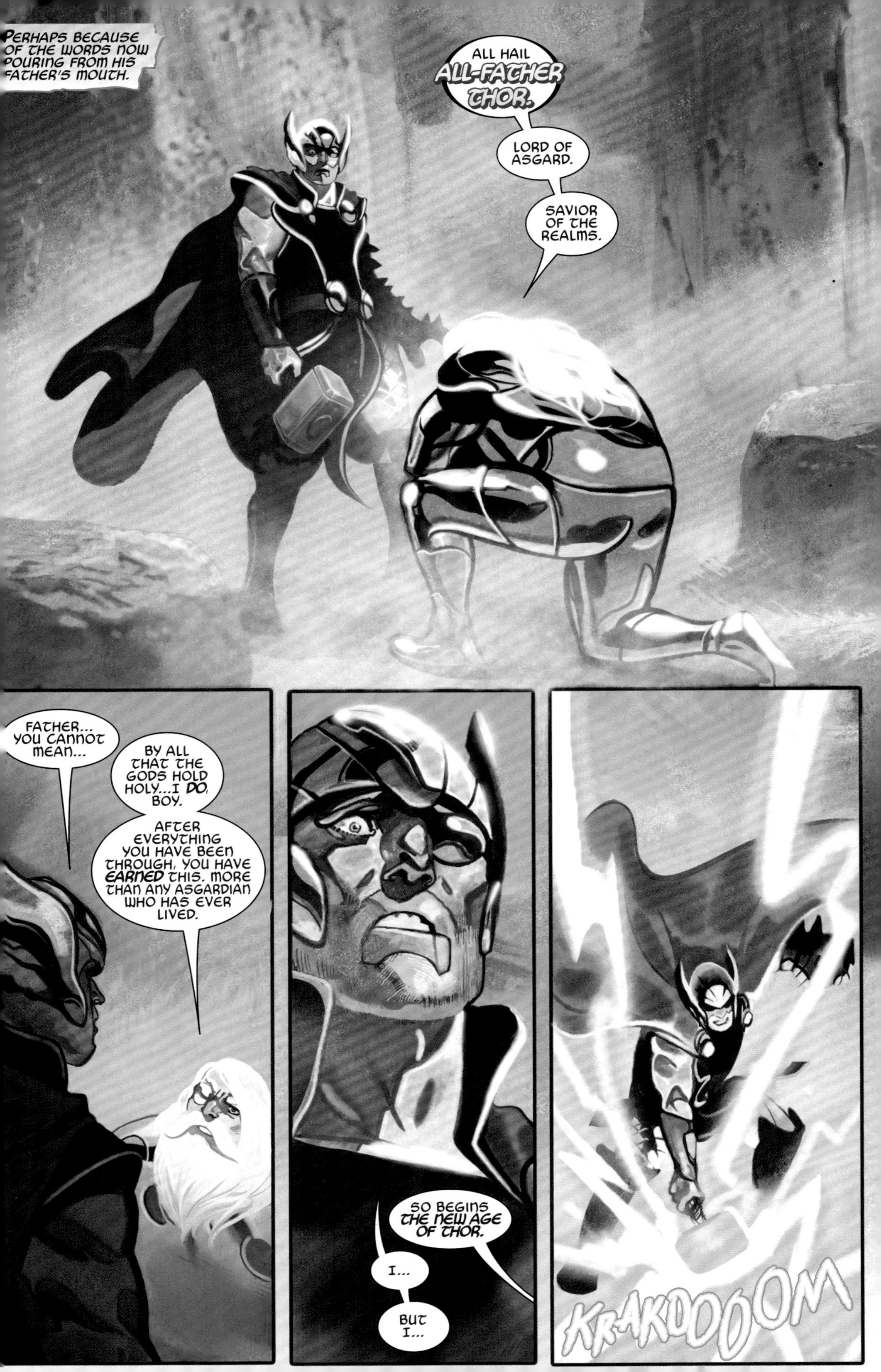
PERHAPS BECAUSE OF THE WORDS NOW POURING FROM HIS FATHER'S MOUTH.
ALL HAIL ALL-FATHER THOR.
LORD OF ASGARD.
SAVIOR OF THE REALMS.
FATHER... YOU CANNOT MEAN...
BY ALL THAT THE GODS HOLD HOLY...I DO, BOY.
AFTER EVERYTHING YOU HAVE BEEN THROUGH, YOU HAVE EARNED THIS. MORE THAN ANY ASGARDIAN WHO HAS EVER LIVED.
SO BEGINS THE NEW AGE OF THOR.
I...
BUT I...
KRAKOOOOOM

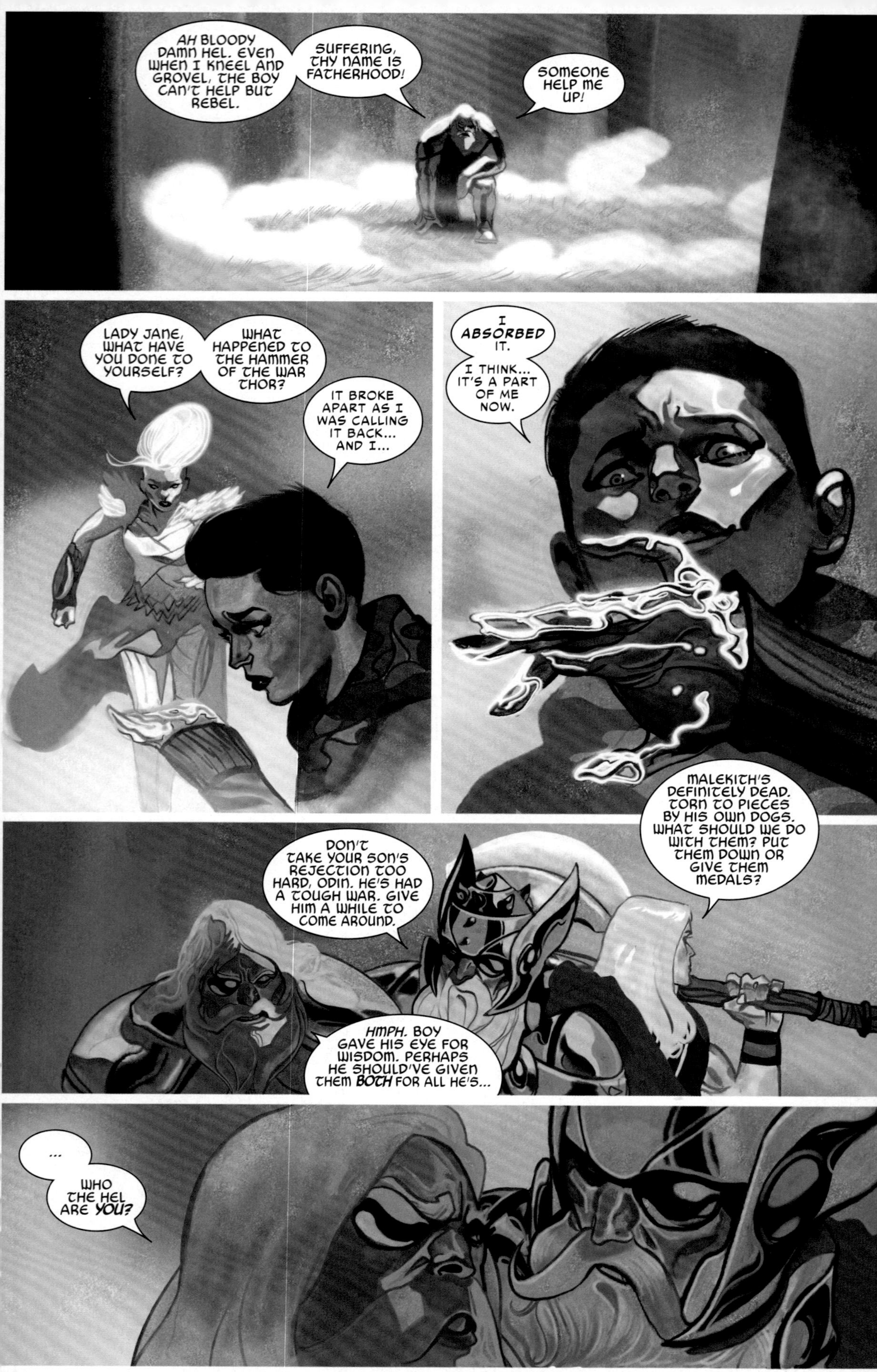
AH BLOODY DAMN HEL. EVEN WHEN I KNEEL AND GROVEL, THE BOY CAN'T HELP BUT REBEL.
SUFFERING, THY NAME IS FATHERHOOD!
SOMEONE HELP ME UP!
LADY JANE, WHAT HAVE YOU DONE TO YOURSELF?
WHAT HAPPENED TO THE HAMMER OF THE WAR THOR?
IT BROKE APART AS I WAS CALLING IT BACK... AND I...
I ABSORBED IT.
I THINK... IT'S A PART OF ME NOW.
MALEKITH'S DEFINITELY DEAD. TORN TO PIECES BY HIS OWN DOGS. WHAT SHOULD WE DO WITH THEM? PUT THEM DOWN OR GIVE THEM MEDALS?
DON'T TAKE YOUR SON'S REJECTION TOO HARD, ODIN. HE'S HAD A TOUGH WAR. GIVE HIM A WHILE TO COME AROUND.
HMPH. BOY GAVE HIS EYE FOR WISDOM. PERHAPS HE SHOULD'VE GIVEN THEM BOTH FOR ALL HE'S...
...
WHO THE HEL ARE YOU?

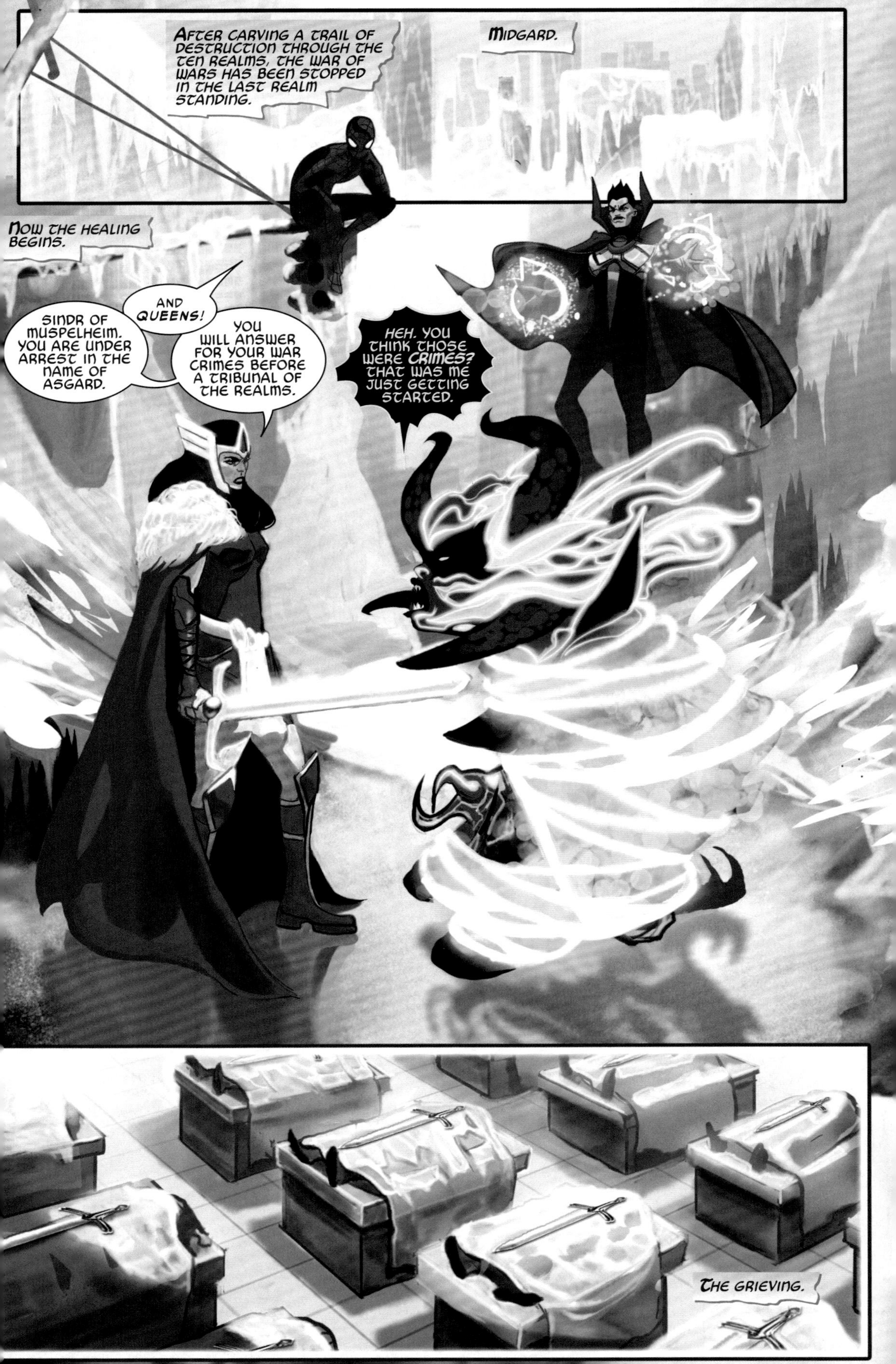
After carving a trail of destruction through the ten realms, the War of Wars has been stopped in the last realm standing.
Midgard.
Now the healing begins.
Sindr of Muspelheim. You are under arrest in the name of Asgard.
And Queens!
You will answer for your war crimes before a tribunal of the realms.
Heh. You think those were crimes? That was me just getting started.
The grieving.

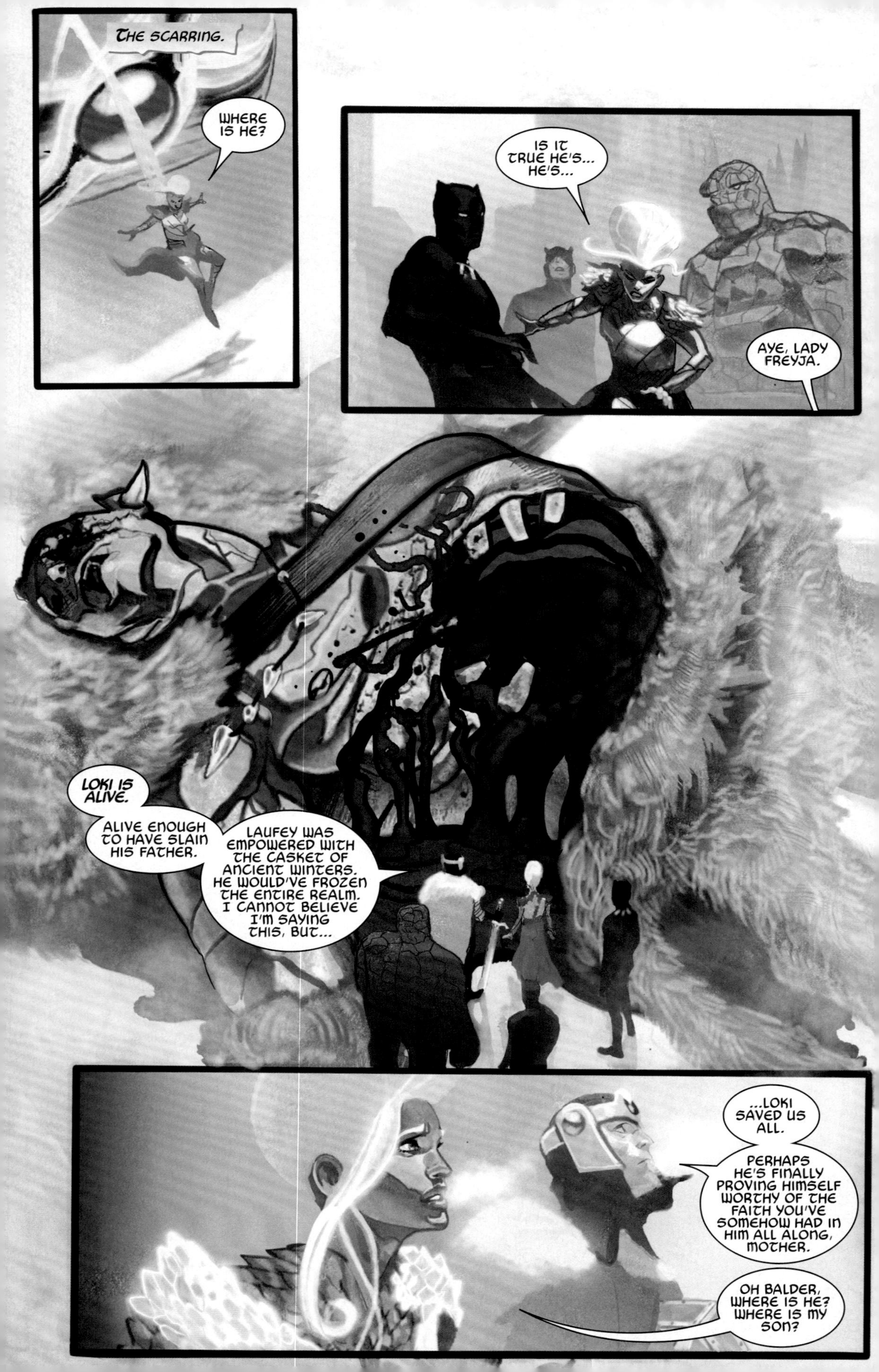
THE SCARRING.
WHERE IS HE?
IS IT TRUE HE'S... HE'S...
AYE, LADY FREYJA.
LOKI IS ALIVE.
ALIVE ENOUGH TO HAVE SLAIN HIS FATHER.
LAUFEY WAS EMPOWERED WITH THE CASKET OF ANCIENT WINTERS. HE WOULD'VE FROZEN THE ENTIRE REALM. I CANNOT BELIEVE I'M SAYING THIS, BUT...
...LOKI SAVED US ALL.
PERHAPS HE'S FINALLY PROVING HIMSELF WORTHY OF THE FAITH YOU'VE SOMEHOW HAD IN HIM ALL ALONG, MOTHER.
OH BALDER, WHERE IS HE? WHERE IS MY SON?

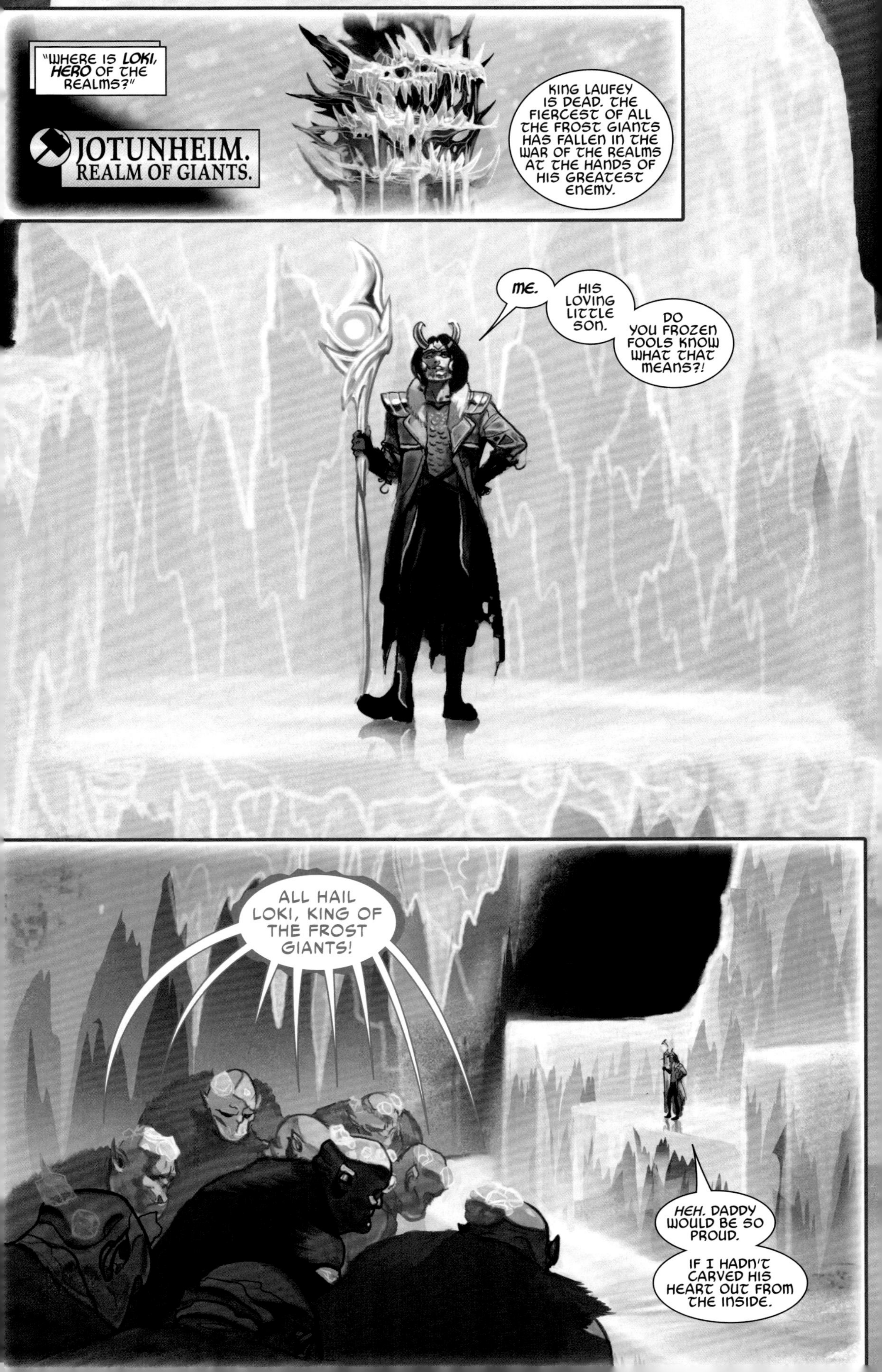
"WHERE IS LOKI, HERO OF THE REALMS?"
JOTUNHEIM. REALM OF GIANTS.
KING LAUFEY IS DEAD. THE FIERCEST OF ALL THE FROST GIANTS HAS FALLEN IN THE WAR OF THE REALMS AT THE HANDS OF HIS GREATEST ENEMY.
ME.
HIS LOVING LITTLE SON.
DO YOU FROZEN FOOLS KNOW WHAT THAT MEANS?!
ALL HAIL LOKI, KING OF THE FROST GIANTS!
HEH. DADDY WOULD BE SO PROUD.
IF I HADN'T CARVED HIS HEART OUT FROM THE INSIDE.

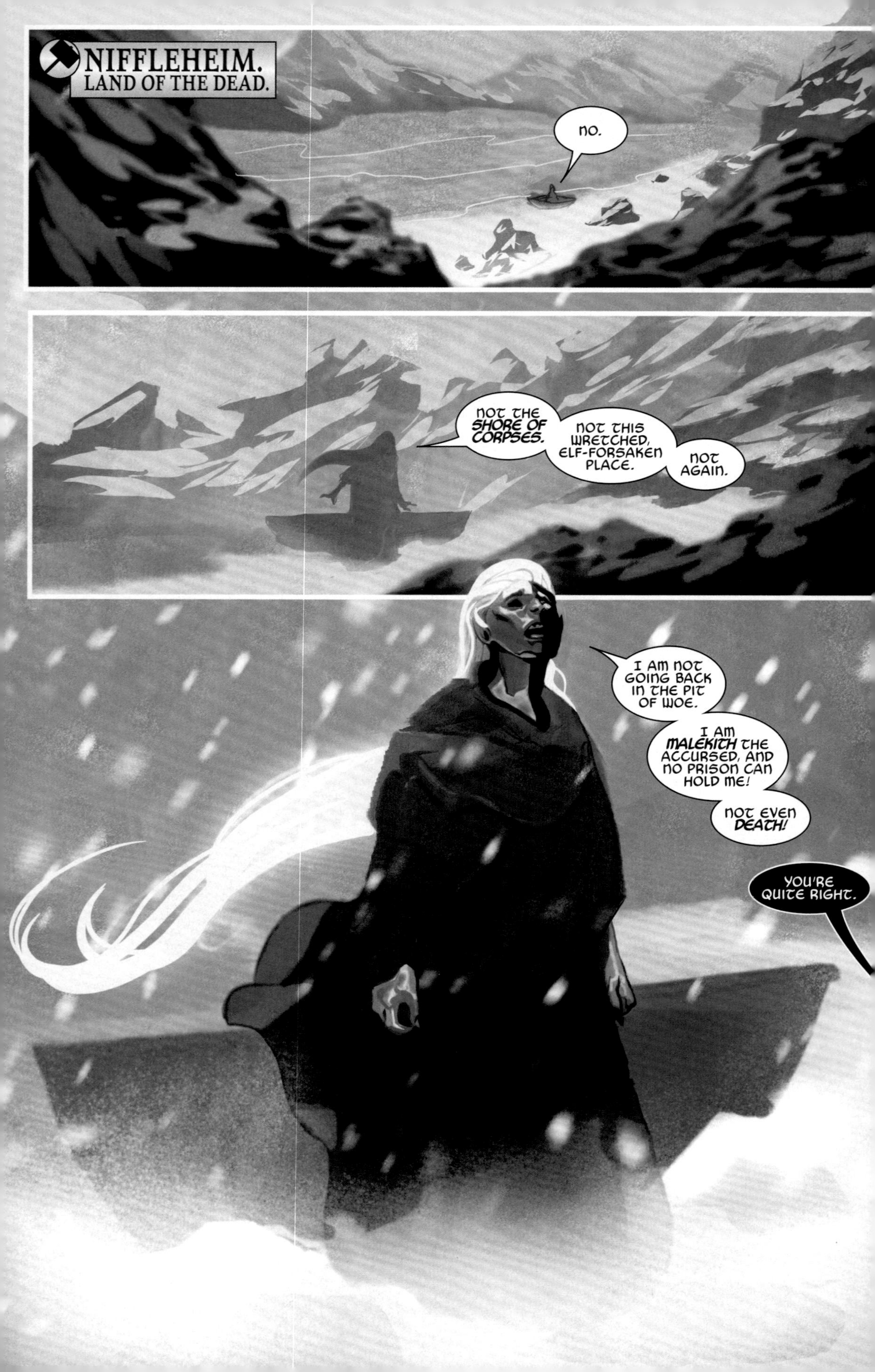
NIFFLEHEIM.
LAND OF THE DEAD.
no.
NOT THE SHORE OF CORPSES.
NOT THIS WRETCHED, ELF-FORSAKEN PLACE.
NOT AGAIN.
I AM NOT GOING BACK IN THE PIT OF WOE.
I AM MALEKITH THE ACCURSED, AND NO PRISON CAN HOLD ME!
NOT EVEN DEATH!
YOU'RE QUITE RIGHT.

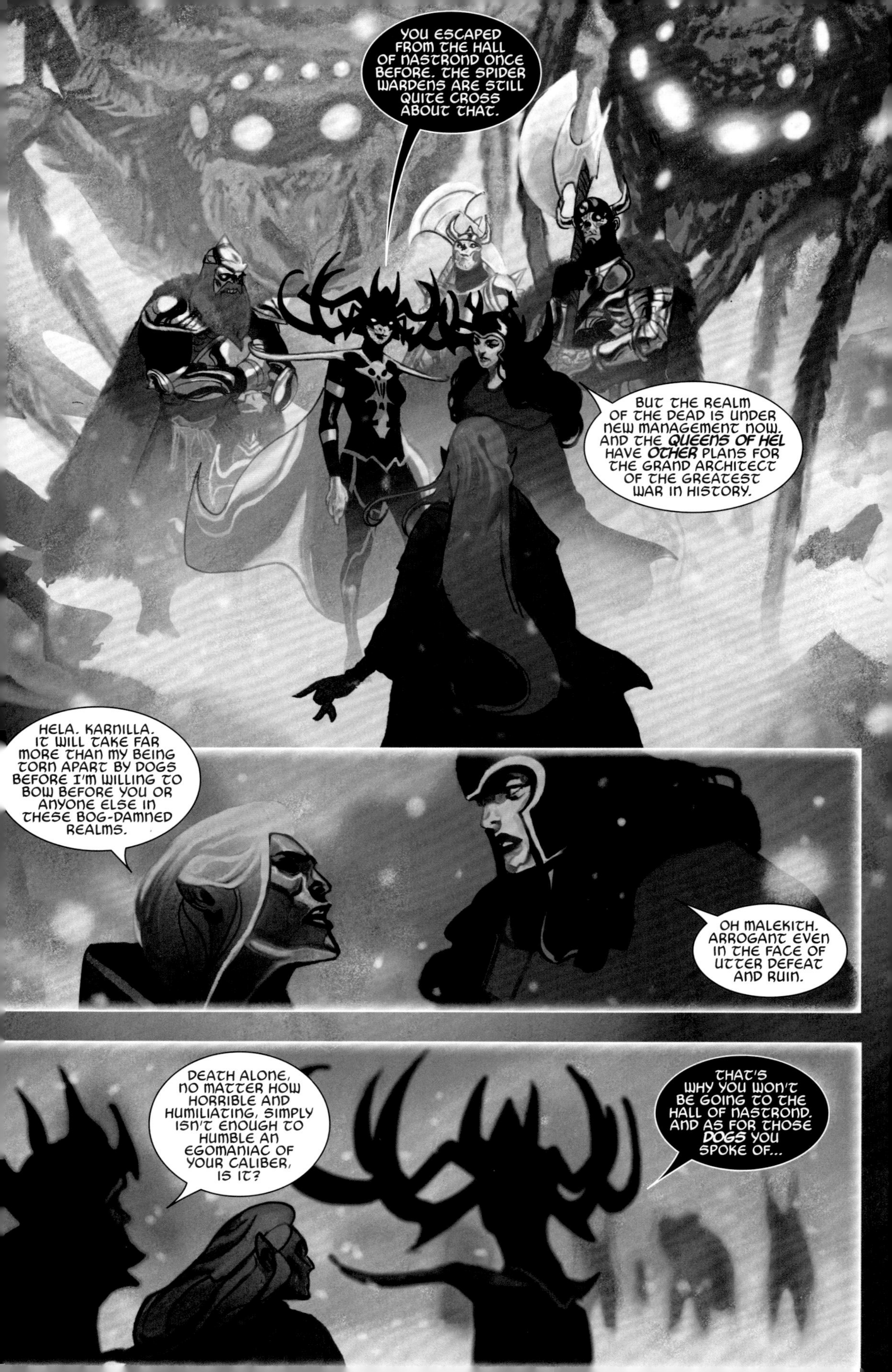
YOU ESCAPED FROM THE HALL OF NASTROND ONCE BEFORE. THE SPIDER WARDENS ARE STILL QUITE CROSS ABOUT THAT.
BUT THE REALM OF THE DEAD IS UNDER NEW MANAGEMENT NOW. AND THE QUEENS OF HEL HAVE OTHER PLANS FOR THE GRAND ARCHITECT OF THE GREATEST WAR IN HISTORY.
HELA. KARNILLA. IT WILL TAKE FAR MORE THAN MY BEING TORN APART BY DOGS BEFORE I'M WILLING TO BOW BEFORE YOU OR ANYONE ELSE IN THESE BOG-DAMNED REALMS.
OH MALEKITH. ARROGANT EVEN IN THE FACE OF UTTER DEFEAT AND RUIN.
DEATH ALONE, NO MATTER HOW HORRIBLE AND HUMILIATING, SIMPLY ISN'T ENOUGH TO HUMBLE AN EGOMANIAC OF YOUR CALIBER, IS IT?
THAT'S WHY YOU WON'T BE GOING TO THE HALL OF NASTROND. AND AS FOR THOSE DOGS YOU SPOKE OF...

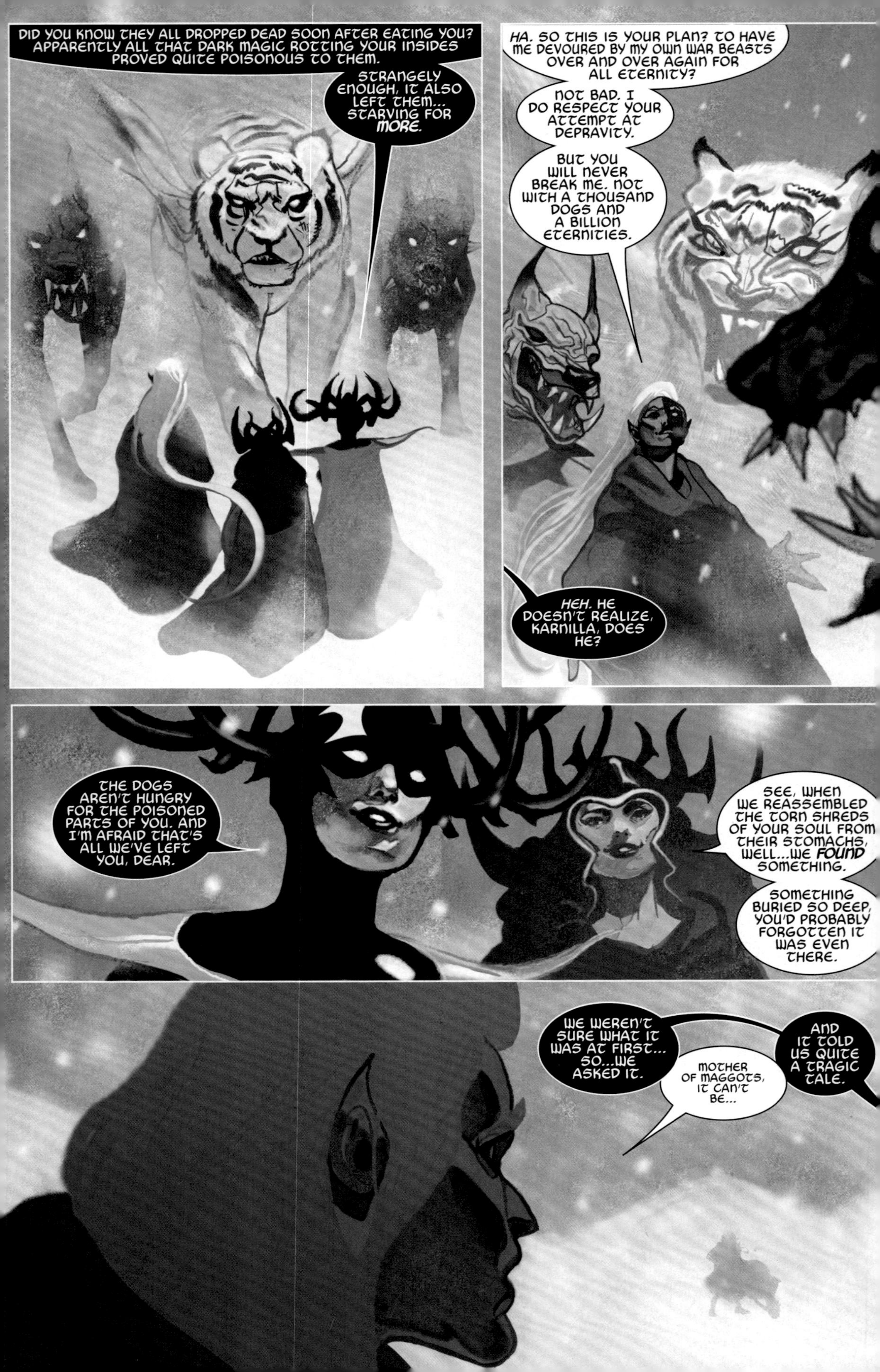
DID YOU KNOW THEY ALL DROPPED DEAD SOON AFTER EATING YOU? APPARENTLY ALL THAT DARK MAGIC ROTTING YOUR INSIDES PROVED QUITE POISONOUS TO THEM.
STRANGELY ENOUGH, IT ALSO LEFT THEM... STARVING FOR *MORE*.
HA. SO THIS IS YOUR PLAN? TO HAVE ME DEVOURED BY MY OWN WAR BEASTS OVER AND OVER AGAIN FOR ALL ETERNITY?
NOT BAD. I DO RESPECT YOUR ATTEMPT AT DEPRAVITY.
BUT YOU WILL NEVER BREAK ME. NOT WITH A THOUSAND DOGS AND A BILLION ETERNITIES.
HEH. HE DOESN'T REALIZE, KARNILLA, DOES HE?
THE DOGS AREN'T HUNGRY FOR THE POISONED PARTS OF YOU. AND I'M AFRAID THAT'S ALL WE'VE LEFT YOU, DEAR.
SEE, WHEN WE REASSEMBLED THE TORN SHREDS OF YOUR SOUL FROM THEIR STOMACHS, WELL...WE *FOUND* SOMETHING.
SOMETHING BURIED SO DEEP, YOU'D PROBABLY FORGOTTEN IT WAS EVEN THERE.
WE WEREN'T SURE WHAT IT WAS AT FIRST... SO...WE ASKED IT.
AND IT TOLD US QUITE A TRAGIC TALE.
MOTHER OF MAGGOTS, IT CAN'T BE...

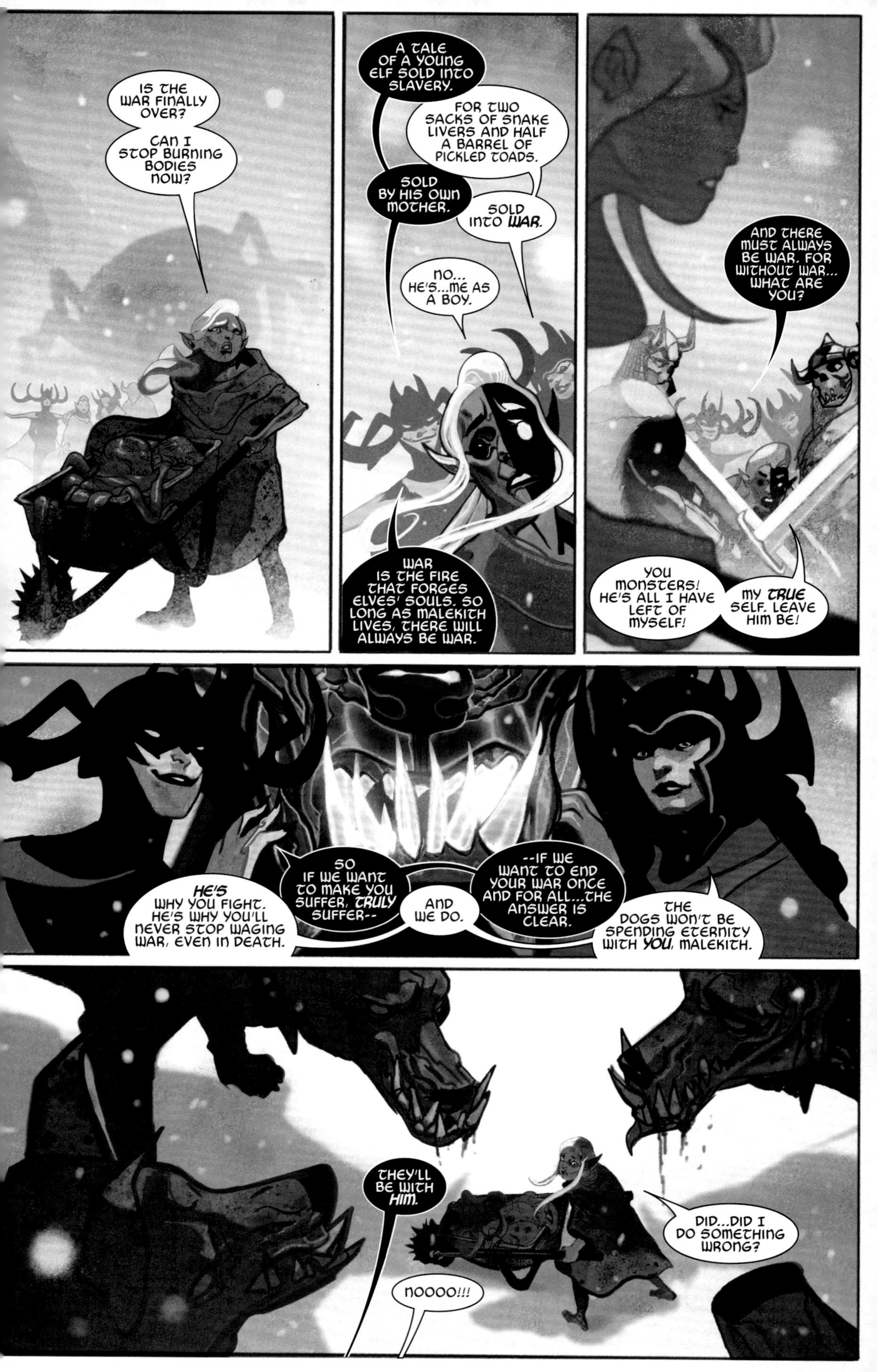

IS THE WAR FINALLY OVER?
CAN I STOP BURNING BODIES NOW?
A TALE OF A YOUNG ELF SOLD INTO SLAVERY.
FOR TWO SACKS OF SNAKE LIVERS AND HALF A BARREL OF PICKLED TOADS.
SOLD BY HIS OWN MOTHER.
SOLD INTO WAR.
NO... HE'S...ME AS A BOY.
WAR IS THE FIRE THAT FORGES ELVES' SOULS. SO LONG AS MALEKITH LIVES, THERE WILL ALWAYS BE WAR.
AND THERE MUST ALWAYS BE WAR. FOR WITHOUT WAR... WHAT ARE YOU?
YOU MONSTERS! HE'S ALL I HAVE LEFT OF MYSELF!
MY TRUE SELF. LEAVE HIM BE!
HE'S WHY YOU FIGHT. HE'S WHY YOU'LL NEVER STOP WAGING WAR, EVEN IN DEATH.
SO IF WE WANT TO MAKE YOU SUFFER, TRULY SUFFER--
AND WE DO.
--IF WE WANT TO END YOUR WAR ONCE AND FOR ALL...THE ANSWER IS CLEAR.
THE DOGS WON'T BE SPENDING ETERNITY WITH YOU, MALEKITH.
THEY'LL BE WITH HIM.
DID...DID I DO SOMETHING WRONG?
NOOOO!!!

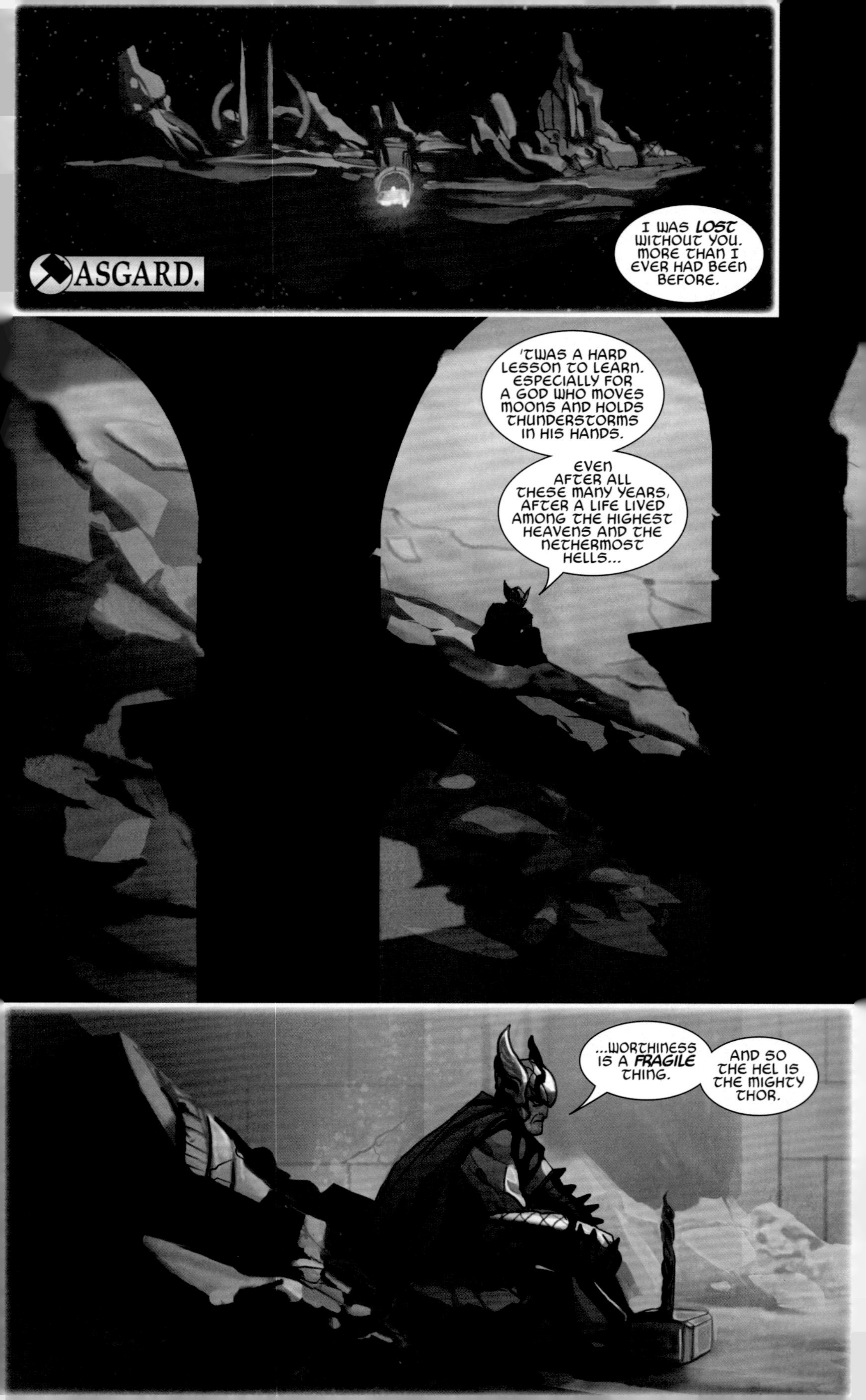
ASGARD.
I WAS LOST WITHOUT YOU. MORE THAN I EVER HAD BEEN BEFORE.
'TWAS A HARD LESSON TO LEARN. ESPECIALLY FOR A GOD WHO MOVES MOONS AND HOLDS THUNDERSTORMS IN HIS HANDS.
EVEN AFTER ALL THESE MANY YEARS, AFTER A LIFE LIVED AMONG THE HIGHEST HEAVENS AND THE NETHERMOST HELLS...
...WORTHINESS IS A FRAGILE THING.
AND SO THE HEL IS THE MIGHTY THOR.

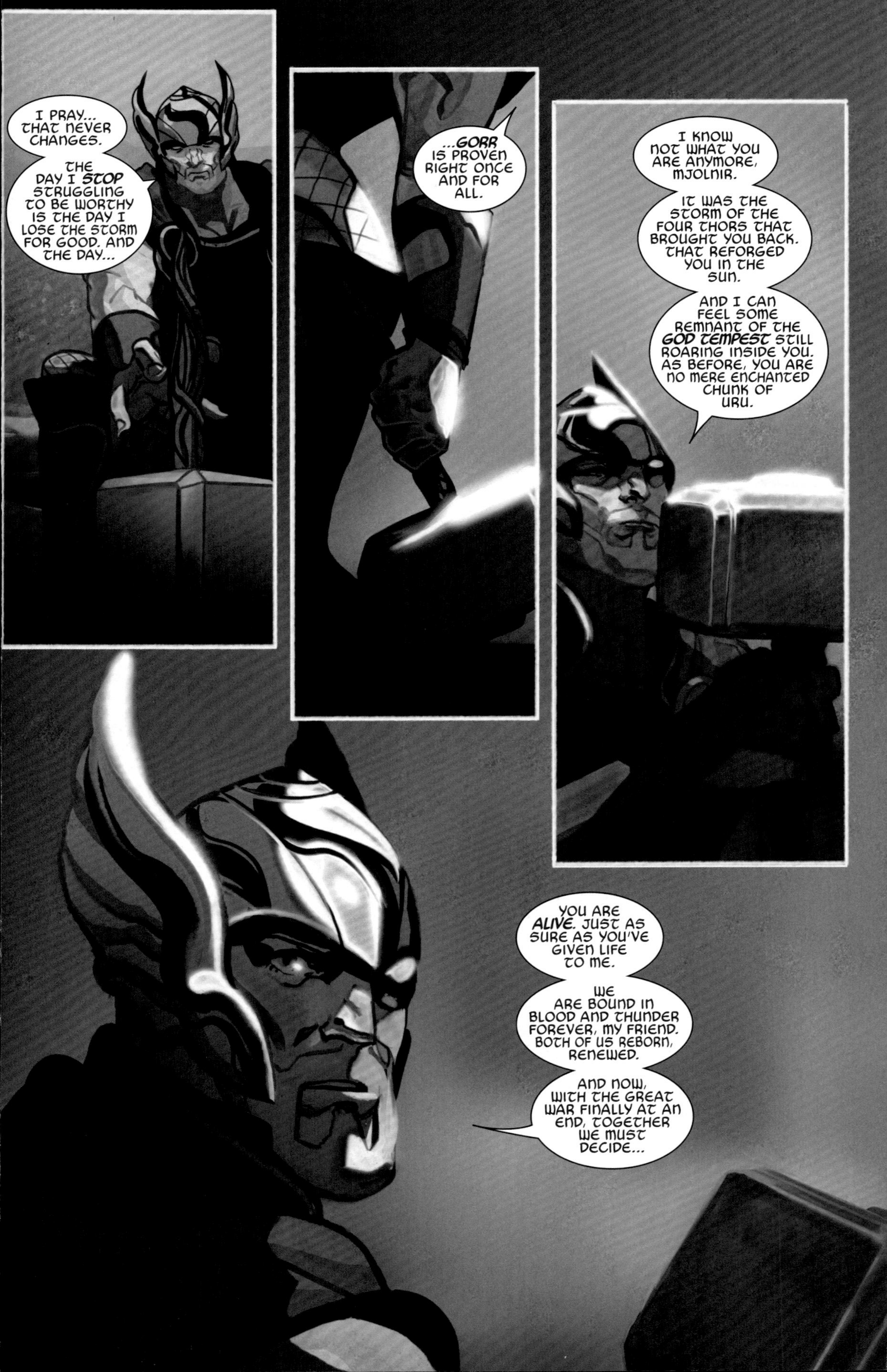
I PRAY... THAT NEVER CHANGES.
THE DAY I STOP STRUGGLING TO BE WORTHY IS THE DAY I LOSE THE STORM FOR GOOD. AND THE DAY...
...GORR IS PROVEN RIGHT ONCE AND FOR ALL.
I KNOW NOT WHAT YOU ARE ANYMORE, MJOLNIR.
IT WAS THE STORM OF THE FOUR THORS THAT BROUGHT YOU BACK. THAT REFORGED YOU IN THE SUN.
AND I CAN FEEL SOME REMNANT OF THE GOD TEMPEST STILL ROARING INSIDE YOU. AS BEFORE, YOU ARE NO MERE ENCHANTED CHUNK OF URU.
YOU ARE ALIVE. JUST AS SURE AS YOU'VE GIVEN LIFE TO ME.
WE ARE BOUND IN BLOOD AND THUNDER FOREVER, MY FRIEND. BOTH OF US REBORN, RENEWED.
AND NOW, WITH THE GREAT WAR FINALLY AT AN END, TOGETHER WE MUST DECIDE...

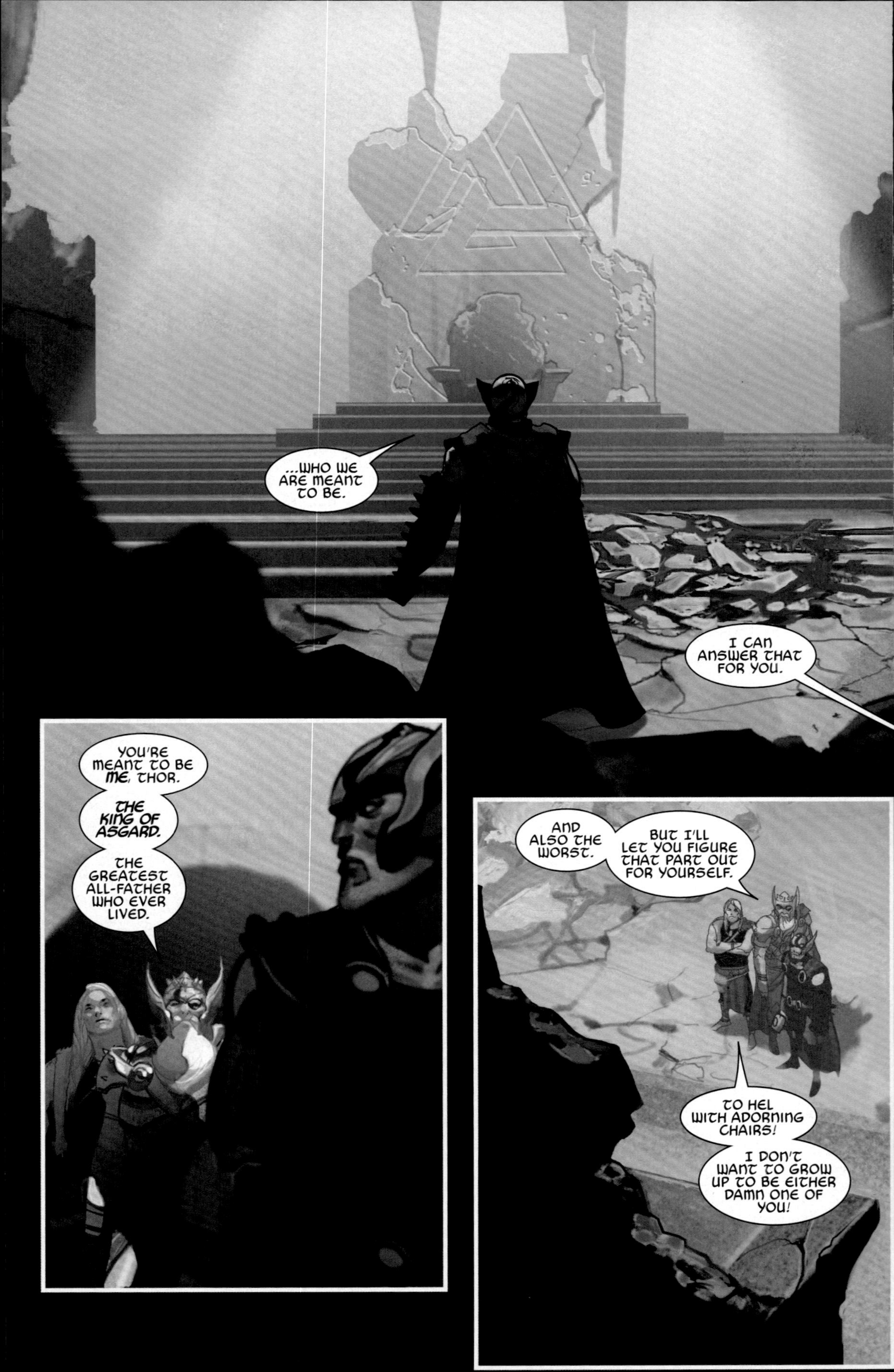
...WHO WE ARE MEANT TO BE.
I CAN ANSWER THAT FOR YOU.
YOU'RE MEANT TO BE *ME*, THOR.
THE KING OF ASGARD.
THE GREATEST ALL-FATHER WHO EVER LIVED.
AND ALSO THE WORST.
BUT I'LL LET YOU FIGURE THAT PART OUT FOR YOURSELF.
TO HEL WITH ADORNING CHAIRS!
I DON'T WANT TO GROW UP TO BE EITHER DAMN ONE OF YOU!

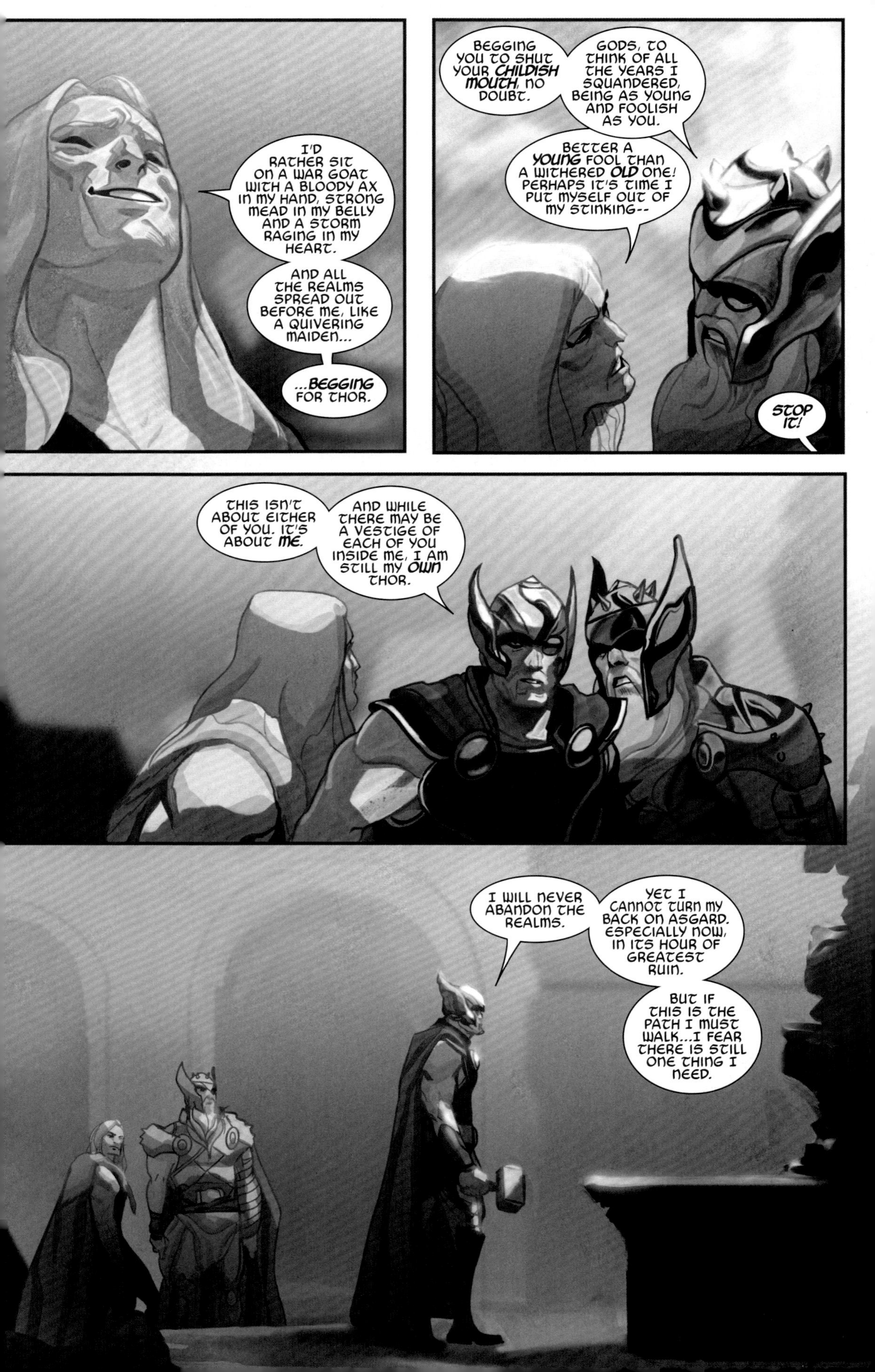
I'D RATHER SIT ON A WAR GOAT WITH A BLOODY AX IN MY HAND, STRONG MEAD IN MY BELLY AND A STORM RAGING IN MY HEART.
AND ALL THE REALMS SPREAD OUT BEFORE ME, LIKE A QUIVERING MAIDEN...
...BEGGING FOR THOR.
BEGGING YOU TO SHUT YOUR CHILDISH MOUTH, NO DOUBT.
GODS, TO THINK OF ALL THE YEARS I SQUANDERED, BEING AS YOUNG AND FOOLISH AS YOU.
BETTER A YOUNG FOOL THAN A WITHERED OLD ONE! PERHAPS IT'S TIME I PUT MYSELF OUT OF MY STINKING--
STOP IT!
THIS ISN'T ABOUT EITHER OF YOU. IT'S ABOUT ME.
AND WHILE THERE MAY BE A VESTIGE OF EACH OF YOU INSIDE ME, I AM STILL MY OWN THOR.
I WILL NEVER ABANDON THE REALMS.
YET I CANNOT TURN MY BACK ON ASGARD. ESPECIALLY NOW, IN ITS HOUR OF GREATEST RUIN.
BUT IF THIS IS THE PATH I MUST WALK...I FEAR THERE IS STILL ONE THING I NEED.

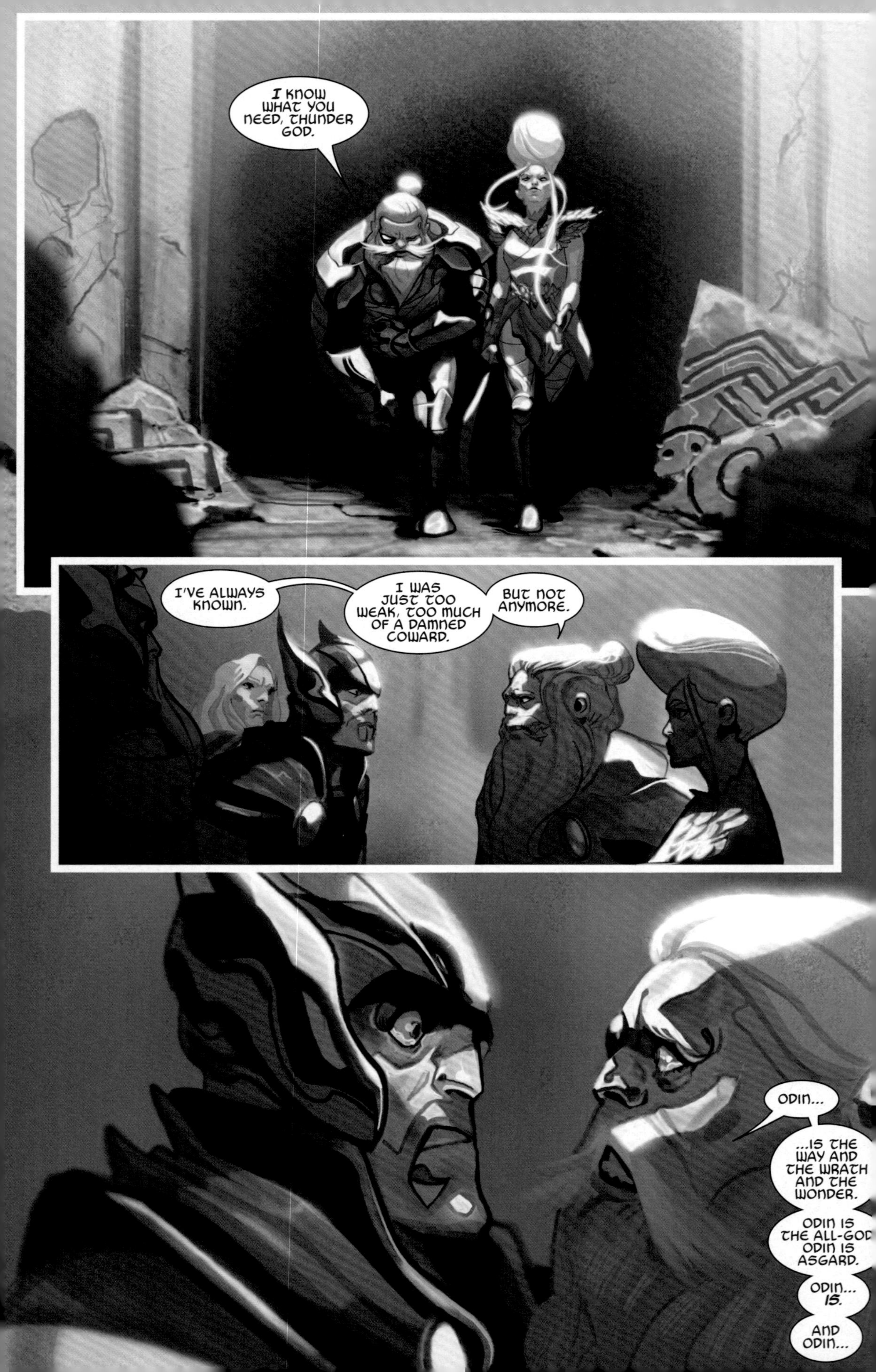
I KNOW WHAT YOU NEED, THUNDER GOD.
I'VE ALWAYS KNOWN.
I WAS JUST TOO WEAK, TOO MUCH OF A DAMNED COWARD.
BUT NOT ANYMORE.
ODIN...
...IS THE WAY AND THE WRATH AND THE WONDER.
ODIN IS THE ALL-GOD. ODIN IS ASGARD.
ODIN... IS.
AND ODIN...

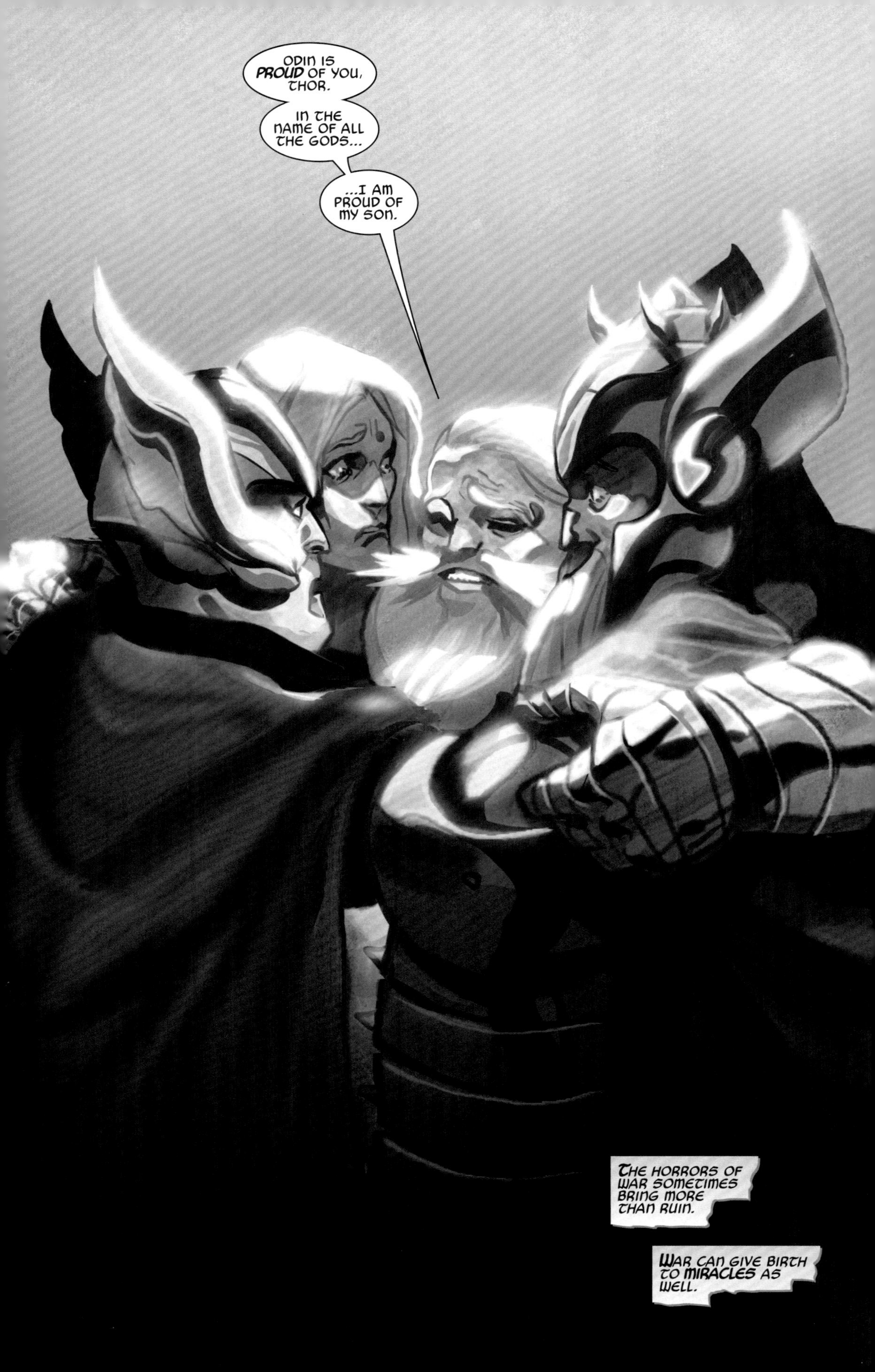
ODIN IS PROUD OF YOU, THOR.
IN THE NAME OF ALL THE GODS...
...I AM PROUD OF MY SON.
THE HORRORS OF WAR SOMETIMES BRING MORE THAN RUIN.
WAR CAN GIVE BIRTH TO MIRACLES AS WELL.

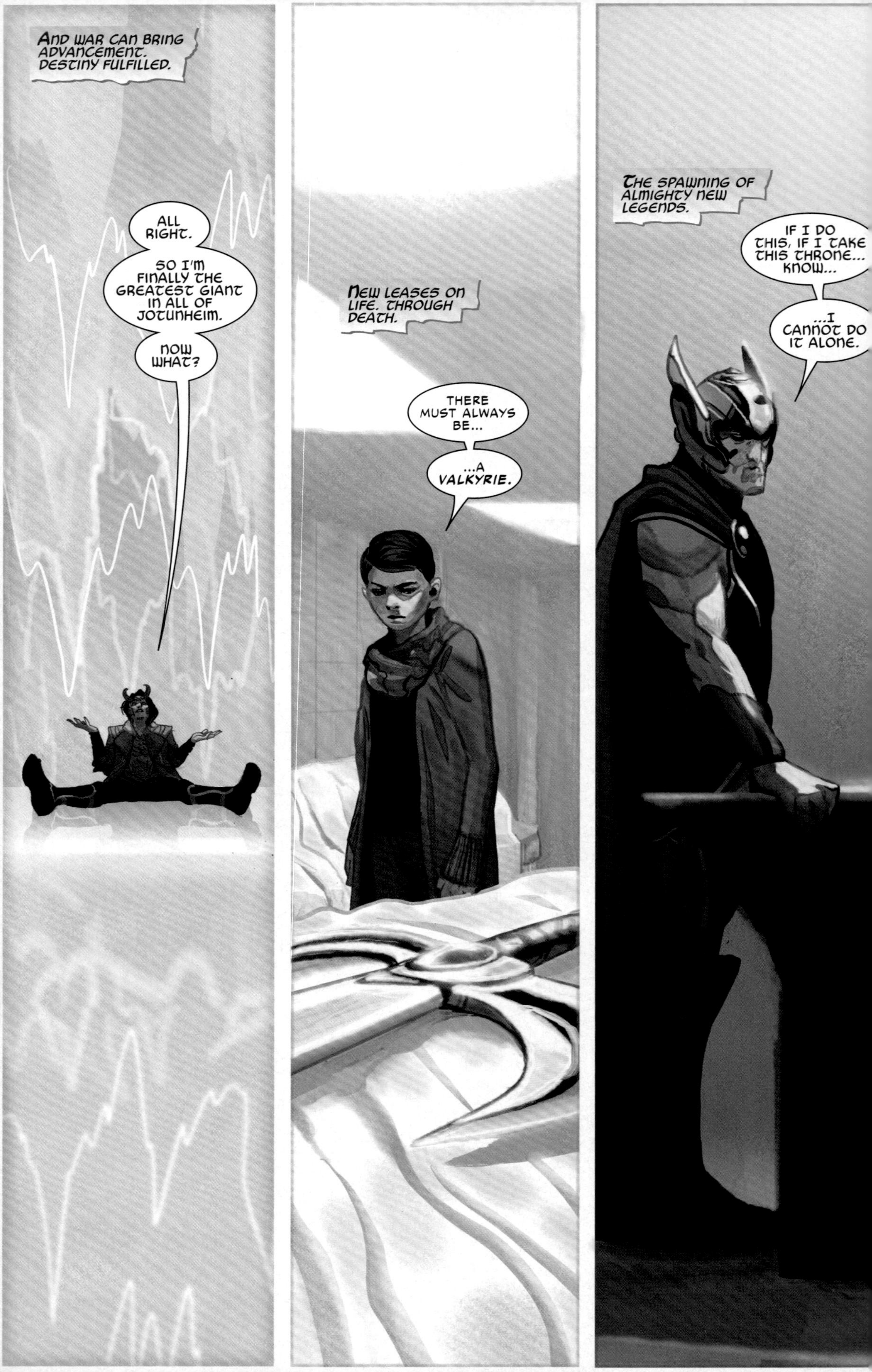
AND WAR CAN BRING ADVANCEMENT. DESTINY FULFILLED.
ALL RIGHT.
SO I'M FINALLY THE GREATEST GIANT IN ALL OF JOTUNHEIM.
NOW WHAT?
NEW LEASES ON LIFE. THROUGH DEATH.
THERE MUST ALWAYS BE...
...A VALKYRIE.
THE SPAWNING OF ALMIGHTY NEW LEGENDS.
IF I DO THIS, IF I TAKE THIS THRONE... KNOW...
...I CANNOT DO IT ALONE.

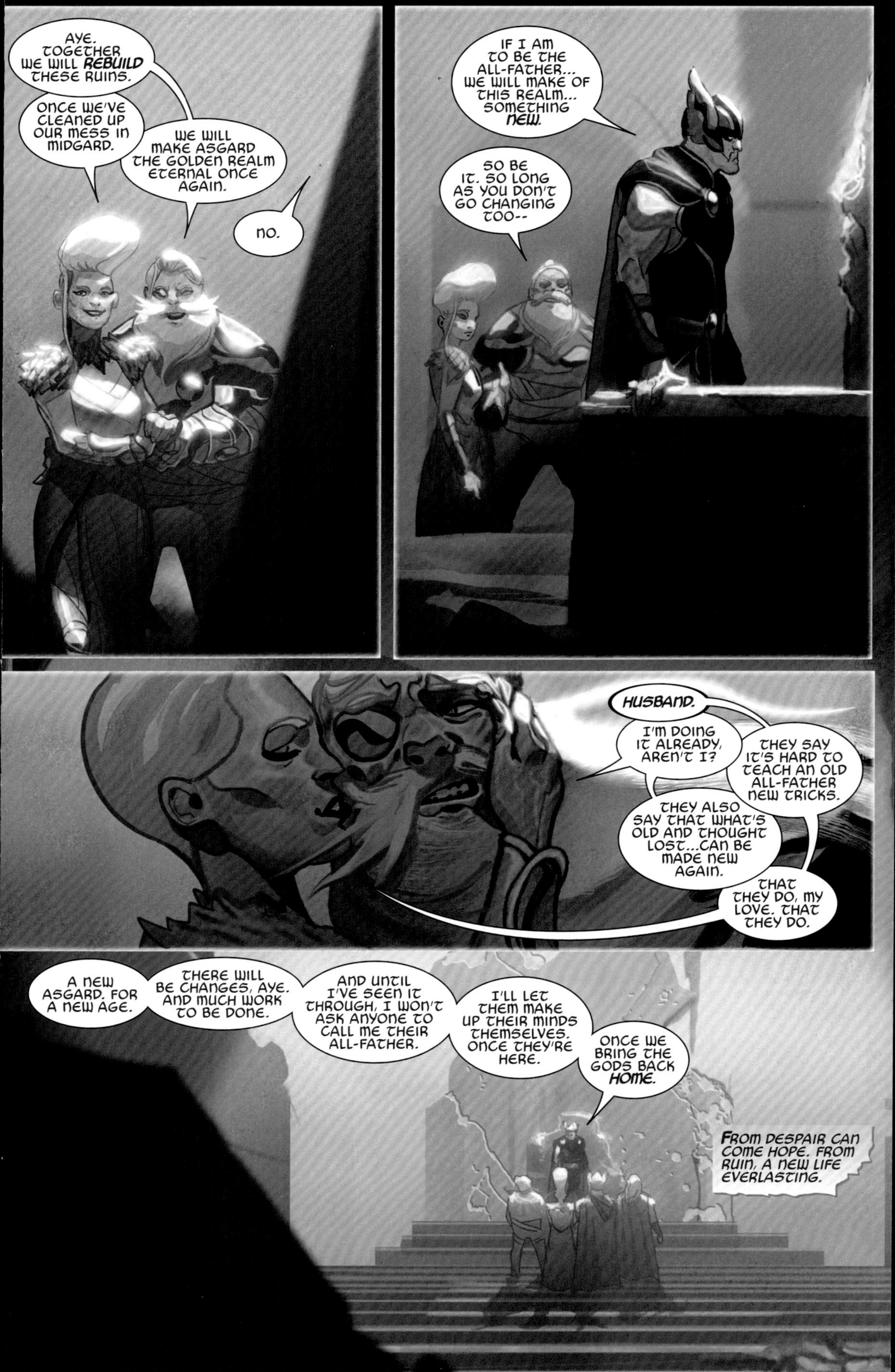
AYE. TOGETHER WE WILL REBUILD THESE RUINS.
ONCE WE'VE CLEANED UP OUR MESS IN MIDGARD.
WE WILL MAKE ASGARD THE GOLDEN REALM ETERNAL ONCE AGAIN.
NO.
IF I AM TO BE THE ALL-FATHER... WE WILL MAKE OF THIS REALM... SOMETHING NEW.
SO BE IT. SO LONG AS YOU DON'T GO CHANGING TOO--
HUSBAND.
I'M DOING IT ALREADY, AREN'T I?
THEY SAY IT'S HARD TO TEACH AN OLD ALL-FATHER NEW TRICKS.
THEY ALSO SAY THAT WHAT'S OLD AND THOUGHT LOST...CAN BE MADE NEW AGAIN.
THAT THEY DO, MY LOVE. THAT THEY DO.
A NEW ASGARD. FOR A NEW AGE.
THERE WILL BE CHANGES, AYE. AND MUCH WORK TO BE DONE.
AND UNTIL I'VE SEEN IT THROUGH, I WON'T ASK ANYONE TO CALL ME THEIR ALL-FATHER.
I'LL LET THEM MAKE UP THEIR MINDS THEMSELVES. ONCE THEY'RE HERE.
ONCE WE BRING THE GODS BACK HOME.
FROM DESPAIR CAN COME HOPE. FROM RUIN, A NEW LIFE EVERLASTING.

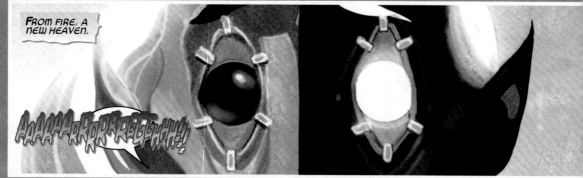

FROM FIRE, A NEW HEAVEN.

AAAAARDRRRGGHH!!!

FROM HORROR, A BEAUTY TO BOGGLE THE MIND AND TAKE THE BREATH AWAY, EVEN AMONG THE BREATHLESS.

NOOOOOOO!!! MAKE IT STOP!!! PLEASE, I BEG YOU, I'LL DO ANYTHING!!!

JUST PLEASE DON'T MAKE ME WATCH!!!

FROM SUFFERING COMES JUSTICE.

HRRRAAAAGGH!!!

NICE TOUCH SEWING HIS EYES OPEN.

YES, I DO BELIEVE WE'VE FOUND THE PERFECT PUNISHMENT FOR THE ARCHITECT OF THE WAR OF THE REALMS.

FORCED TO LOOK UPON HIS GREATEST HORROR FOR ALL ETERNITY. I BELIEVE THIS CALLS FOR A TOAST.

FROM SIN, DIVINE RETRIBUTION.

HERE'S TO MALEKITH THE ACCURSED. LONG MAY HE SUFFER.

INDEED.

AND HERE'S TO MALEKITH THE ELF BOY, THE CORPSE BURNER, THE WAR SLAVE...

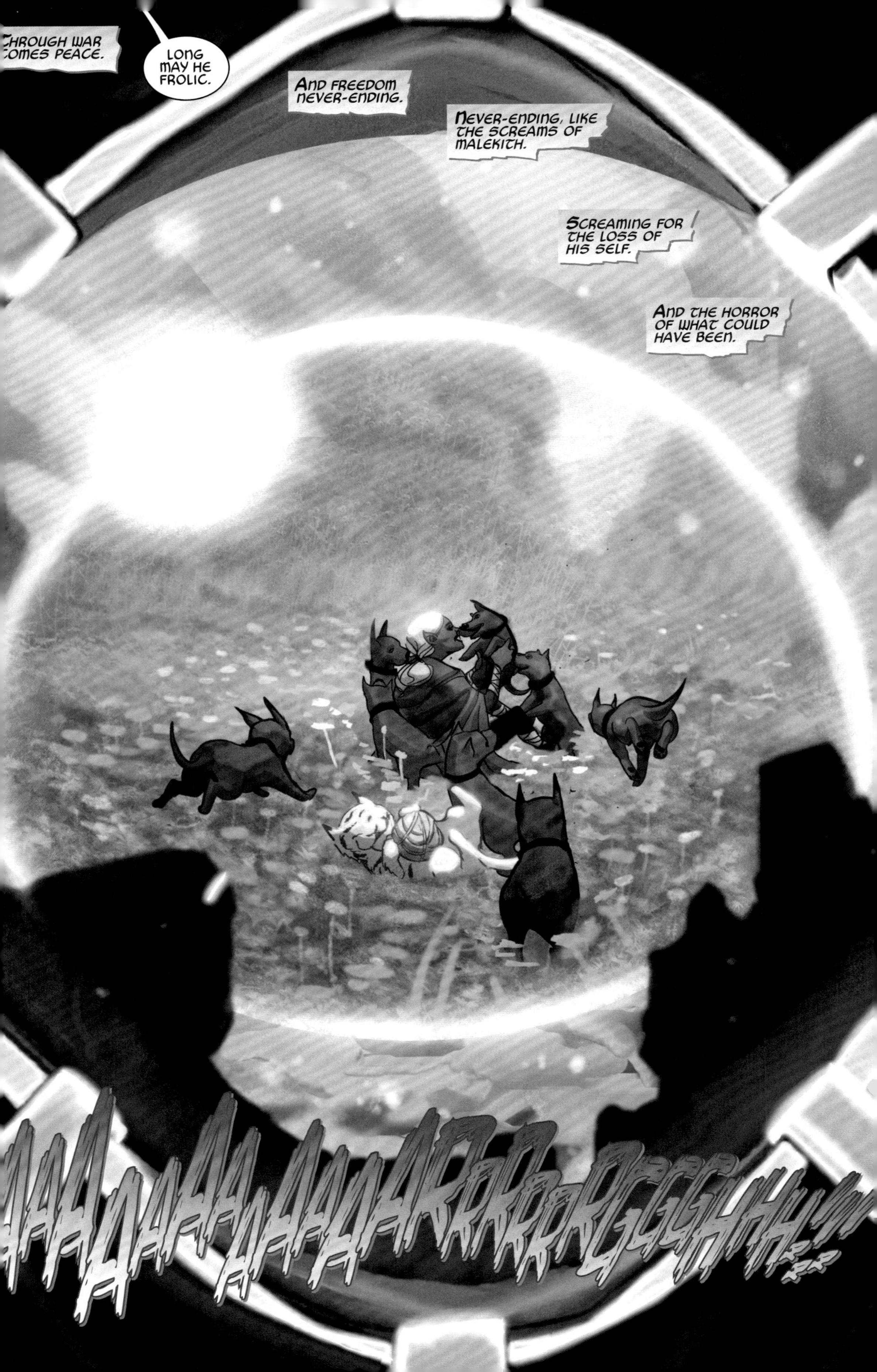
THROUGH WAR COMES PEACE.
LONG MAY HE FROLIC.
AND FREEDOM NEVER-ENDING.
NEVER-ENDING, LIKE THE SCREAMS OF MALEKITH.
SCREAMING FOR THE LOSS OF HIS SELF.
AND THE HORROR OF WHAT COULD HAVE BEEN.
AAAAAAAAAAAAARRRRRRGGHH!

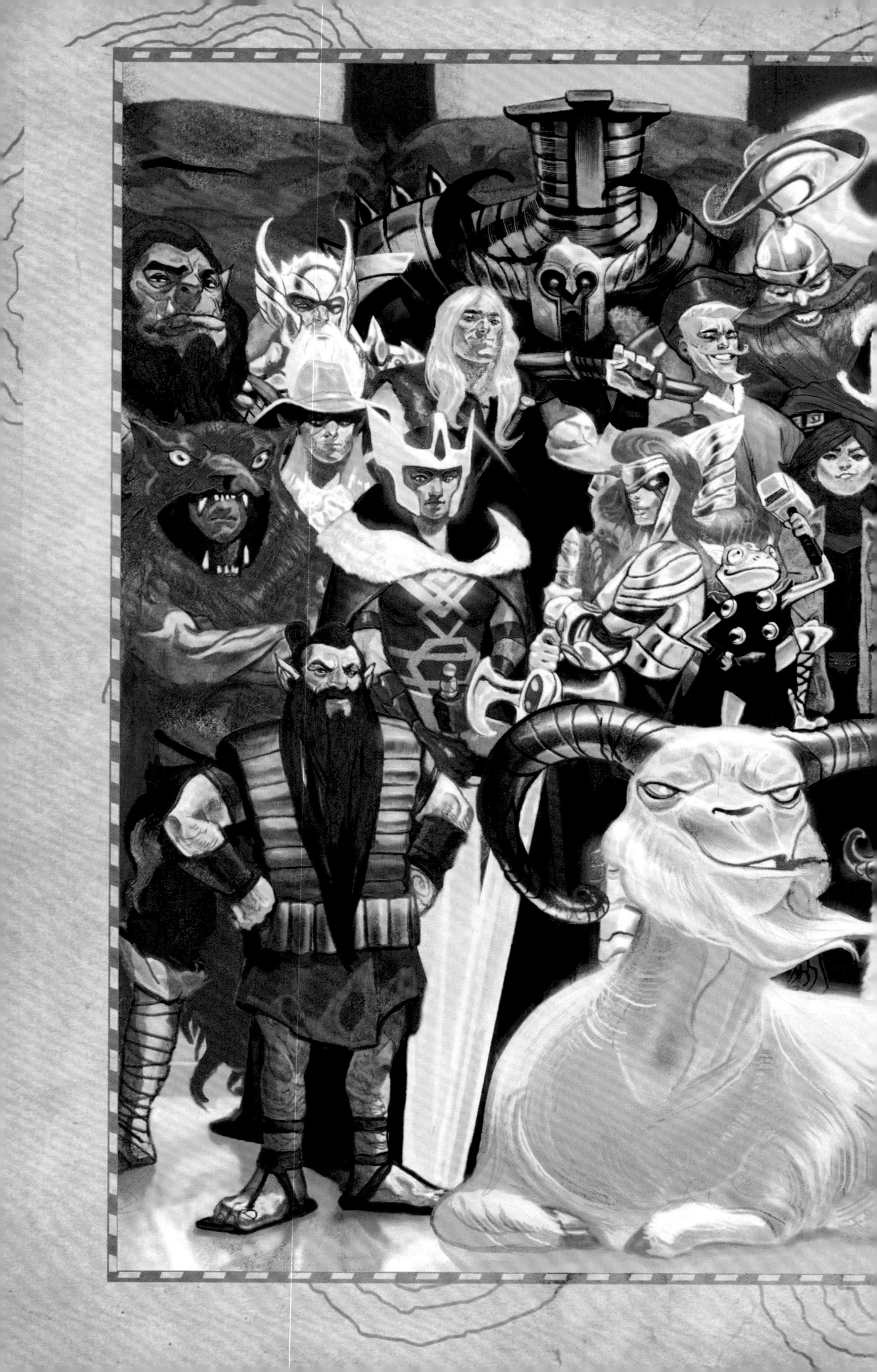

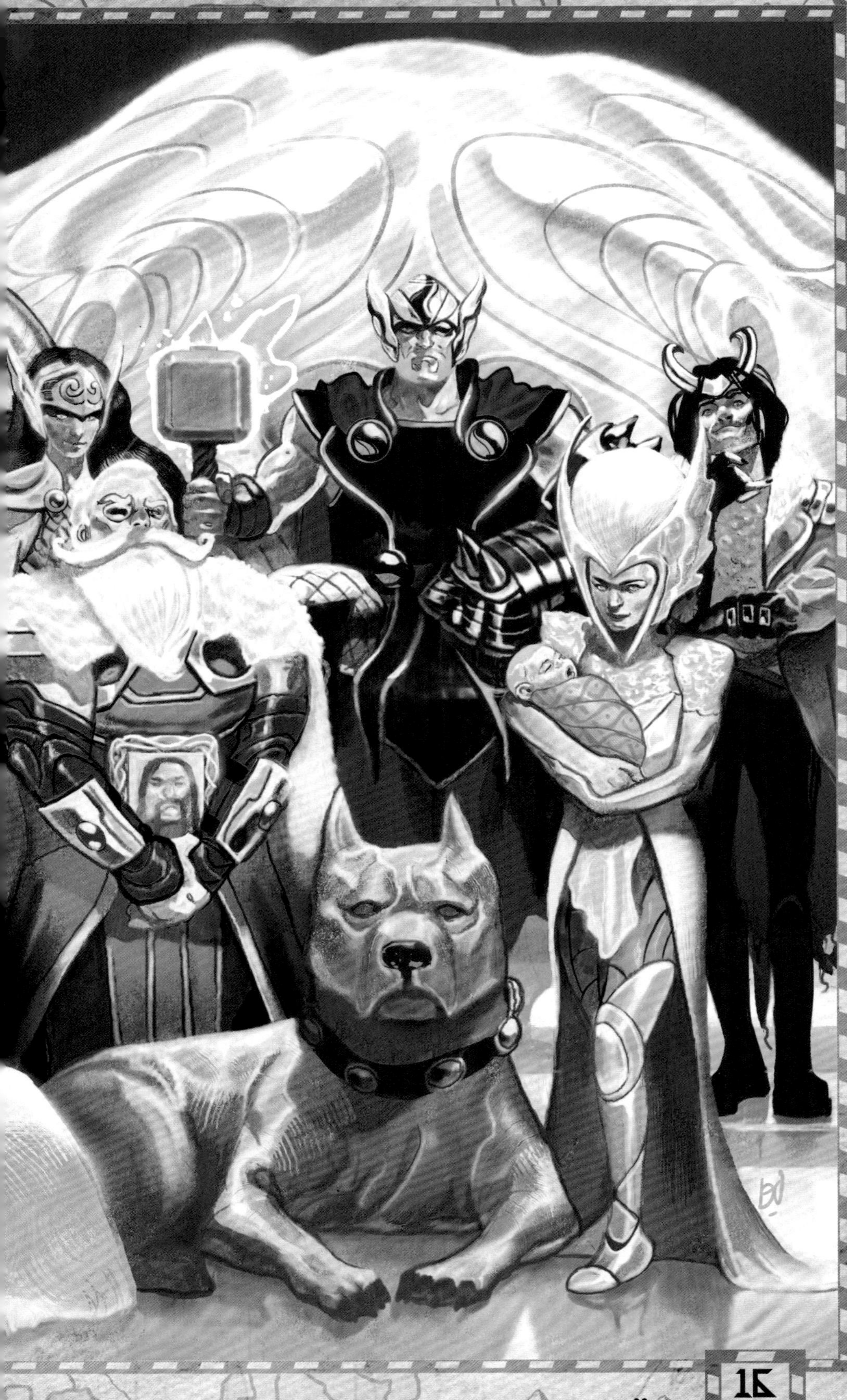

"ONCE UPON A TIME IN ASGARD"

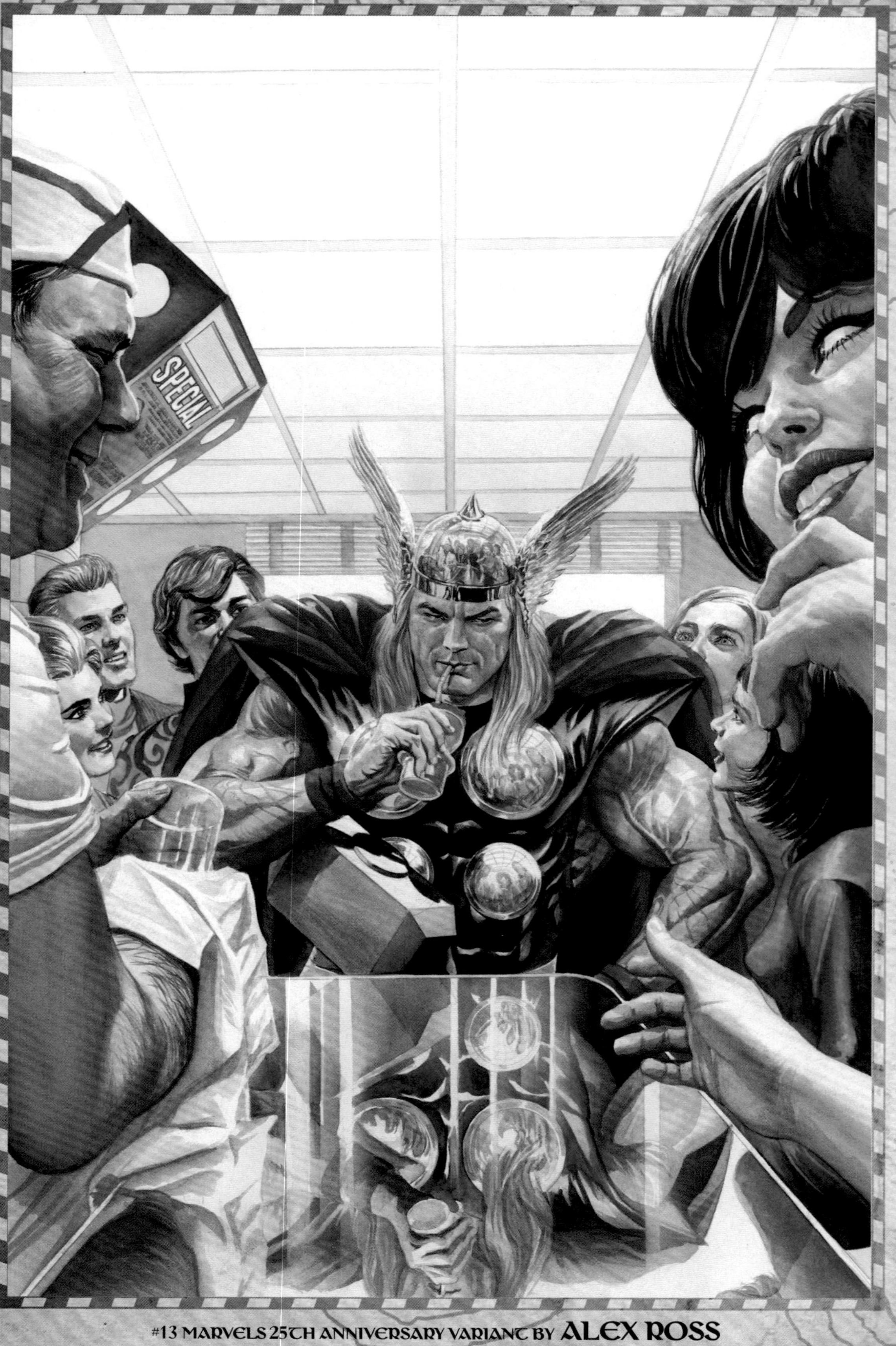
SPECIAL

#13 MARVELS 25TH ANNIVERSARY VARIANT BY ALEX ROSS

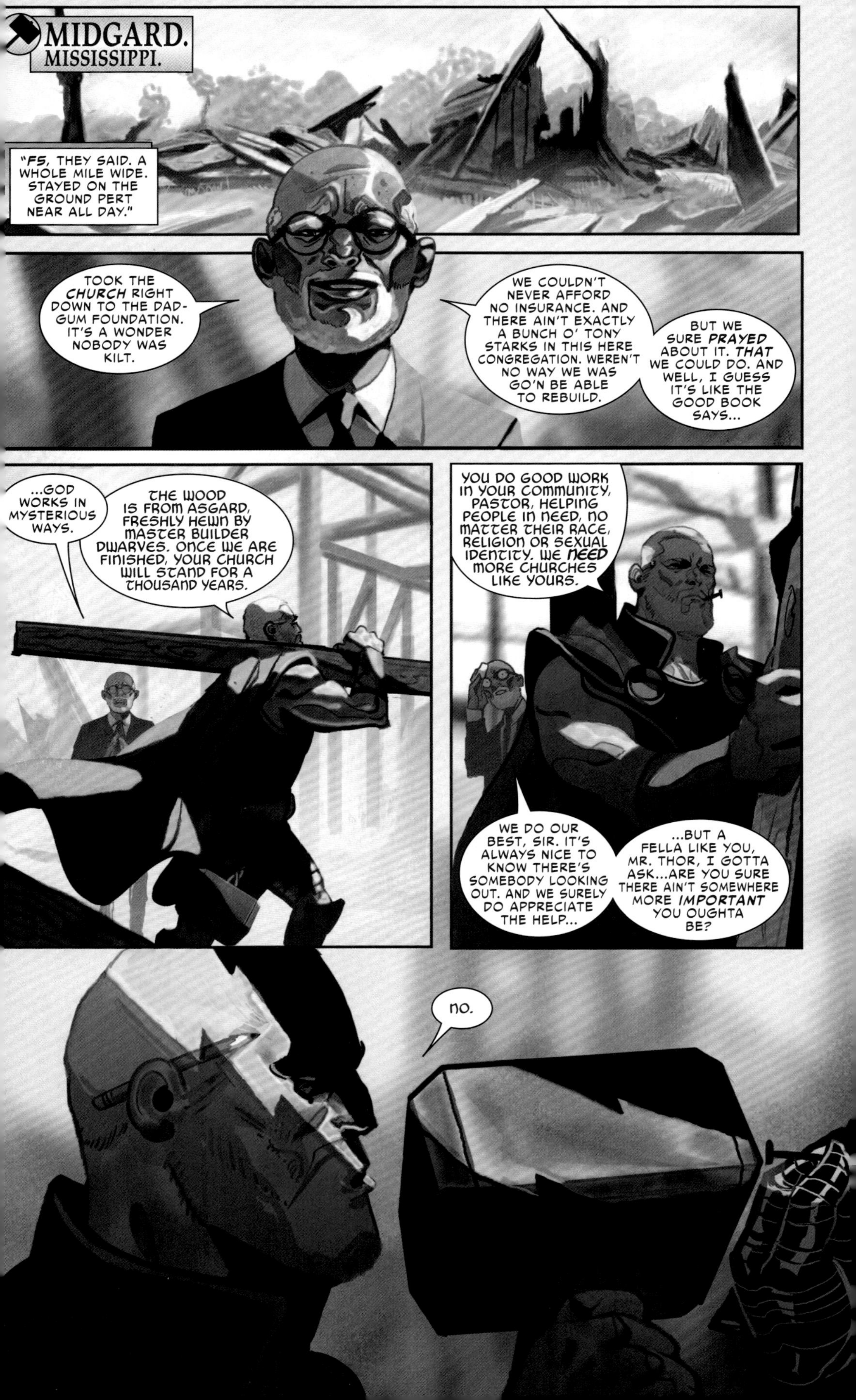
MIDGARD.
MISSISSIPPI.
"F5, THEY SAID. A WHOLE MILE WIDE. STAYED ON THE GROUND PERT NEAR ALL DAY."
TOOK THE CHURCH RIGHT DOWN TO THE DAD-GUM FOUNDATION. IT'S A WONDER NOBODY WAS KILT.
WE COULDN'T NEVER AFFORD NO INSURANCE. AND THERE AIN'T EXACTLY A BUNCH O' TONY STARKS IN THIS HERE CONGREGATION. WEREN'T NO WAY WE WAS GO'N BE ABLE TO REBUILD.
BUT WE SURE PRAYED ABOUT IT. THAT WE COULD DO. AND WELL, I GUESS IT'S LIKE THE GOOD BOOK SAYS...
...GOD WORKS IN MYSTERIOUS WAYS.
THE WOOD IS FROM ASGARD, FRESHLY HEWN BY MASTER BUILDER DWARVES. ONCE WE ARE FINISHED, YOUR CHURCH WILL STAND FOR A THOUSAND YEARS.
YOU DO GOOD WORK IN YOUR COMMUNITY, PASTOR, HELPING PEOPLE IN NEED, NO MATTER THEIR RACE, RELIGION OR SEXUAL IDENTITY. WE NEED MORE CHURCHES LIKE YOURS.
WE DO OUR BEST, SIR. IT'S ALWAYS NICE TO KNOW THERE'S SOMEBODY LOOKING OUT. AND WE SURELY DO APPRECIATE THE HELP...
...BUT A FELLA LIKE YOU, MR. THOR, I GOTTA ASK...ARE YOU SURE THERE AIN'T SOMEWHERE MORE IMPORTANT YOU OUGHTA BE?
no.

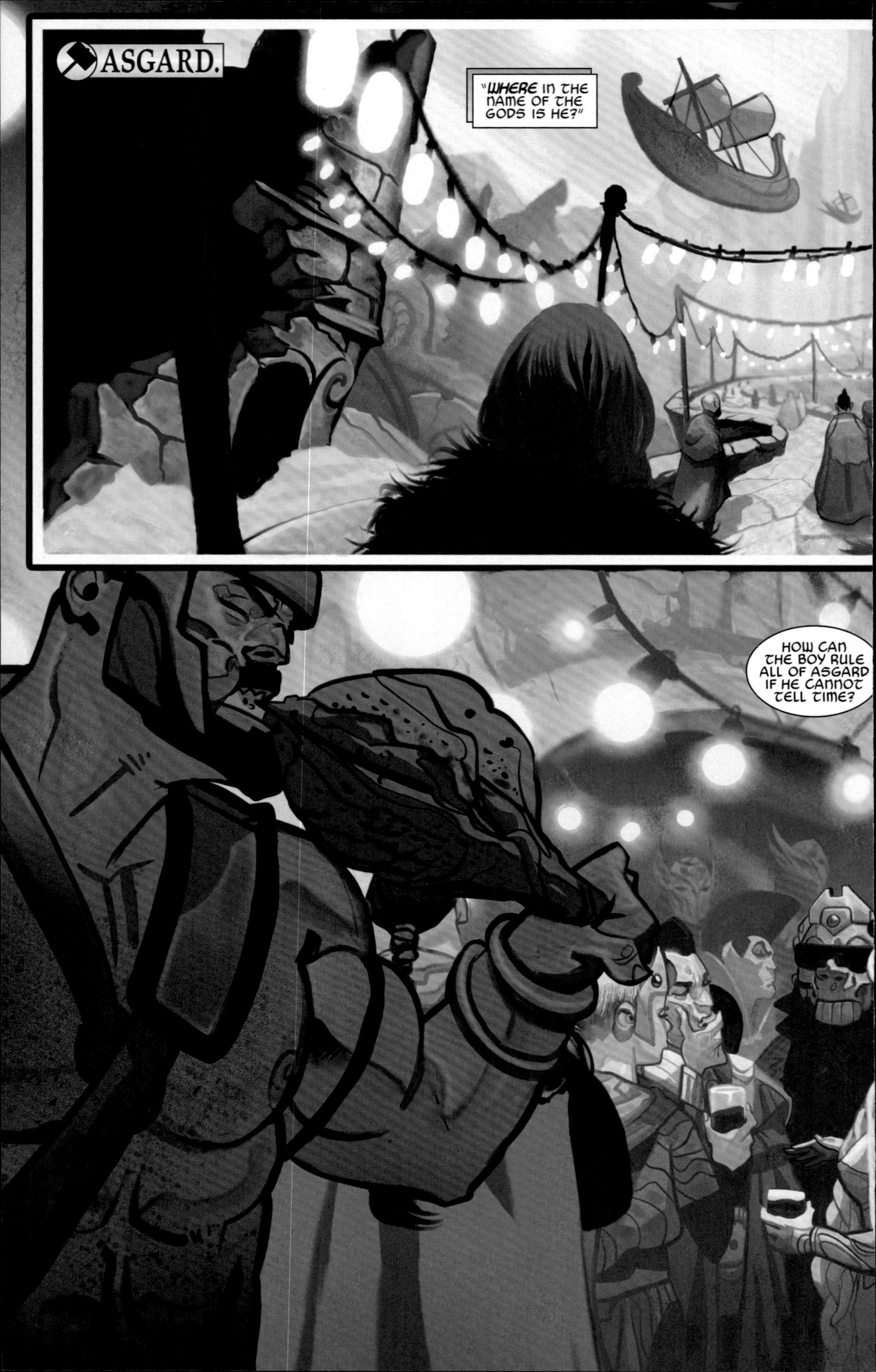
ASGARD.
"WHERE IN THE NAME OF THE GODS IS HE?"
HOW CAN THE BOY RULE ALL OF ASGARD IF HE CANNOT TELL TIME?

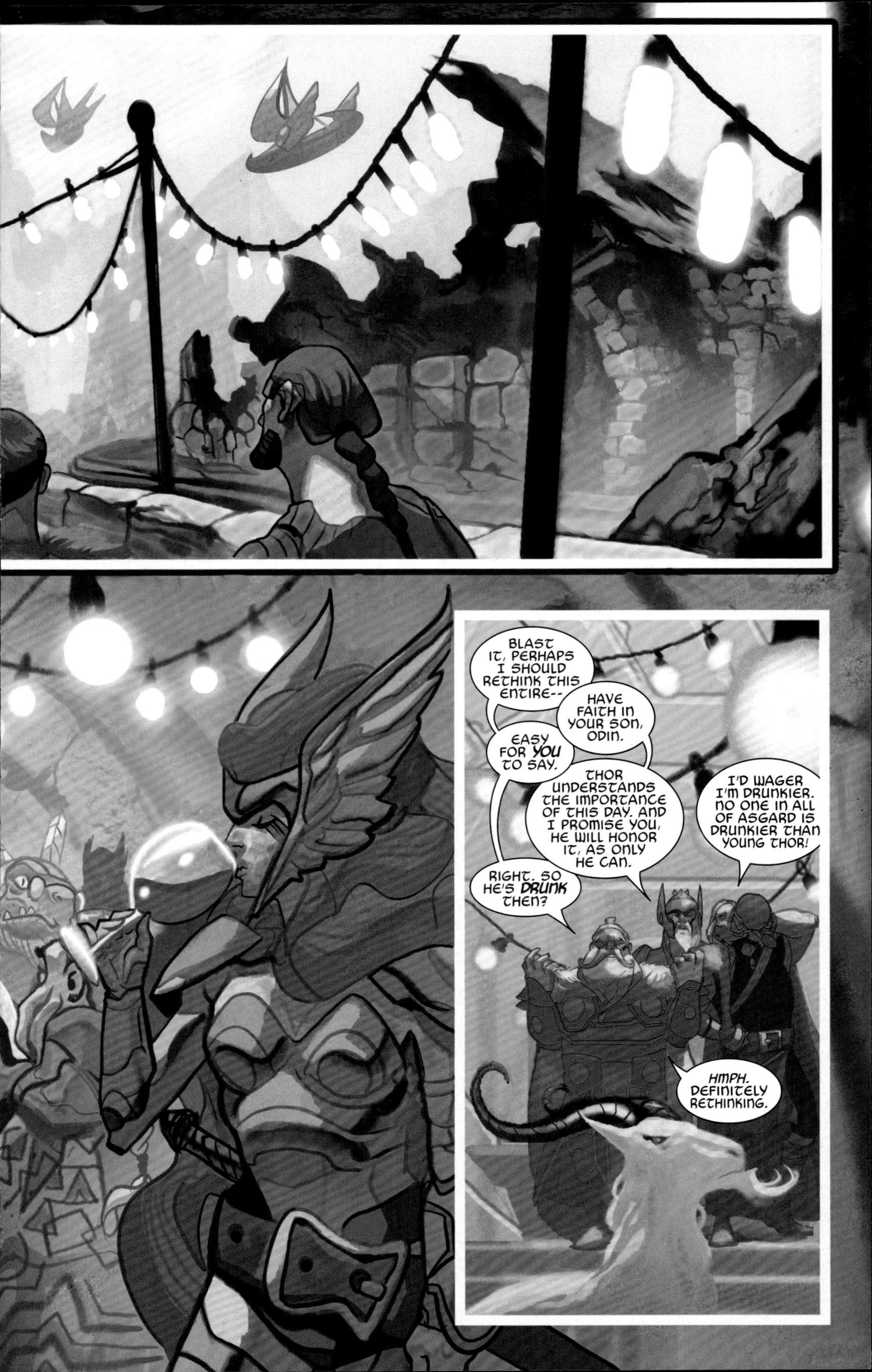
BLAST IT, PERHAPS I SHOULD RETHINK THIS ENTIRE--
HAVE FAITH IN YOUR SON, ODIN.
EASY FOR YOU TO SAY.
THOR UNDERSTANDS THE IMPORTANCE OF THIS DAY. AND I PROMISE YOU, HE WILL HONOR IT, AS ONLY HE CAN.
RIGHT. SO HE'S DRUNK THEN?
I'D WAGER I'M DRUNKIER. NO ONE IN ALL OF ASGARD IS DRUNKIER THAN YOUNG THOR!
HMPH. DEFINITELY RETHINKING.

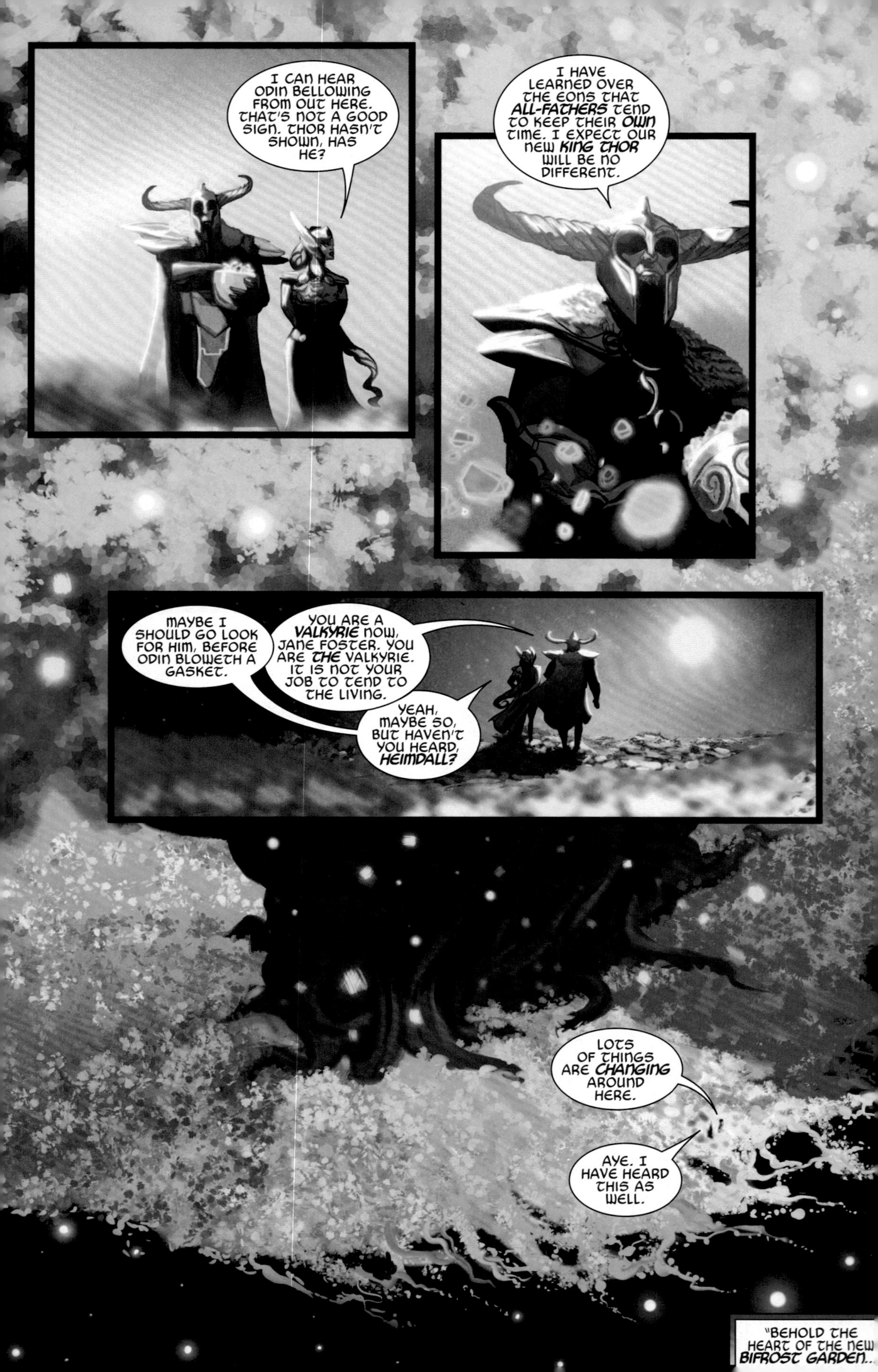
I CAN HEAR ODIN BELLOWING FROM OUT HERE. THAT'S NOT A GOOD SIGN. THOR HASN'T SHOWN, HAS HE?
I HAVE LEARNED OVER THE EONS THAT ALL-FATHERS TEND TO KEEP THEIR OWN TIME. I EXPECT OUR NEW KING THOR WILL BE NO DIFFERENT.
MAYBE I SHOULD GO LOOK FOR HIM, BEFORE ODIN BLOWETH A GASKET.
YOU ARE A VALKYRIE NOW, JANE FOSTER. YOU ARE THE VALKYRIE. IT IS NOT YOUR JOB TO TEND TO THE LIVING.
YEAH, MAYBE SO, BUT HAVEN'T YOU HEARD, HEIMDALL?
LOTS OF THINGS ARE CHANGING AROUND HERE.
AYE. I HAVE HEARD THIS AS WELL.
"BEHOLD THE HEART OF THE NEW BIFROST GARDEN...

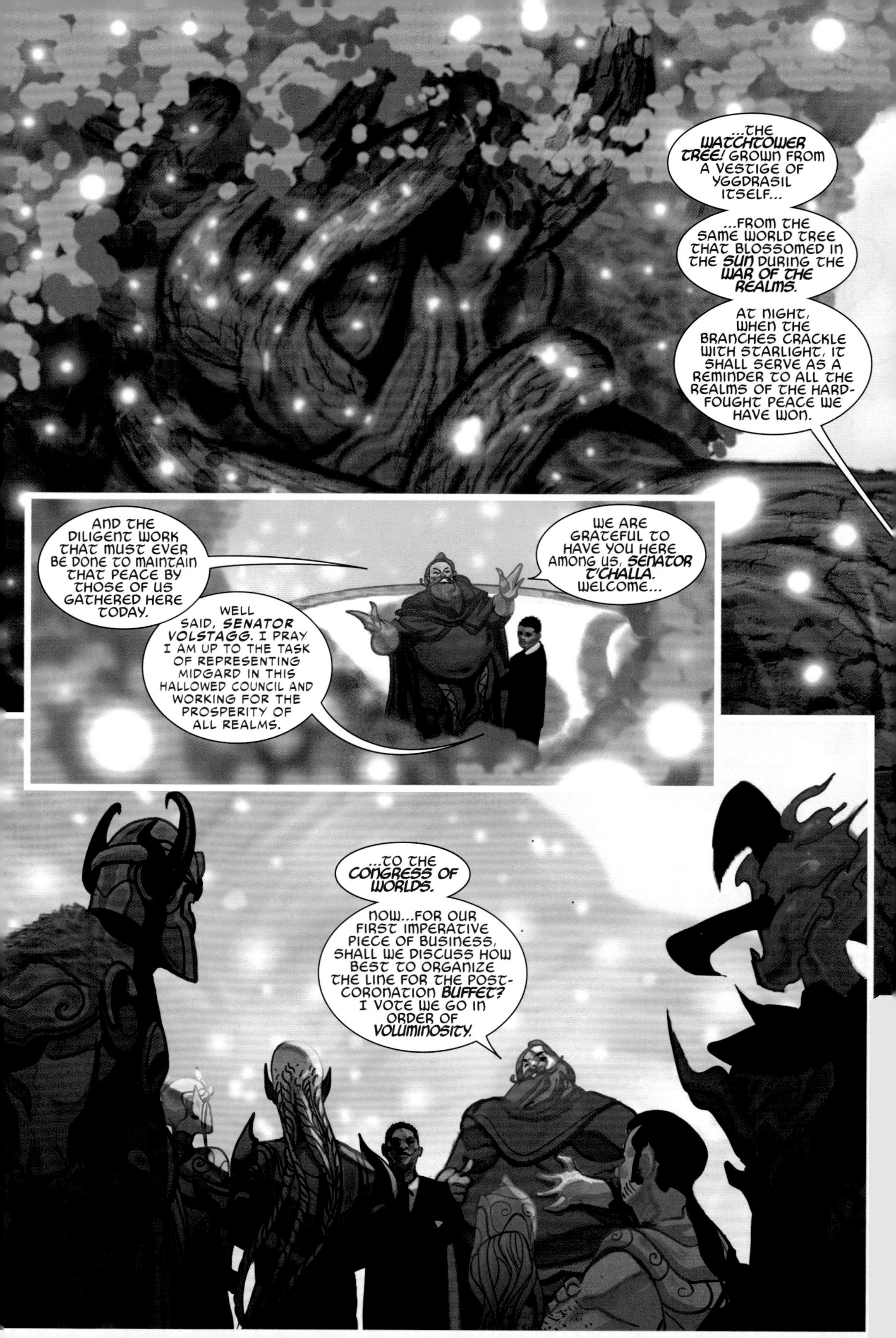
...THE WATCHTOWER TREE! GROWN FROM A VESTIGE OF YGGDRASIL ITSELF...
...FROM THE SAME WORLD TREE THAT BLOSSOMED IN THE SUN DURING THE WAR OF THE REALMS.
AT NIGHT, WHEN THE BRANCHES CRACKLE WITH STARLIGHT, IT SHALL SERVE AS A REMINDER TO ALL THE REALMS OF THE HARD-FOUGHT PEACE WE HAVE WON.
AND THE DILIGENT WORK THAT MUST EVER BE DONE TO MAINTAIN THAT PEACE BY THOSE OF US GATHERED HERE TODAY.
WELL SAID, SENATOR VOLSTAGG. I PRAY I AM UP TO THE TASK OF REPRESENTING MIDGARD IN THIS HALLOWED COUNCIL AND WORKING FOR THE PROSPERITY OF ALL REALMS.
WE ARE GRATEFUL TO HAVE YOU HERE AMONG US, SENATOR T'CHALLA. WELCOME...
...TO THE CONGRESS OF WORLDS.
NOW...FOR OUR FIRST IMPERATIVE PIECE OF BUSINESS, SHALL WE DISCUSS HOW BEST TO ORGANIZE THE LINE FOR THE POST-CORONATION BUFFET? I VOTE WE GO IN ORDER OF VOLUMINOSITY.

TROLLS HARD AT WORK REBUILDING THE TOWERS OF ASGARD...

...IN RETURN FOR A PLACE OF THEIR OWN HERE IN THE *REALM ETERNAL.* THIS IS SOMETHING I NEVER IMAGINED I WOULD SEE.

AYE, BILL. ALL-FATHER THOR'S FIRST DECISION, TO MAKE PEACE WITH THE TROLLS, WOULD APPEAR TO BE A WISE ONE.

SO...HORSE AND FROG SAY...*THORI* NO MORE MURDER TROLLS?

YES. APOLOGIES, THORI, BUT IT WOULD APPEAR YOUR TROLL-MURDERING DAYS ARE BEHIND YOU, MY FRIEND.

THORI IS... VERY...*ANGRY* ABOUT THIS. GRRR.

IS THIS WHAT *PEACE* FEELS LIKE? LIKE A WET STING IN THE EYE?

PEACE AT LAST. THA[NK] THE DOG GODS.

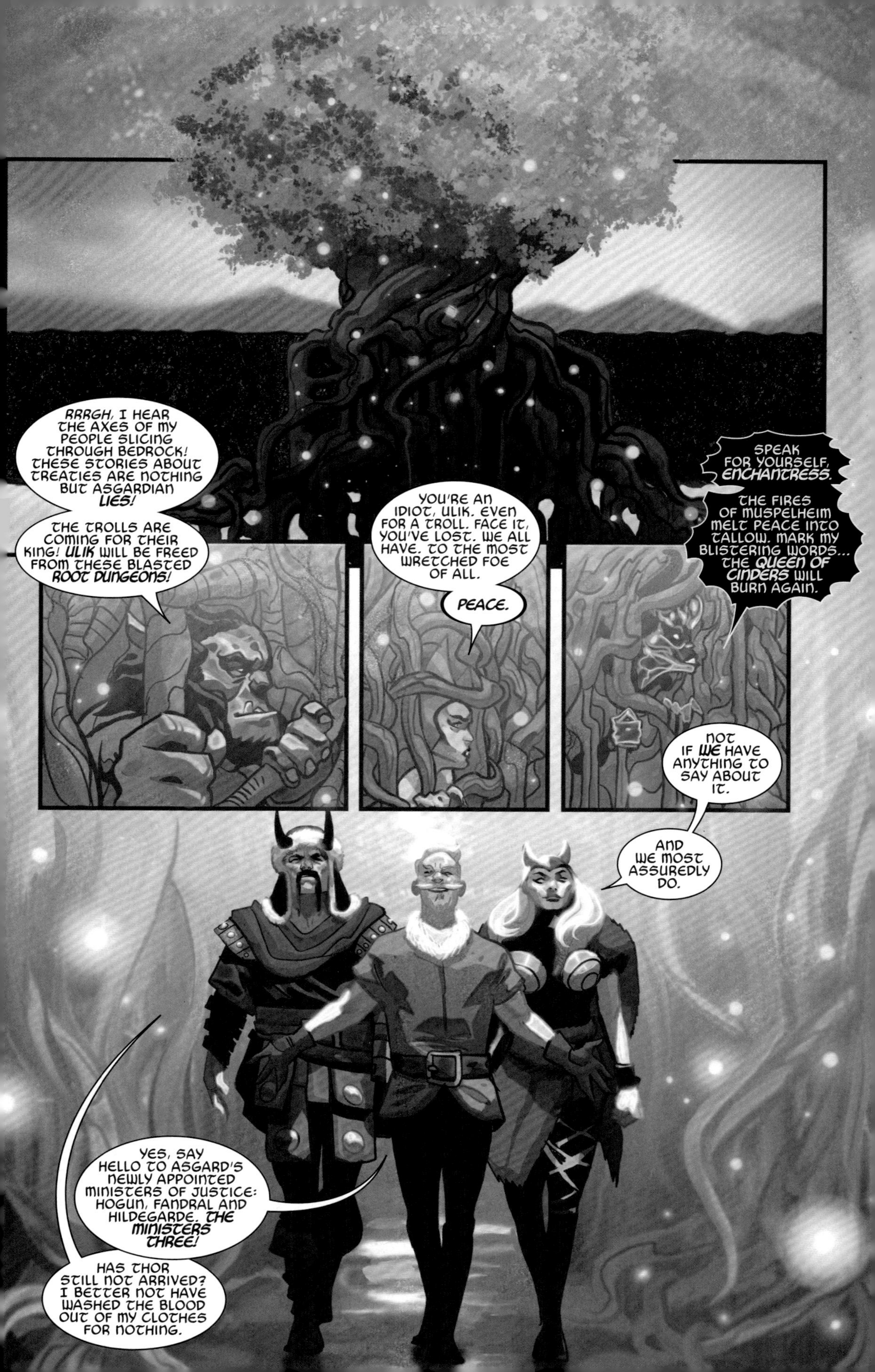
RRRGH, I HEAR THE AXES OF MY PEOPLE SLICING THROUGH BEDROCK! THESE STORIES ABOUT TREATIES ARE NOTHING BUT ASGARDIAN LIES!
THE TROLLS ARE COMING FOR THEIR KING! ULIK WILL BE FREED FROM THESE BLASTED ROOT DUNGEONS!
YOU'RE AN IDIOT, ULIK. EVEN FOR A TROLL. FACE IT, YOU'VE LOST. WE ALL HAVE. TO THE MOST WRETCHED FOE OF ALL.
PEACE.
SPEAK FOR YOURSELF, ENCHANTRESS.
THE FIRES OF MUSPELHEIM MELT PEACE INTO TALLOW. MARK MY BLISTERING WORDS... THE QUEEN OF CINDERS WILL BURN AGAIN.
NOT IF WE HAVE ANYTHING TO SAY ABOUT IT.
AND WE MOST ASSUREDLY DO.
YES, SAY HELLO TO ASGARD'S NEWLY APPOINTED MINISTERS OF JUSTICE: HOGUN, FANDRAL AND HILDEGARDE. THE MINISTERS THREE!
HAS THOR STILL NOT ARRIVED? I BETTER NOT HAVE WASHED THE BLOOD OUT OF MY CLOTHES FOR NOTHING.

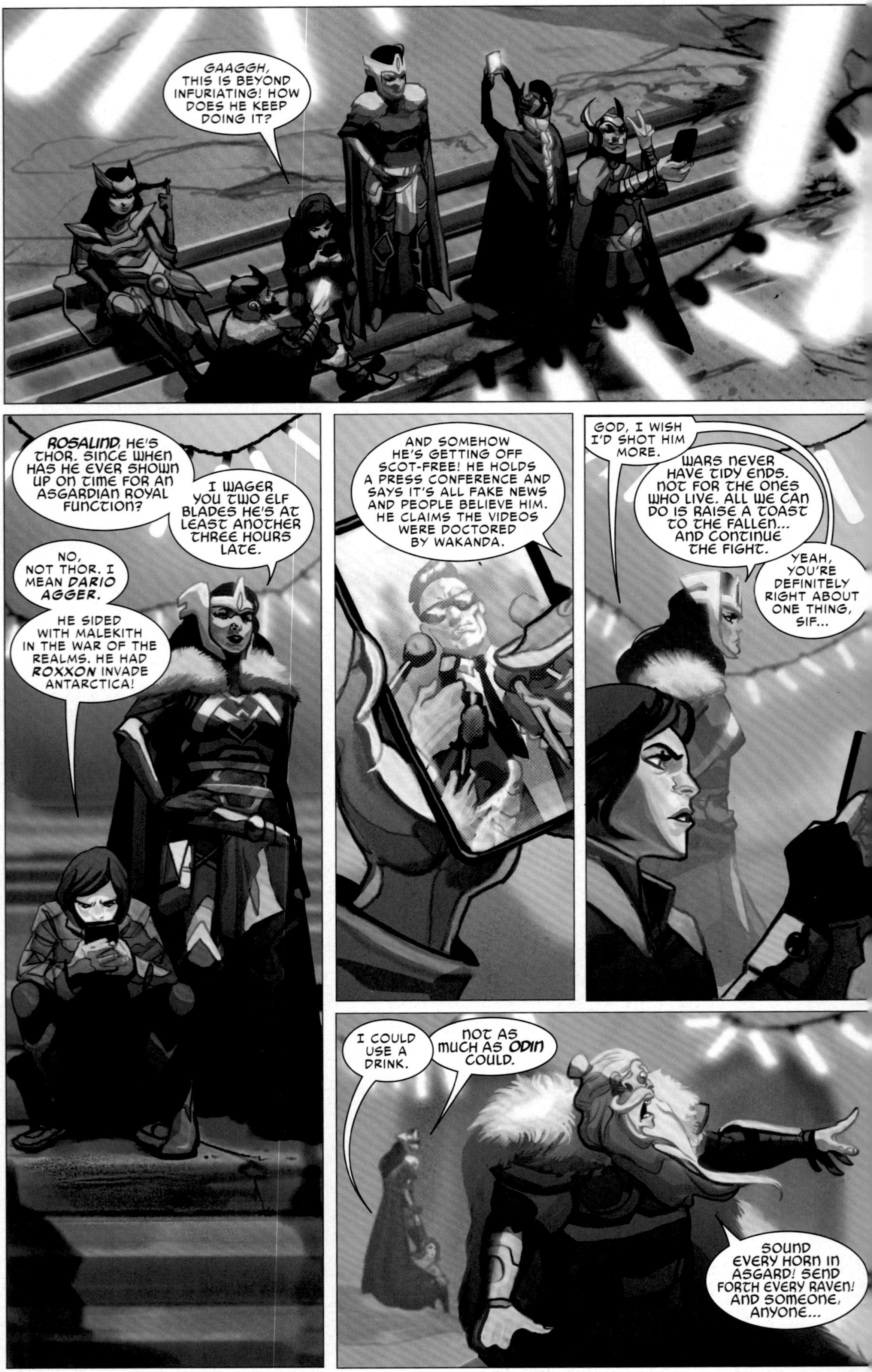
GAAGGH, THIS IS BEYOND INFURIATING! HOW DOES HE KEEP DOING IT?
ROSALIND, HE'S THOR. SINCE WHEN HAS HE EVER SHOWN UP ON TIME FOR AN ASGARDIAN ROYAL FUNCTION?
I WAGER YOU TWO ELF BLADES HE'S AT LEAST ANOTHER THREE HOURS LATE.
NO, NOT THOR. I MEAN DARIO AGGER.
HE SIDED WITH MALEKITH IN THE WAR OF THE REALMS. HE HAD ROXXON INVADE ANTARCTICA!
AND SOMEHOW HE'S GETTING OFF SCOT-FREE! HE HOLDS A PRESS CONFERENCE AND SAYS IT'S ALL FAKE NEWS AND PEOPLE BELIEVE HIM. HE CLAIMS THE VIDEOS WERE DOCTORED BY WAKANDA.
GOD, I WISH I'D SHOT HIM MORE.
WARS NEVER HAVE TIDY ENDS. NOT FOR THE ONES WHO LIVE. ALL WE CAN DO IS RAISE A TOAST TO THE FALLEN... AND CONTINUE THE FIGHT.
YEAH, YOU'RE DEFINITELY RIGHT ABOUT ONE THING, SIF...
I COULD USE A DRINK.
NOT AS MUCH AS ODIN COULD.
SOUND EVERY HORN IN ASGARD! SEND FORTH EVERY RAVEN! AND SOMEONE, ANYONE...

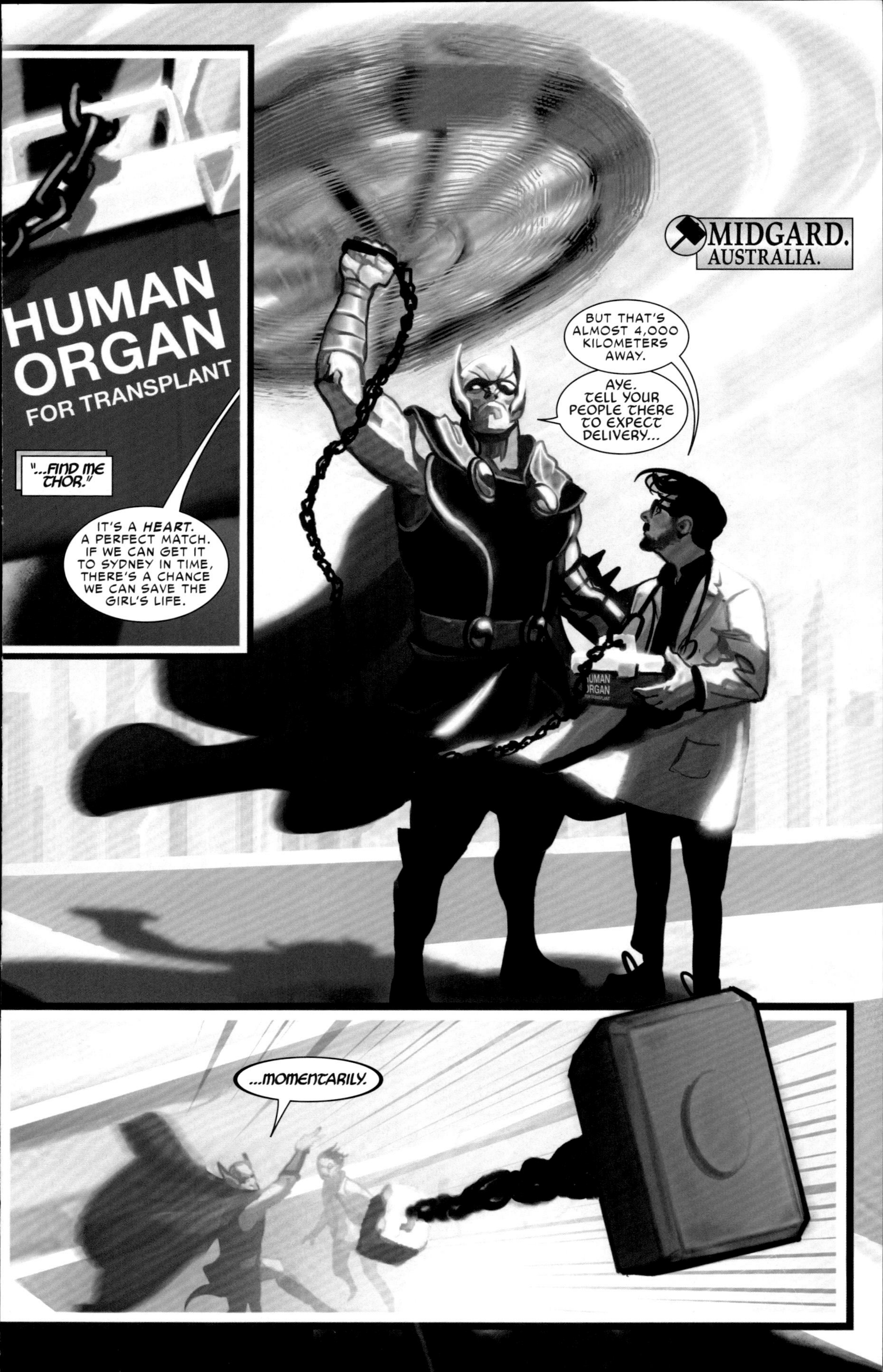
HUMAN ORGAN FOR TRANSPLANT
"...FIND ME THOR."
IT'S A HEART. A PERFECT MATCH. IF WE CAN GET IT TO SYDNEY IN TIME, THERE'S A CHANCE WE CAN SAVE THE GIRL'S LIFE.
MIDGARD. AUSTRALIA.
BUT THAT'S ALMOST 4,000 KILOMETERS AWAY.
AYE. TELL YOUR PEOPLE THERE TO EXPECT DELIVERY...
...MOMENTARILY.

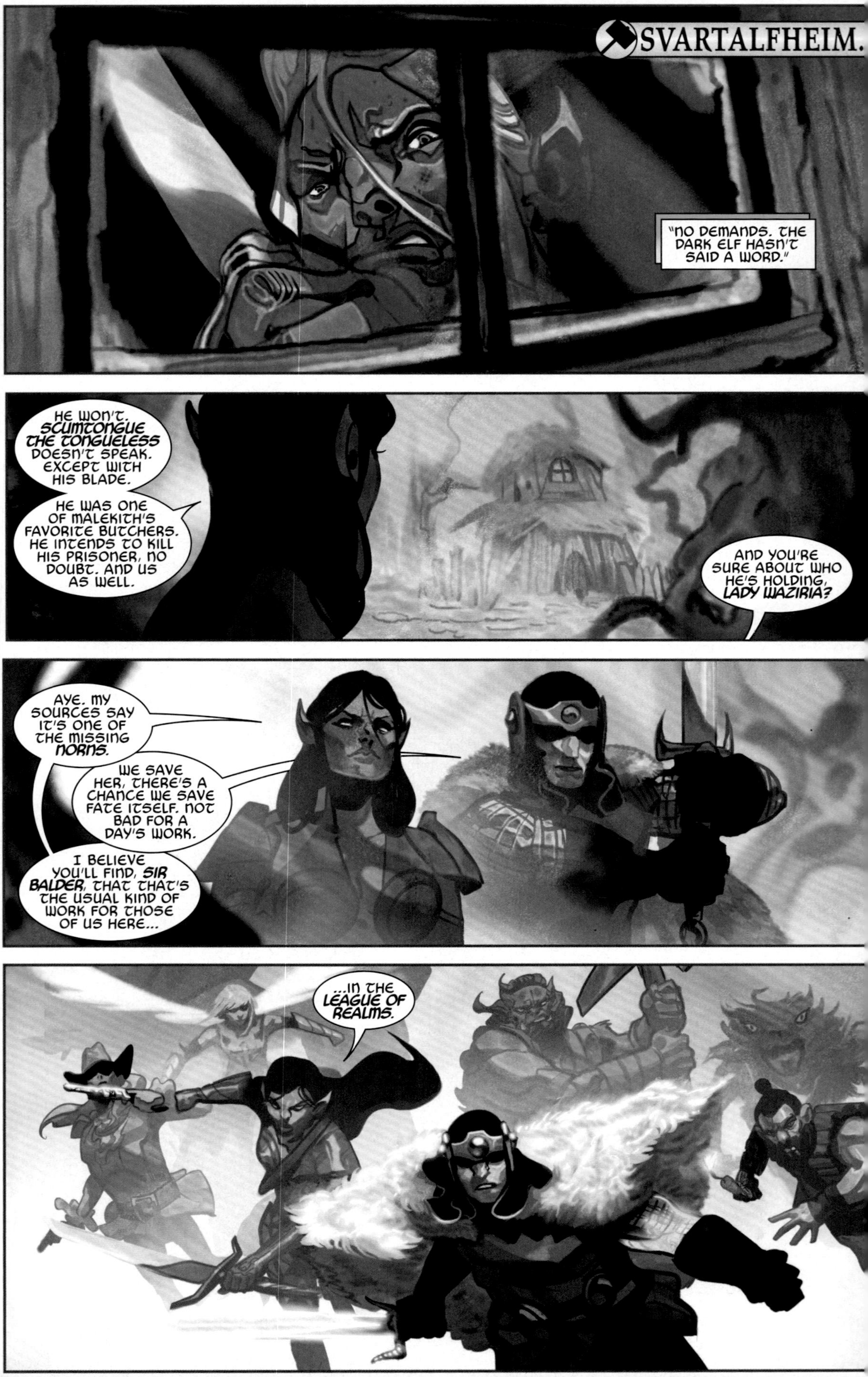
SVARTALFHEIM.
"NO DEMANDS. THE DARK ELF HASN'T SAID A WORD."
HE WON'T. SCUMTONGUE THE TONGUELESS DOESN'T SPEAK. EXCEPT WITH HIS BLADE.
HE WAS ONE OF MALEKITH'S FAVORITE BUTCHERS. HE INTENDS TO KILL HIS PRISONER, NO DOUBT. AND US AS WELL.
AND YOU'RE SURE ABOUT WHO HE'S HOLDING, LADY WAZIRIA?
AYE. MY SOURCES SAY IT'S ONE OF THE MISSING NORNS.
WE SAVE HER, THERE'S A CHANCE WE SAVE FATE ITSELF. NOT BAD FOR A DAY'S WORK.
I BELIEVE YOU'LL FIND, SIR BALDER, THAT THAT'S THE USUAL KIND OF WORK FOR THOSE OF US HERE...
...IN THE LEAGUE OF REALMS.

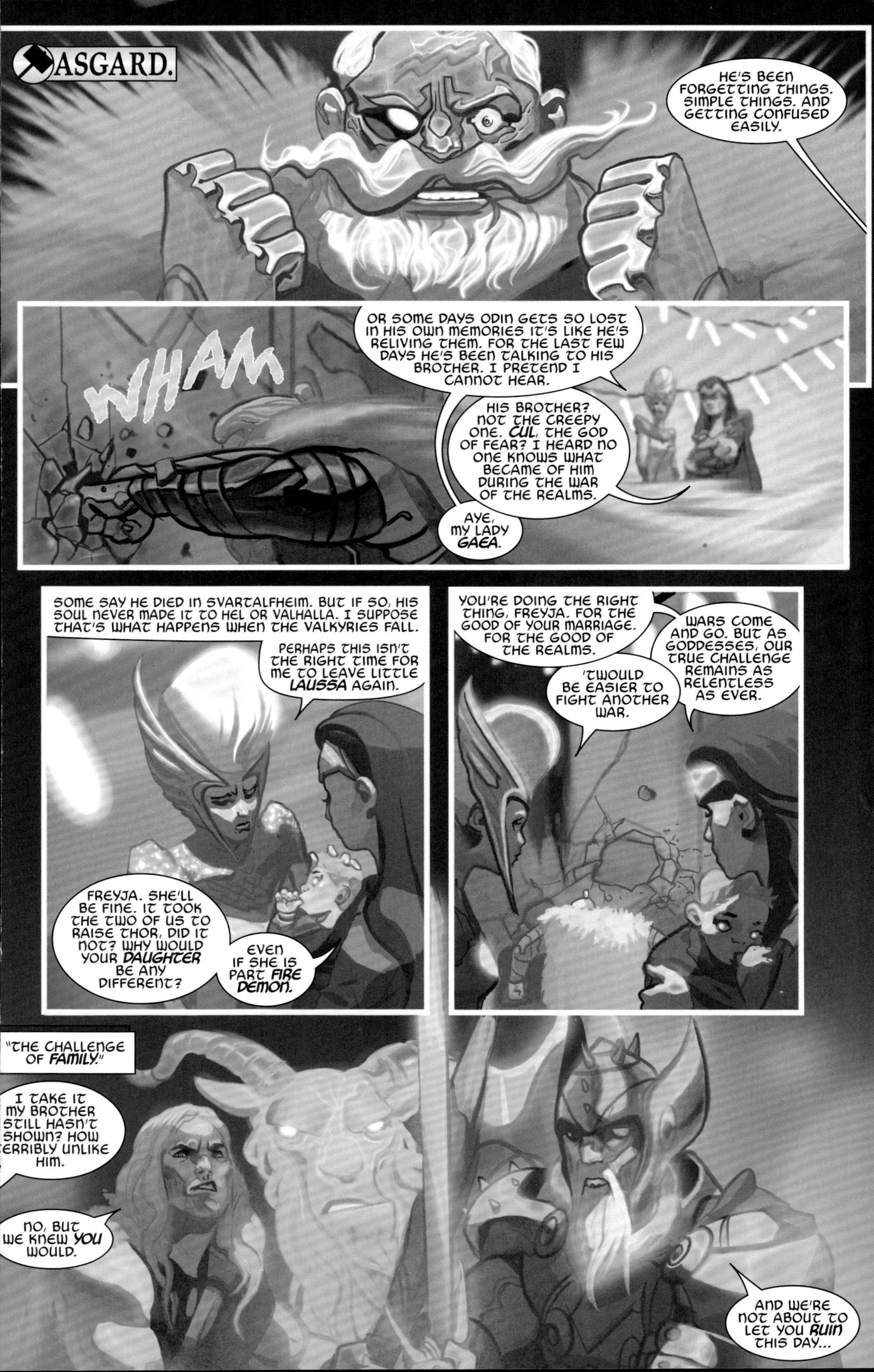
ASGARD.
HE'S BEEN FORGETTING THINGS. SIMPLE THINGS. AND GETTING CONFUSED EASILY.
WHAM
OR SOME DAYS ODIN GETS SO LOST IN HIS OWN MEMORIES IT'S LIKE HE'S RELIVING THEM. FOR THE LAST FEW DAYS HE'S BEEN TALKING TO HIS BROTHER. I PRETEND I CANNOT HEAR.
HIS BROTHER? NOT THE CREEPY ONE. CUL, THE GOD OF FEAR? I HEARD NO ONE KNOWS WHAT BECAME OF HIM DURING THE WAR OF THE REALMS.
AYE, MY LADY GAEA.
SOME SAY HE DIED IN SVARTALFHEIM. BUT IF SO, HIS SOUL NEVER MADE IT TO HEL OR VALHALLA. I SUPPOSE THAT'S WHAT HAPPENS WHEN THE VALKYRIES FALL.
PERHAPS THIS ISN'T THE RIGHT TIME FOR ME TO LEAVE LITTLE LAUSSA AGAIN.
FREYJA. SHE'LL BE FINE. IT TOOK THE TWO OF US TO RAISE THOR, DID IT NOT? WHY WOULD YOUR DAUGHTER BE ANY DIFFERENT?
EVEN IF SHE IS PART FIRE DEMON.
YOU'RE DOING THE RIGHT THING, FREYJA. FOR THE GOOD OF YOUR MARRIAGE. FOR THE GOOD OF THE REALMS.
WARS COME AND GO. BUT AS GODDESSES, OUR TRUE CHALLENGE REMAINS AS RELENTLESS AS EVER.
'TWOULD BE EASIER TO FIGHT ANOTHER WAR.
"THE CHALLENGE OF FAMILY."
I TAKE IT MY BROTHER STILL HASN'T SHOWN? HOW TERRIBLY UNLIKE HIM.
NO, BUT WE KNEW YOU WOULD.
AND WE'RE NOT ABOUT TO LET YOU RUIN THIS DAY...

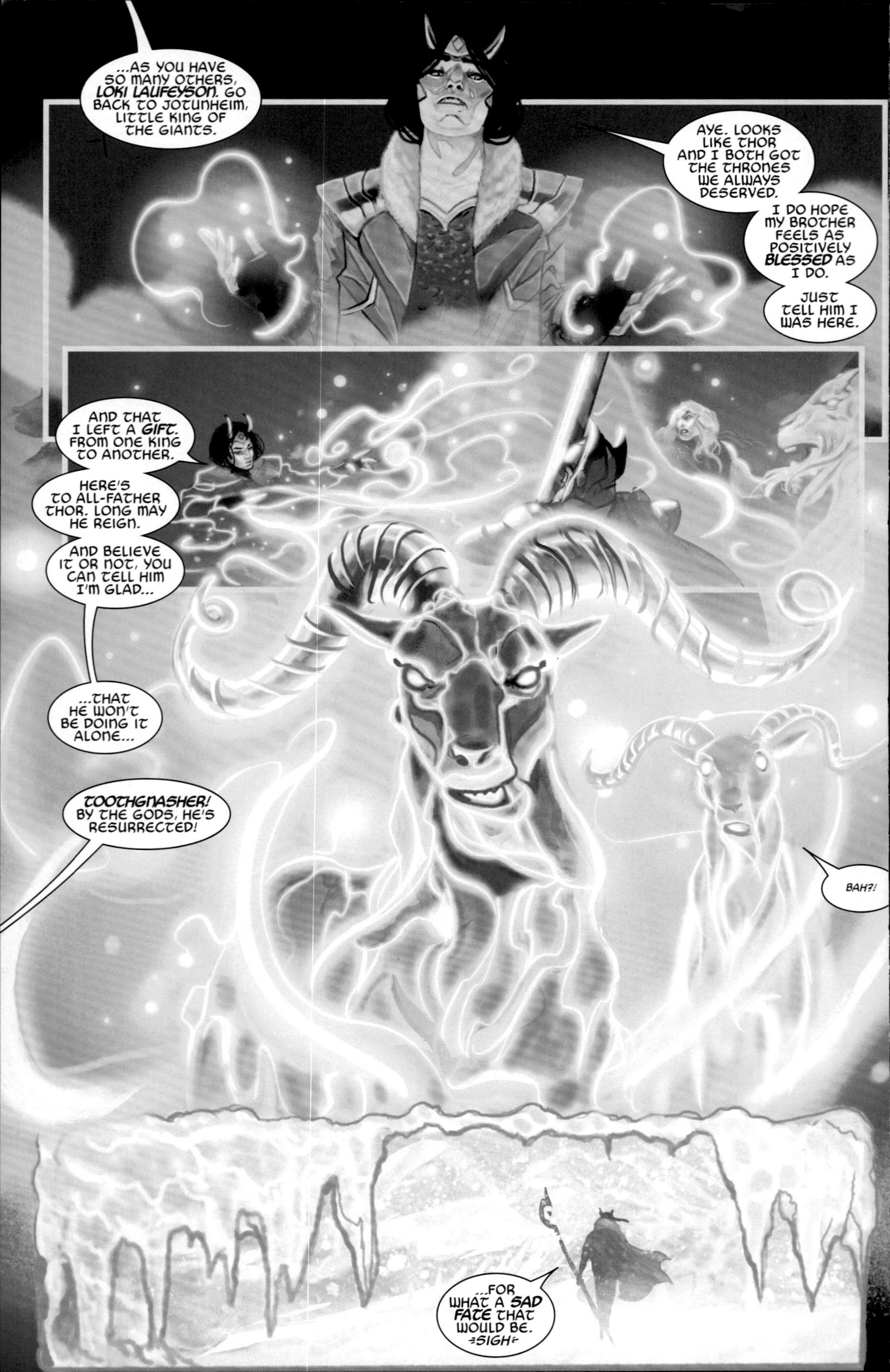
...AS YOU HAVE SO MANY OTHERS, LOKI LAUFEYSON. GO BACK TO JOTUNHEIM, LITTLE KING OF THE GIANTS.
AYE. LOOKS LIKE THOR AND I BOTH GOT THE THRONES WE ALWAYS DESERVED.
I DO HOPE MY BROTHER FEELS AS POSITIVELY BLESSED AS I DO.
JUST TELL HIM I WAS HERE.
AND THAT I LEFT A GIFT. FROM ONE KING TO ANOTHER.
HERE'S TO ALL-FATHER THOR. LONG MAY HE REIGN.
AND BELIEVE IT OR NOT, YOU CAN TELL HIM I'M GLAD...
...THAT HE WON'T BE DOING IT ALONE...
TOOTHGNASHER! BY THE GODS, HE'S RESURRECTED!
BAH?!
...FOR WHAT A SAD FATE THAT WOULD BE.
=SIGH=

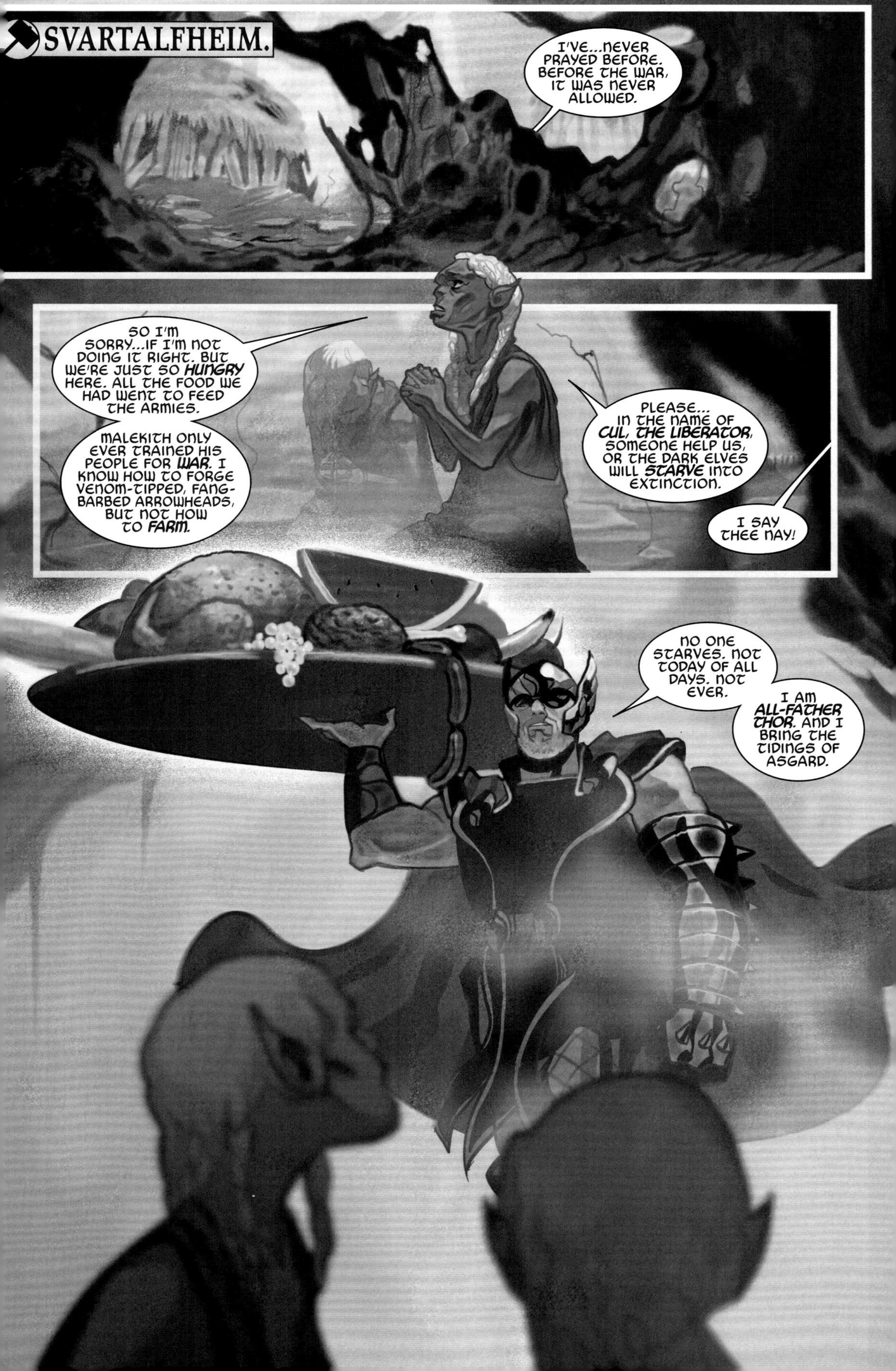
SVARTALFHEIM.
I'VE...NEVER PRAYED BEFORE. BEFORE THE WAR, IT WAS NEVER ALLOWED.
SO I'M SORRY...IF I'M NOT DOING IT RIGHT. BUT WE'RE JUST SO HUNGRY HERE. ALL THE FOOD WE HAD WENT TO FEED THE ARMIES.
MALEKITH ONLY EVER TRAINED HIS PEOPLE FOR WAR. I KNOW HOW TO FORGE VENOM-TIPPED, FANG-BARBED ARROWHEADS, BUT NOT HOW TO FARM.
PLEASE... IN THE NAME OF CUL, THE LIBERATOR, SOMEONE HELP US, OR THE DARK ELVES WILL STARVE INTO EXTINCTION.
I SAY THEE NAY!
NO ONE STARVES. NOT TODAY OF ALL DAYS. NOT EVER.
I AM ALL-FATHER THOR. AND I BRING THE TIDINGS OF ASGARD.

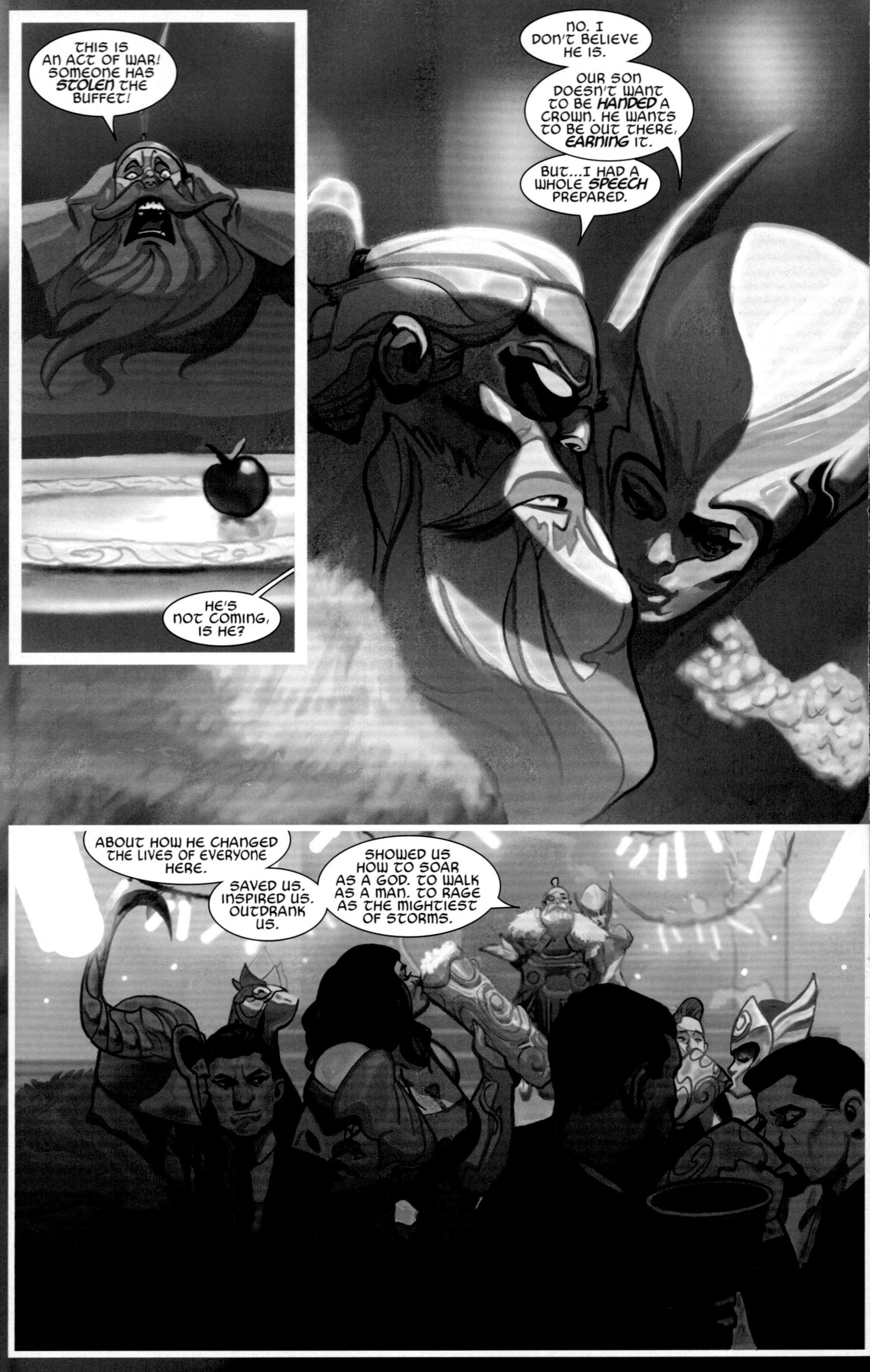
THIS IS AN ACT OF WAR! SOMEONE HAS STOLEN THE BUFFET!
HE'S NOT COMING, IS HE?
NO. I DON'T BELIEVE HE IS.
OUR SON DOESN'T WANT TO BE HANDED A CROWN. HE WANTS TO BE OUT THERE, EARNING IT.
BUT...I HAD A WHOLE SPEECH PREPARED.
ABOUT HOW HE CHANGED THE LIVES OF EVERYONE HERE.
SAVED US. INSPIRED US. OUTDRANK US.
SHOWED US HOW TO SOAR AS A GOD. TO WALK AS A MAN. TO RAGE AS THE MIGHTIEST OF STORMS.

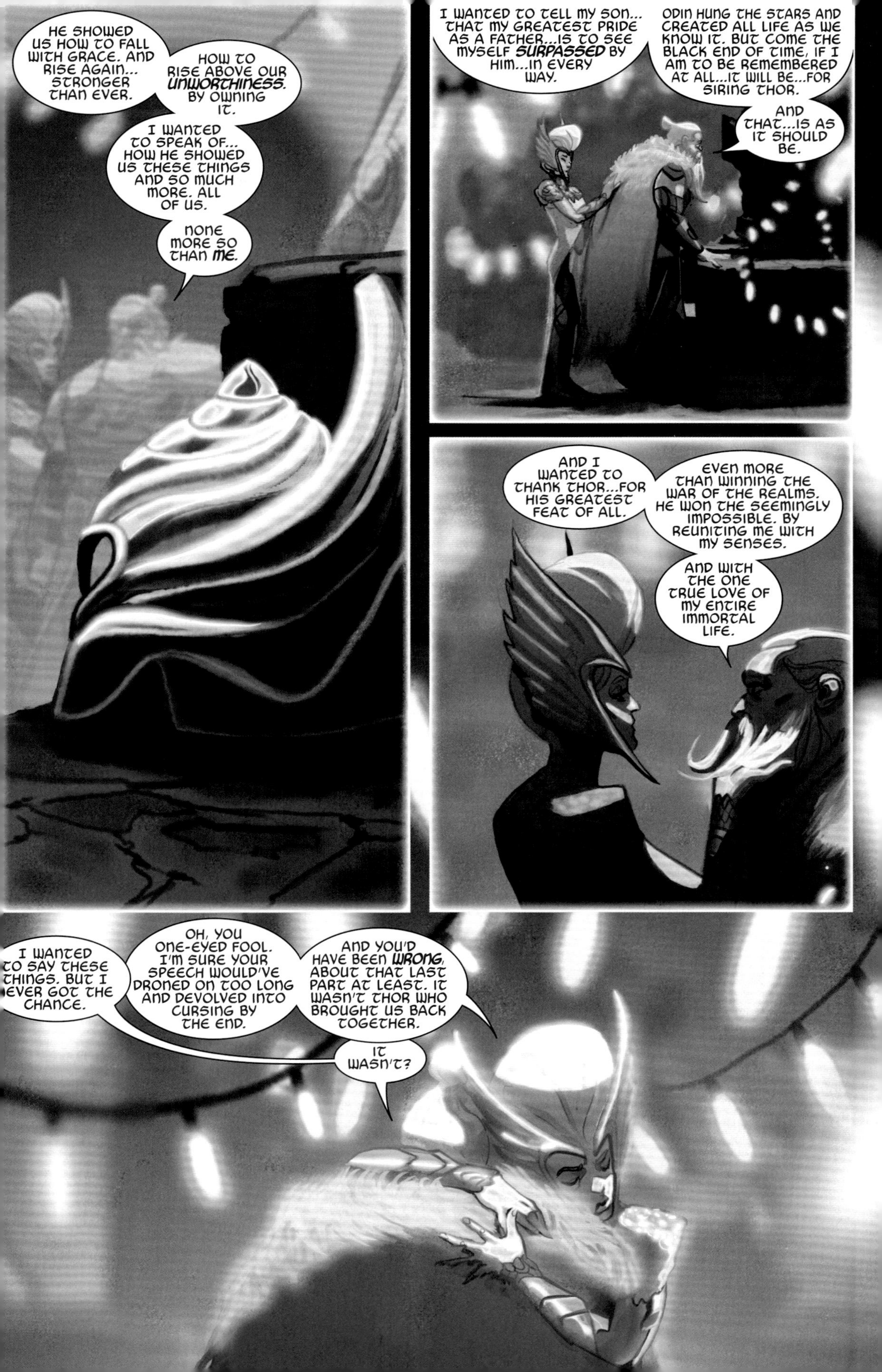
HE SHOWED US HOW TO FALL WITH GRACE. AND RISE AGAIN... STRONGER THAN EVER.
HOW TO RISE ABOVE OUR UNWORTHINESS. BY OWNING IT.
I WANTED TO SPEAK OF... HOW HE SHOWED US THESE THINGS AND SO MUCH MORE. ALL OF US.
NONE MORE SO THAN ME.
I WANTED TO TELL MY SON... THAT MY GREATEST PRIDE AS A FATHER...IS TO SEE MYSELF SURPASSED BY HIM...IN EVERY WAY.
ODIN HUNG THE STARS AND CREATED ALL LIFE AS WE KNOW IT. BUT COME THE BLACK END OF TIME, IF I AM TO BE REMEMBERED AT ALL...IT WILL BE...FOR SIRING THOR.
AND THAT...IS AS IT SHOULD BE.
AND I WANTED TO THANK THOR...FOR HIS GREATEST FEAT OF ALL.
EVEN MORE THAN WINNING THE WAR OF THE REALMS. HE WON THE SEEMINGLY IMPOSSIBLE. BY REUNITING ME WITH MY SENSES.
AND WITH THE ONE TRUE LOVE OF MY ENTIRE IMMORTAL LIFE.
I WANTED TO SAY THESE THINGS. BUT I NEVER GOT THE CHANCE.
OH, YOU ONE-EYED FOOL. I'M SURE YOUR SPEECH WOULD'VE DRONED ON TOO LONG AND DEVOLVED INTO CURSING BY THE END.
AND YOU'D HAVE BEEN WRONG, ABOUT THAT LAST PART AT LEAST. IT WASN'T THOR WHO BROUGHT US BACK TOGETHER.
IT WASN'T?

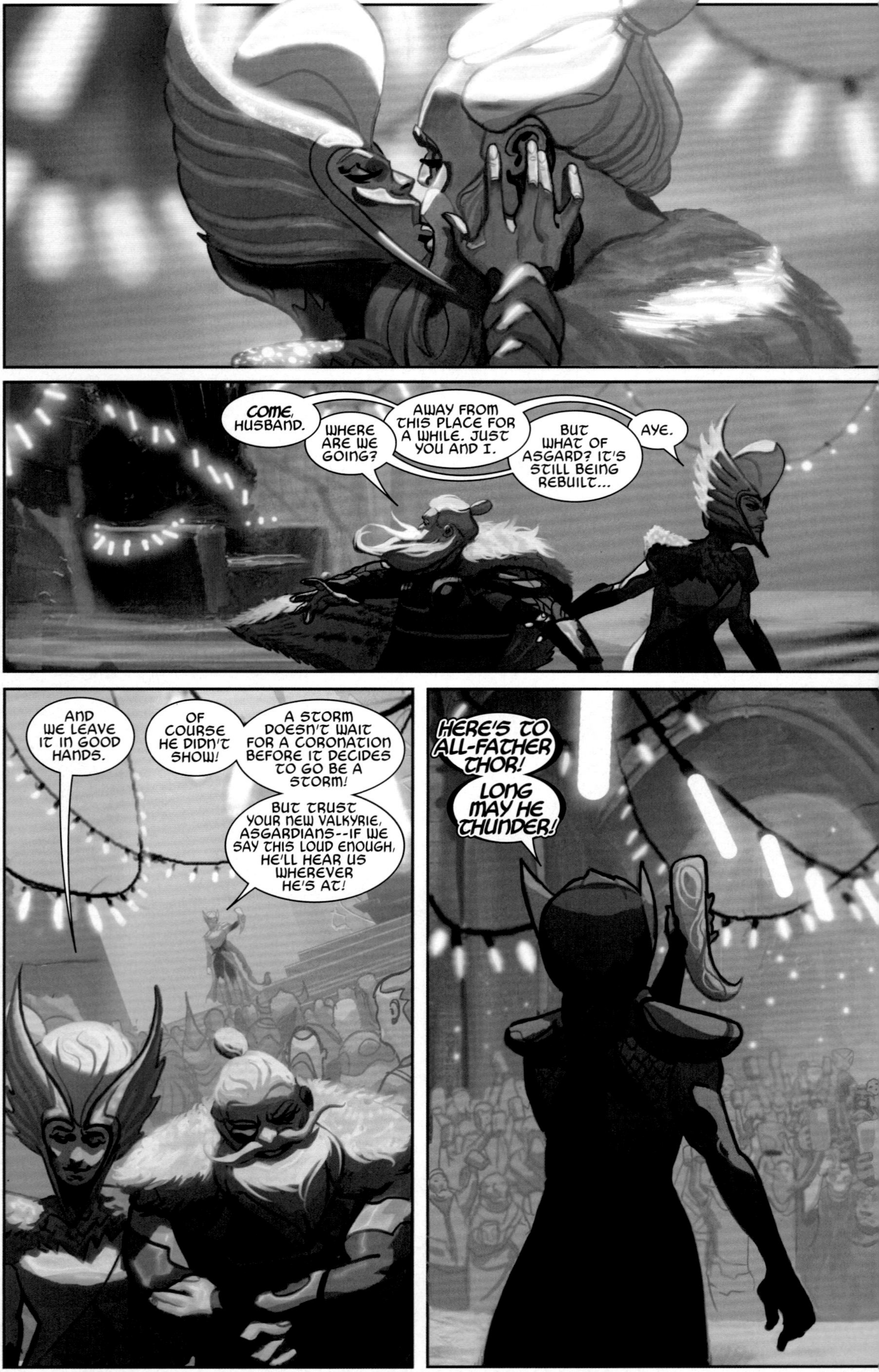
COME, HUSBAND.
WHERE ARE WE GOING?
AWAY FROM THIS PLACE FOR A WHILE. JUST YOU AND I.
BUT WHAT OF ASGARD? IT'S STILL BEING REBUILT...
AYE.
AND WE LEAVE IT IN GOOD HANDS.
OF COURSE HE DIDN'T SHOW!
A STORM DOESN'T WAIT FOR A CORONATION BEFORE IT DECIDES TO GO BE A STORM!
BUT TRUST YOUR NEW VALKYRIE, ASGARDIANS--IF WE SAY THIS LOUD ENOUGH, HE'LL HEAR US WHEREVER HE'S AT!
HERE'S TO ALL-FATHER THOR!
LONG MAY HE THUNDER!

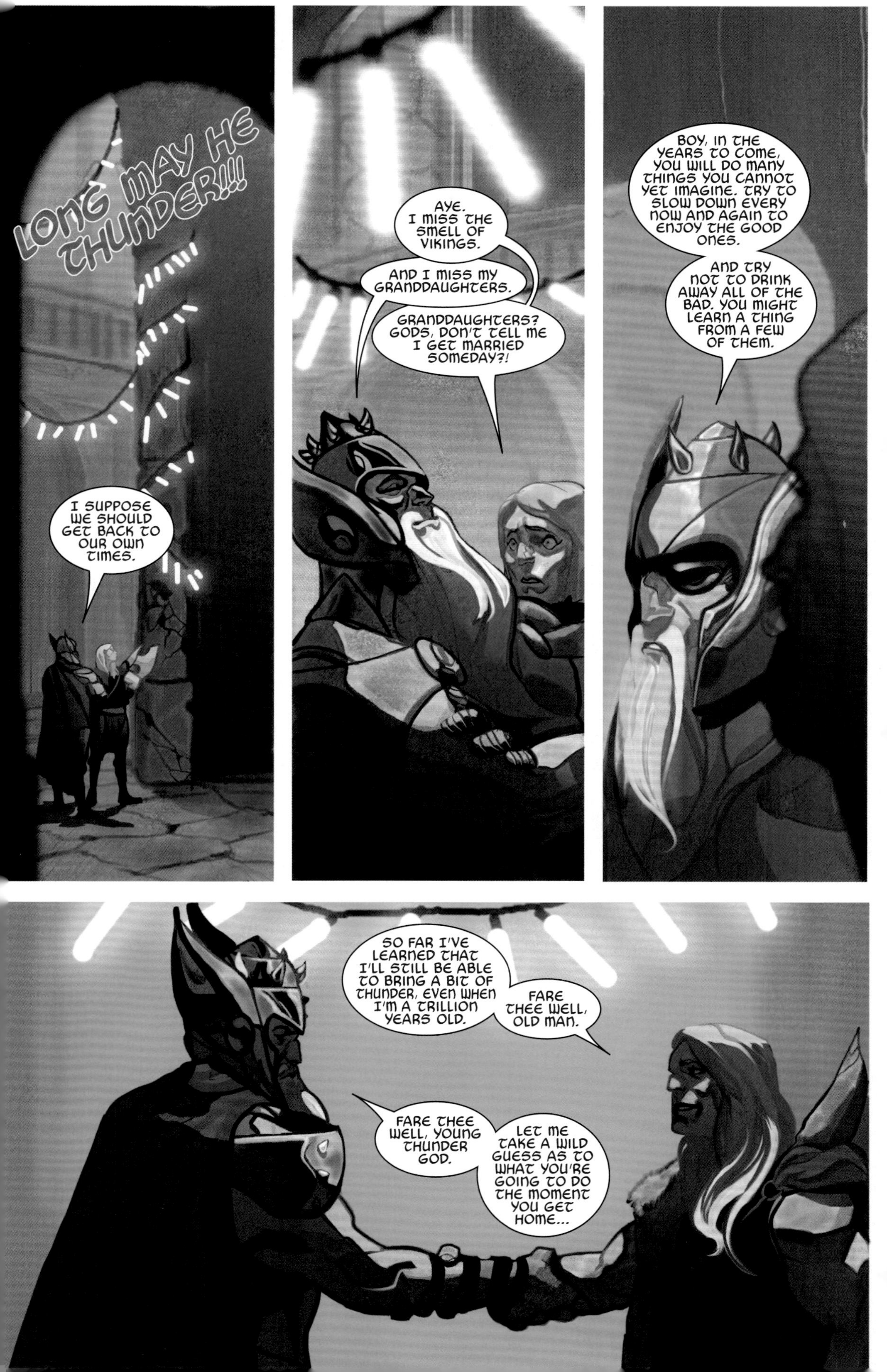
LONG MAY HE THUNDER!!!
I SUPPOSE WE SHOULD GET BACK TO OUR OWN TIMES.
AYE. I MISS THE SMELL OF VIKINGS.
AND I MISS MY GRANDDAUGHTERS.
GRANDDAUGHTERS? GODS, DON'T TELL ME I GET MARRIED SOMEDAY?!
BOY, IN THE YEARS TO COME, YOU WILL DO MANY THINGS YOU CANNOT YET IMAGINE. TRY TO SLOW DOWN EVERY NOW AND AGAIN TO ENJOY THE GOOD ONES.
AND TRY NOT TO DRINK AWAY ALL OF THE BAD. YOU MIGHT LEARN A THING FROM A FEW OF THEM.
SO FAR I'VE LEARNED THAT I'LL STILL BE ABLE TO BRING A BIT OF THUNDER, EVEN WHEN I'M A TRILLION YEARS OLD.
FARE THEE WELL, OLD MAN.
FARE THEE WELL, YOUNG THUNDER GOD.
LET ME TAKE A WILD GUESS AS TO WHAT YOU'RE GOING TO DO THE MOMENT YOU GET HOME...

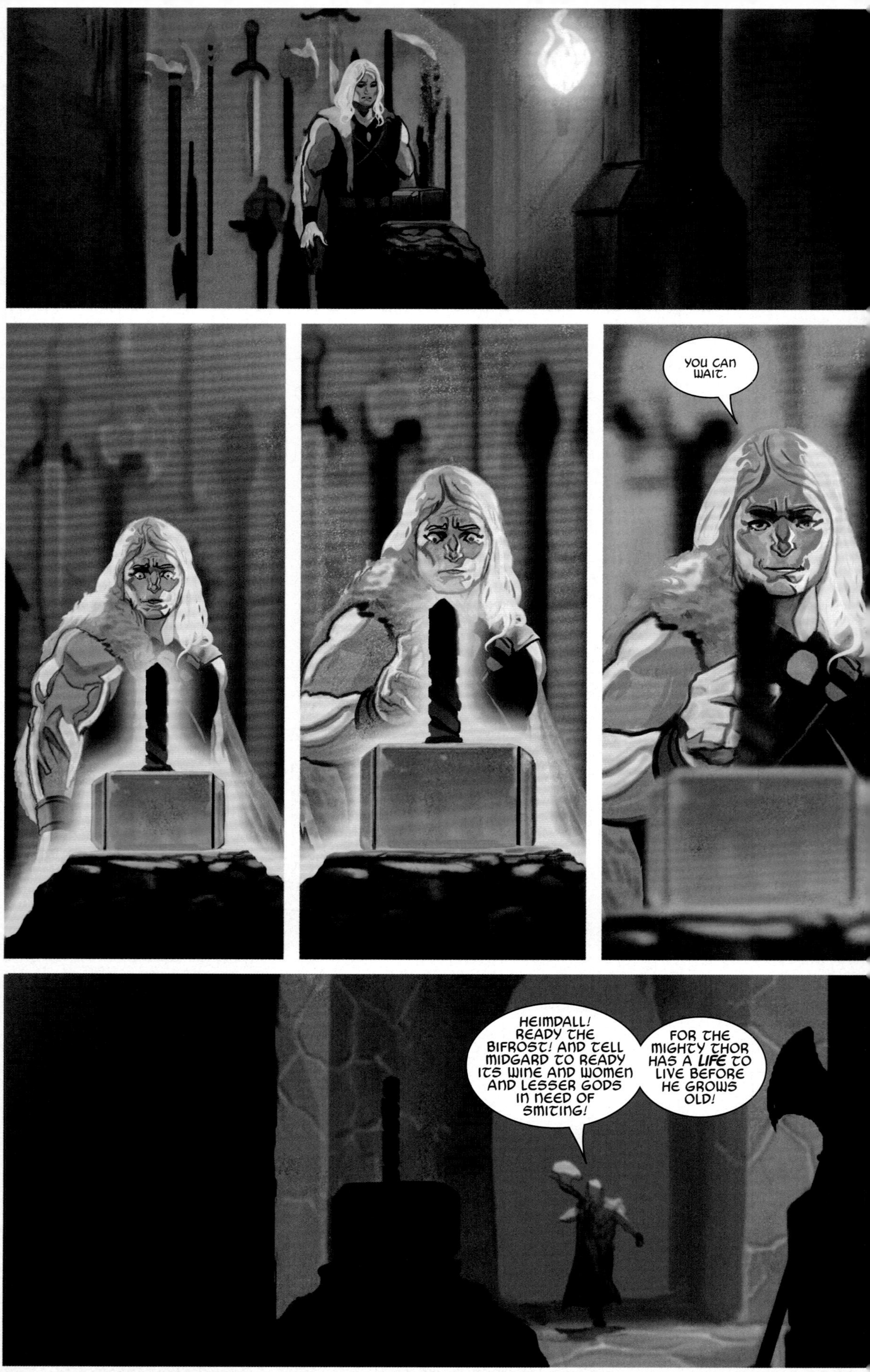
YOU CAN WAIT.
HEIMDALL! READY THE BIFROST! AND TELL MIDGARD TO READY ITS WINE AND WOMEN AND LESSER GODS IN NEED OF SMITING!
FOR THE MIGHTY THOR HAS A LIFE TO LIVE BEFORE HE GROWS OLD!

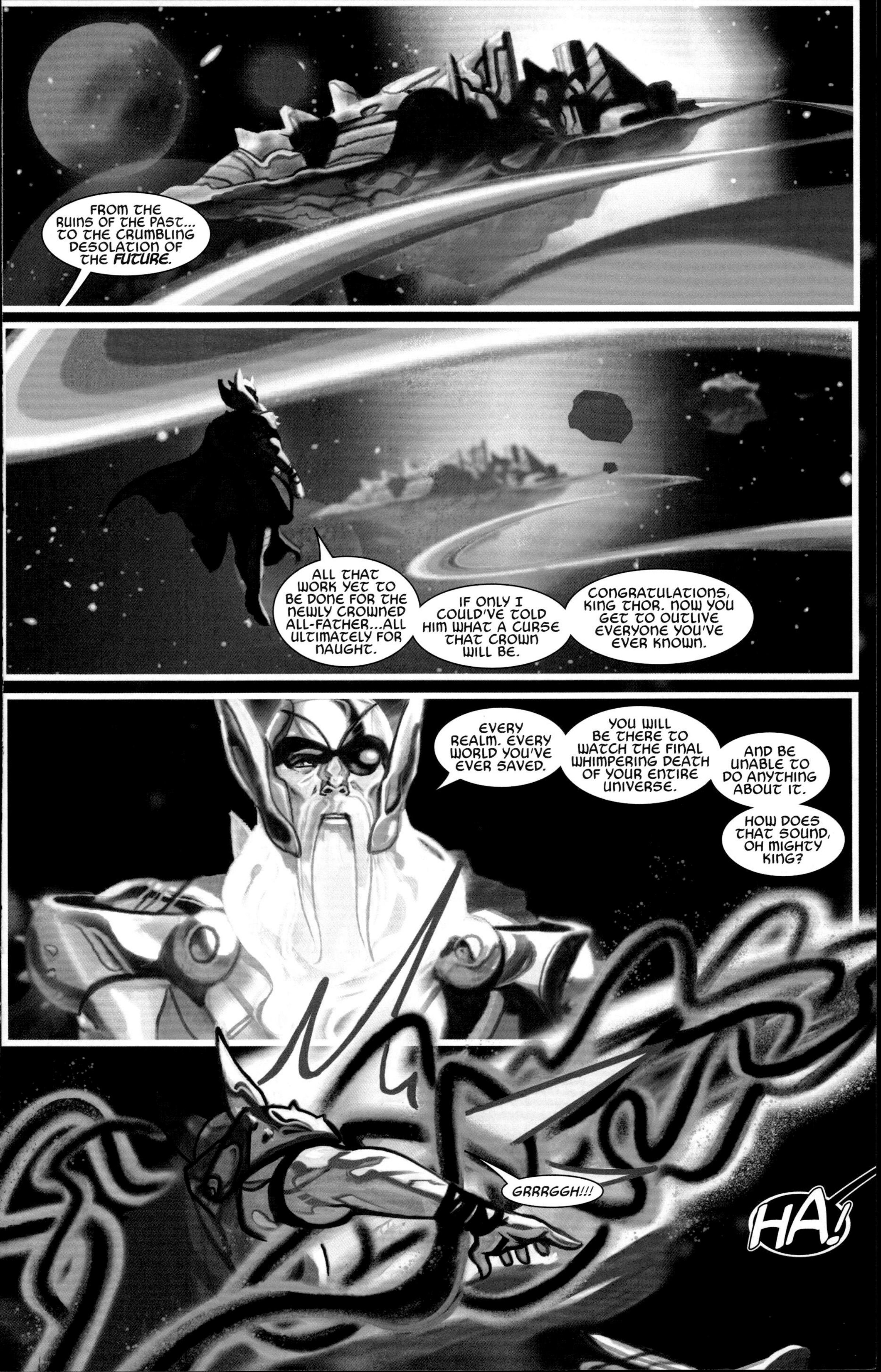
FROM THE RUINS OF THE PAST... TO THE CRUMBLING DESOLATION OF THE *FUTURE*.
ALL THAT WORK YET TO BE DONE FOR THE NEWLY CROWNED ALL-FATHER...ALL ULTIMATELY FOR NAUGHT.
IF ONLY I COULD'VE TOLD HIM WHAT A CURSE THAT CROWN WILL BE.
CONGRATULATIONS, KING THOR. NOW YOU GET TO OUTLIVE EVERYONE YOU'VE EVER KNOWN.
EVERY REALM. EVERY WORLD YOU'VE EVER SAVED.
YOU WILL BE THERE TO WATCH THE FINAL WHIMPERING DEATH OF YOUR ENTIRE UNIVERSE.
AND BE UNABLE TO DO ANYTHING ABOUT IT.
HOW DOES THAT SOUND, OH MIGHTY KING?
GRRRGGH!!!
HA!

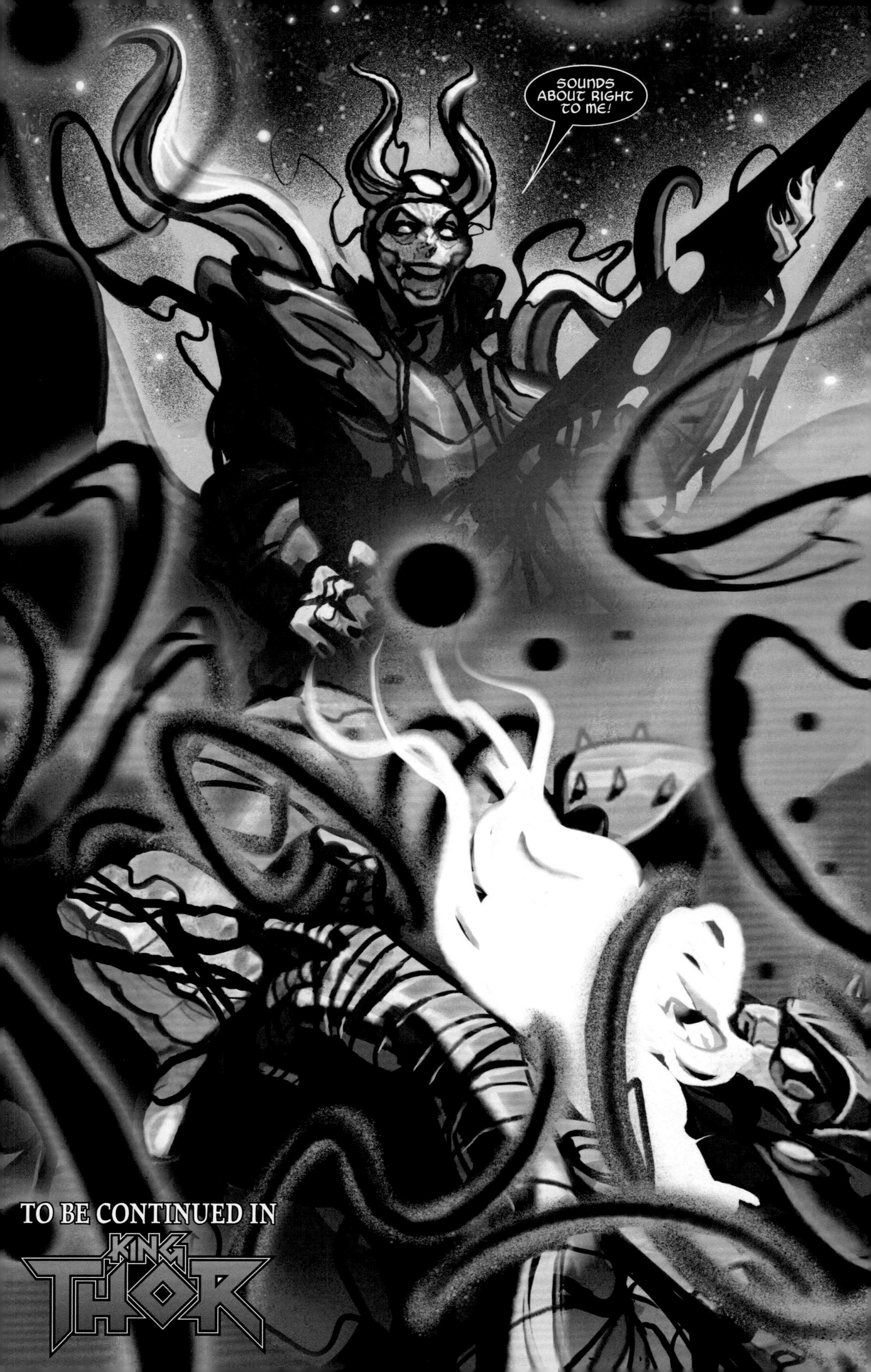
SOUNDS ABOUT RIGHT TO ME!
TO BE CONTINUED IN
KING THOR

Well. This is an ending for me. Of sorts. With this issue, I've now taken our present-day Thor just about as far as I ever will. He's survived a God Butcher, unworthiness and the war of wars to become the one-eyed, one-armed, Mjolnir-toting king of Asgard. Sounds familiar, doesn't it? Who knows what wild new adventures lie in store for All-Father Thor. Well, I've got at least a little idea what's coming for our God of Thunder. But more on that in a minute.

I'll save my seven years' worth of thanks and blubbery goodbyes for a few months from now. But I do want to take this moment to bid a very heartfelt adieu to Mike del Mundo. I've been very spoiled when it comes to artists on my THOR run, going back to Esad Ribić at the beginning and continuing on through Russell Dauterman and Olivier Coipel — all artistic heavyweights at the peak of their prowess, each with their own wildly imaginative and distinctive style. That's a tough group to follow. But Mike took the Asgardian baton with this latest volume, with the rebirth of Thor Odinson, and very much made the character his own. Made Thor's entire world his own. No one in comics or anywhere else is going to out-imagine Mike del Mundo. The wild life, pure uncut passion and beautiful weirdness he injects into his pages has filled me each and every month with complete and utter joy, awe and gratitude. Thank you, Mike. It's been a thunderous pleasure.

So where do we go from here? Well, back to the very beginning in one sense. And all the way to the dark and dismal end in another. The end of everything that's ever been or ever will be. The last Thor story. That's what awaits you in the pages of KING THOR #1, along with the triumphant return of Esad Ribić and maybe a few other old friends as well…as I try to say goodbye in style.

It's the end of my run on THOR. And I've decided that when I leave…I'm going to take the whole universe with me.

Join me in the fire, won't you?

Stay worthy.

Jason Aaron
KC, August 2019

This book has been such an amazing ride. I really feel like my art flourished throughout my run, and I am so proud of what I was able to accomplish. It's all because of the complex, fun, emotional, action-packed scenes and intimate moments that Jason writes. I've been truly spoiled by how Jason crafts this beautiful story and am super blessed to be a part of his epic run. So many standout moments, from Toothgrinder driving Thor's boat to Odin and Thor's father-son scenes, the battle scene with Juggernaut, Balder's monster truck, Loki and his father's relationship. There's Roz melting away a Frost Giant, Thanos and Hela's breakup, Thor's torture scene with the Angels, and I can't forget that murderous dog, Thori. There are so many other scenes to name. Thank you, Jason, for making me a part of your story — it's really been surreal, and I hope we can do it again. WEIRDWORLD gave me a small fix of your talent and it left me wanting more. I finally got it with THOR.

Thanks to Wil Moss and Sarah Brunstad for an amazing job at calling the plays in this book and making sure each detail was carefully looked at with love, and also for guiding me through this whole process.

Joe Sabino, your lettering is impeccable. Thank you!

Marco, I couldn't have finished this book without you. You're the best at setting the stage and laying down that lighting. Also love the names you make up in the layers palette.

I'm gonna miss this book… Bring on the thunder!

Regards,
Mike del Mundo

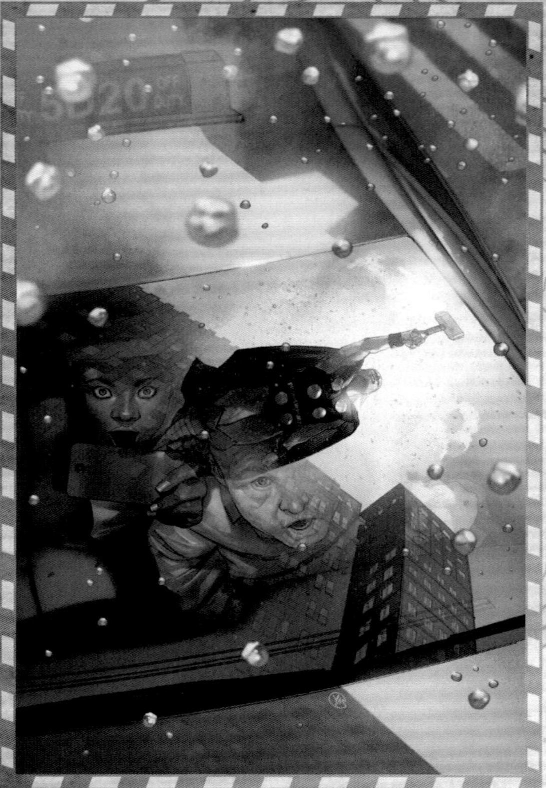

#14 MARVELS 25TH TRIUTE VARIANT BY
YASMINE PUTRI

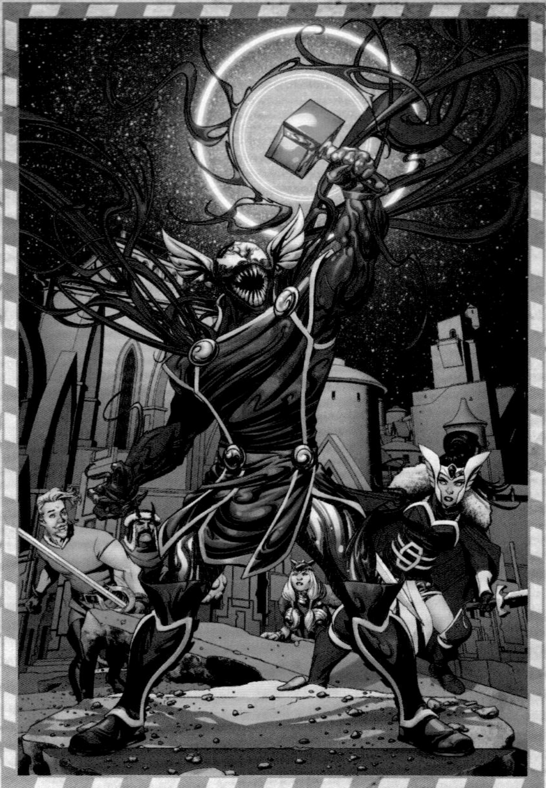

#15 CARNAGE-IZED VARIANT BY
MIKE McKONE
& NOLAN WOODARD

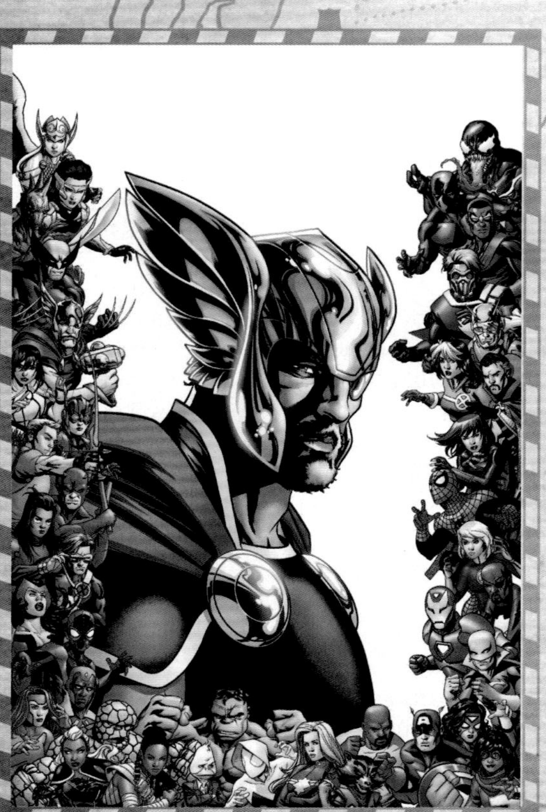

#16 80TH FRAME VARIANT BY
MIKE McKONE
& EDGAR DELGADO

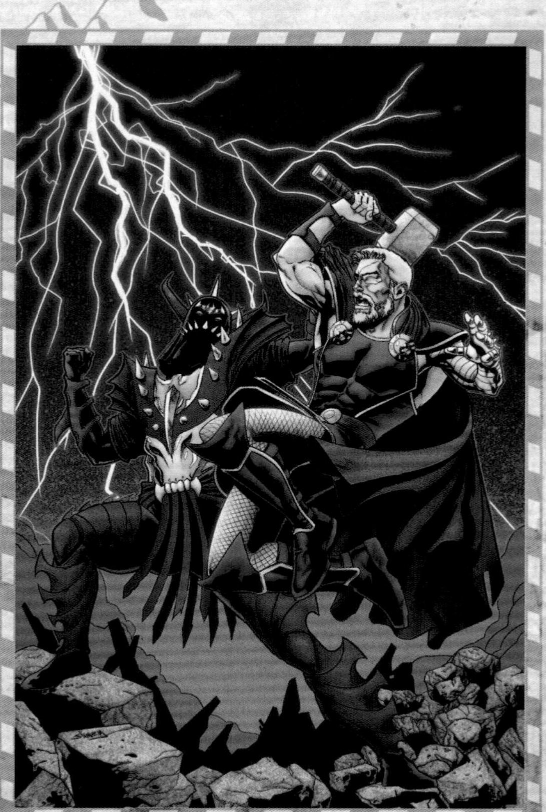

#16 BRING ON THE BAD GUYS VARIANT BY
WILL SLINEY
& MORRY HOLLOWELL

THOR
THOR
THOR
THOR
Writer • Artist • Inker • Colors • Cover
THE WAR OF THE REALMS
THOR
Writer • Artist • Inker • Colors • Cover
THE WAR OF THE REALMS
THOR
Writer • Artist • Inker • Colors • Cover
THE WAR OF THE REALMS
THOR
Writer • Artist • Inker • Colors • Cover
THE WAR OF THE REALMS
THOR

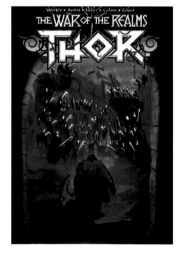

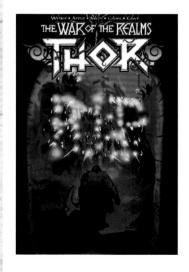

#12 & #13 COVER SKETCHES BY MIKE DEL MUNDO

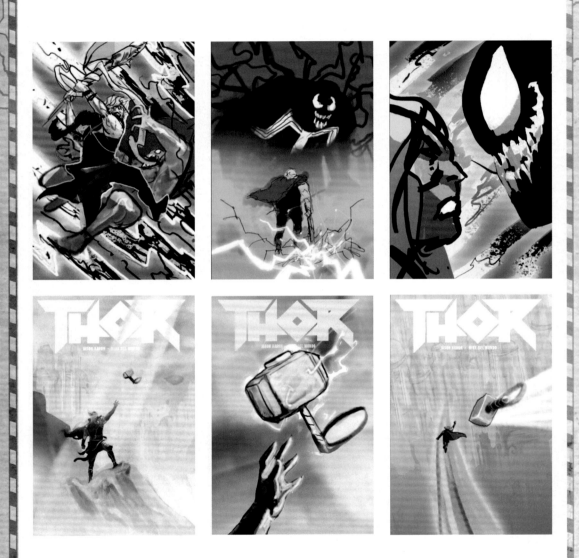

#14 & #15 COVER SKETCHES BY MIKE DEL MUNDO

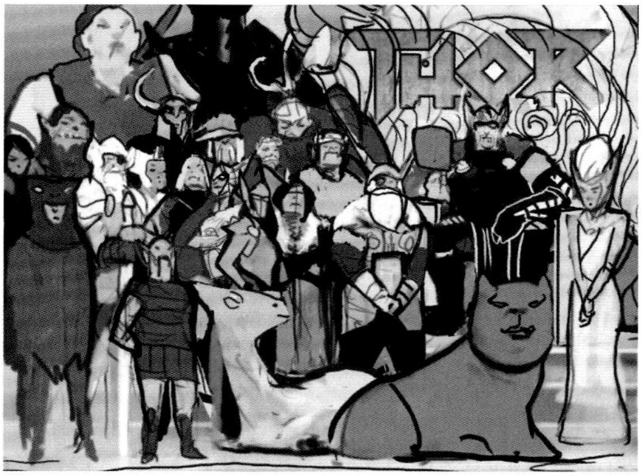
THOR

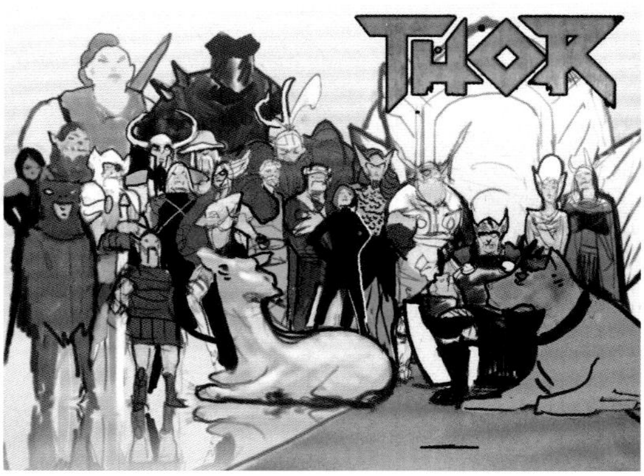
THOR

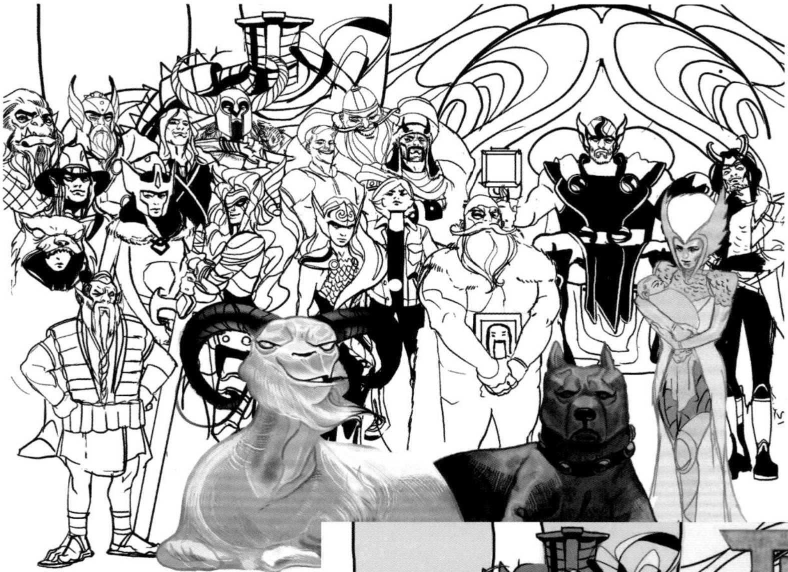

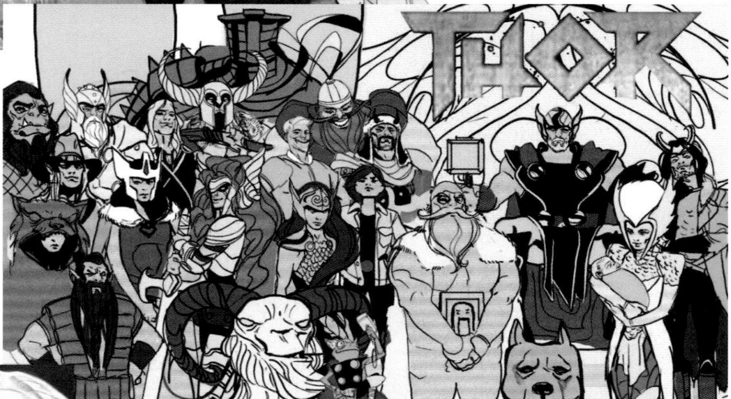
THOR

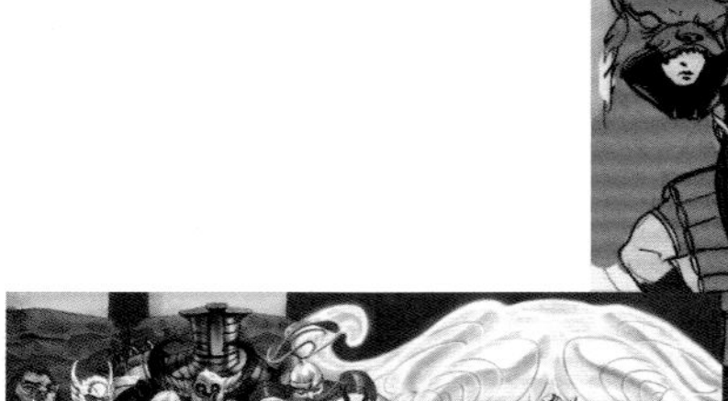

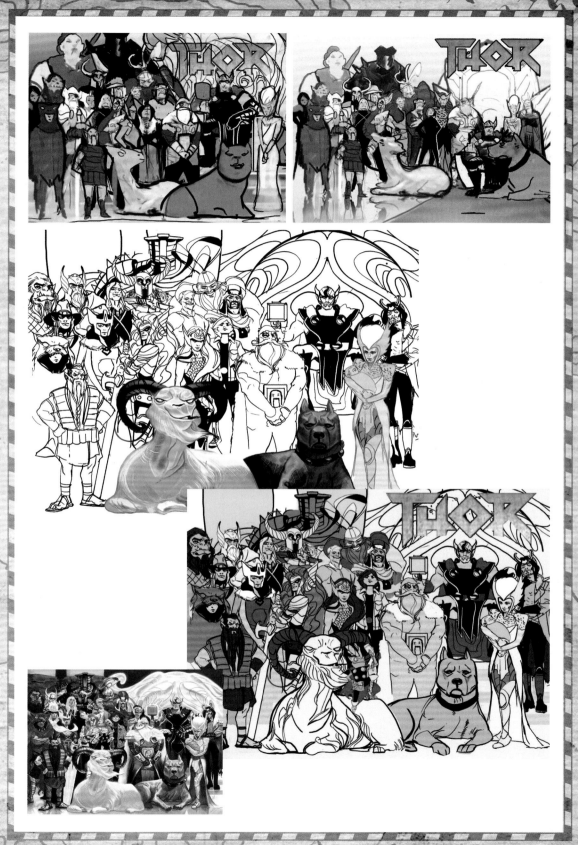

#16 COVER PROCESS BY MIKE DEL MUNDO

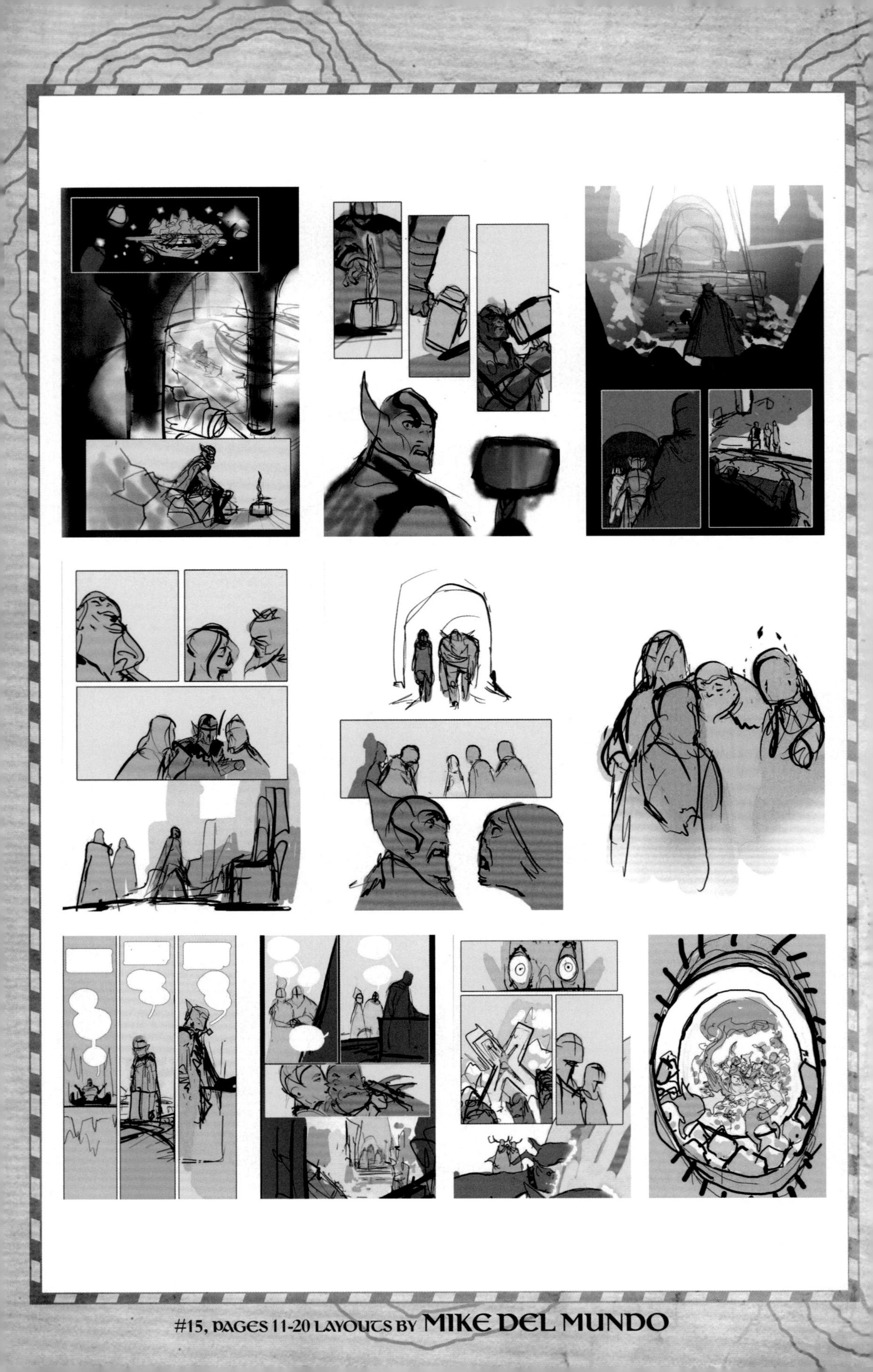

#15, PAGES 11-20 LAYOUTS BY **MIKE DEL MUNDO**

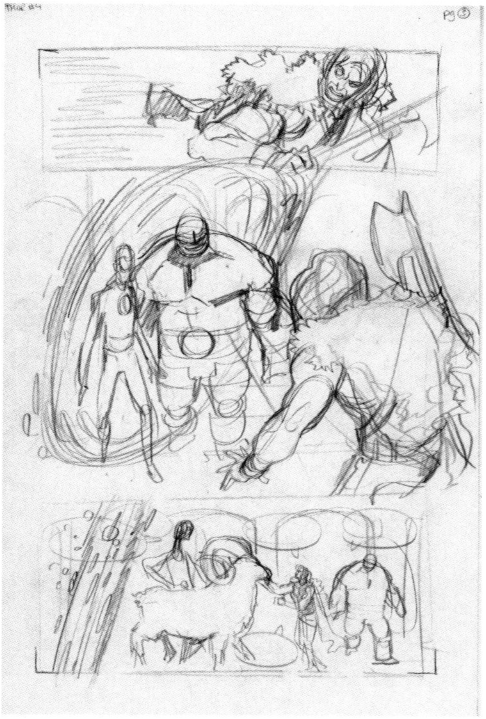

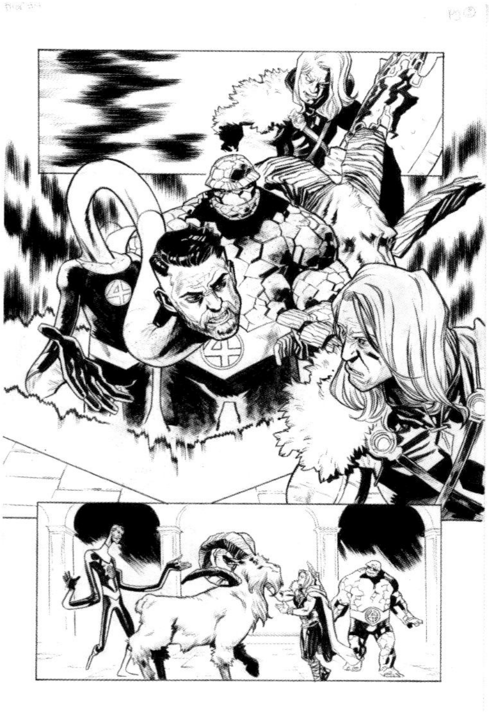

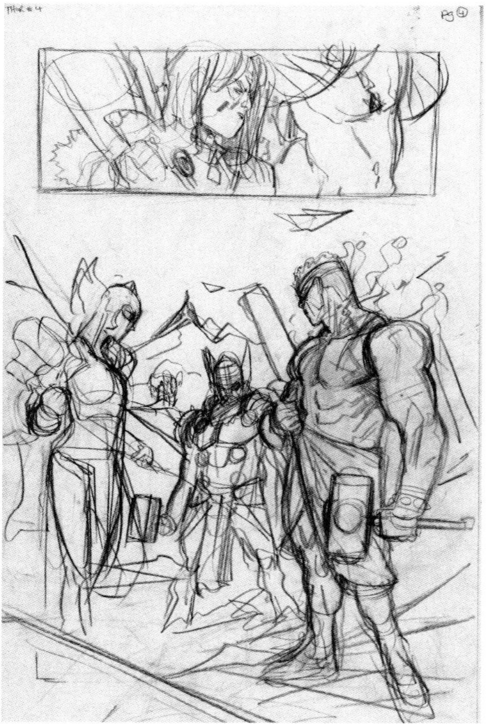

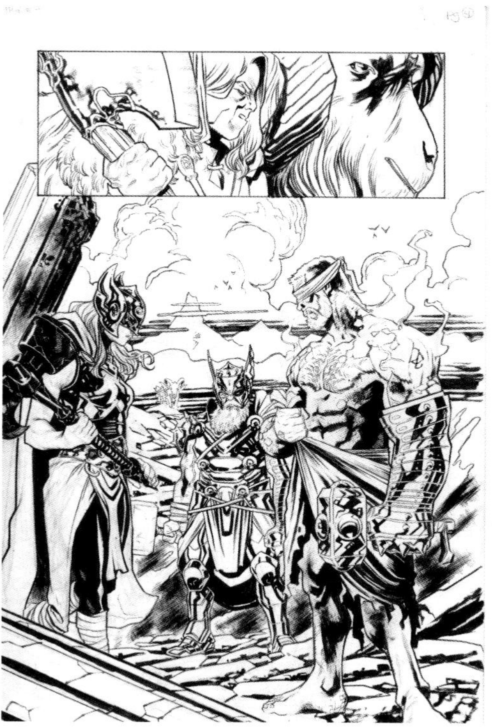

#14, PAGES 3 & 4 ART PROCESS BY SCOTT HEPBURN

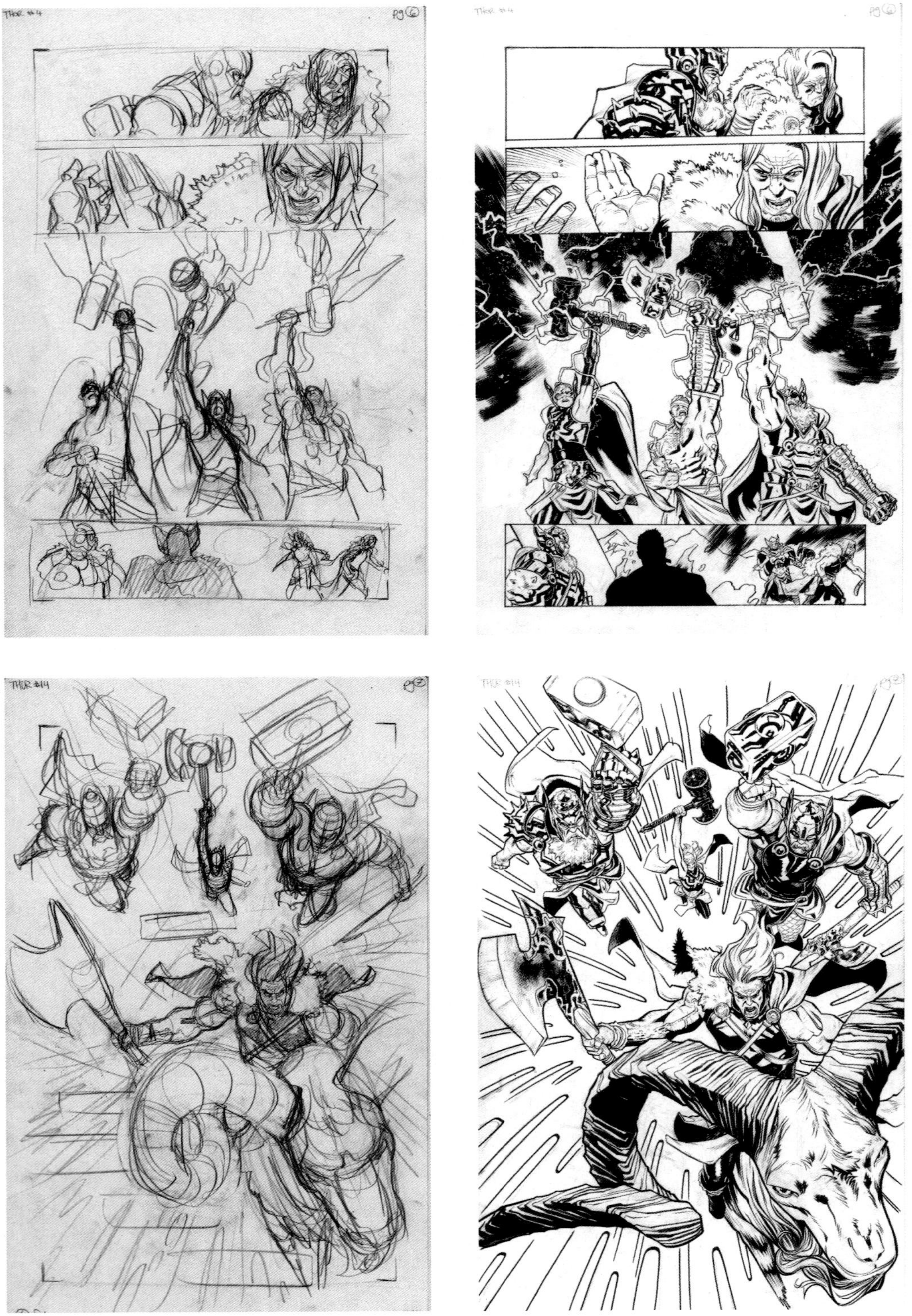

#14, PAGES 6 & 7 ART PROCESS BY SCOTT HEPBURN